REMEMBERING SIMPLIFIED HANZI – BOOK 1

BY THE SAME AUTHORS

Remembering Traditional Hanzi: How Not to Forget the Meaning and Writing of Chinese Characters, Book 1. Honolulu: University of Hawai'i Press, 2009

REMEMBERING
SIMPLIFIED HANZI

*How Not to Forget the Meaning
and Writing of Chinese Characters*

Book 1

James W. Heisig

Timothy W. Richardson

University of Hawai'i Press
HONOLULU

14 13 12 11   6 5 4 3 2

Library of Congress Cataloging-in-Publication Data

Heisig, James W., 1944-
    Remembering simplified Hanzi : book 1 : how not to forget the meaning and
    writing of Chinese characters / James W. Heisig ; Timothy W. Richardson.
    p. cm.
    Includes indexes.
    ISBN 978-0-8248-3323-7 (pbk. : alk. paper)
    1. Chinese language--Simplified characters. 2. Chinese language--study and
    teaching. I. Richardson, Timothy W. II. Title. III. Title: How not to forget the
    meaning and writing of Chinese characters.
PL1175.H45 2008
495.1—dc22
                                                    2008032998

The typesetting for this book was done at the Nanzan Institute for Religion and Culture.

University of Hawai'i Press books are printed on acid-free paper and meet the guidelines
for permanence and durability of the Council on Library Resources.

CONTENTS

INTRODUCTION

THE AIM OF THIS course is to help you teach yourself, as quickly and efficiently as possible, the meaning and writing of the 3,000 most commonly used Chinese characters. The course is intended not only for beginners, but also for more advanced students looking for some way to systematize what they already know and gain relief from the constant frustration of forgetting how to write the characters. By showing how to break down the complexities of the characters into their basic elements, assigning meanings to those elements, and arranging the characters in a unique and rational order, the method aims to make use of the structural properties of the writing system itself to reduce the burden on memory.

The 55 lessons that make up Book 1 cover the 1,000 most commonly used characters in the Chinese writing system, plus another 500 included either because they are needed to preserve the logical ordering of the material or because they are especially easy to learn at this early stage. Book 2 will add another 1,500 characters for a total of 3,000—all of them selected on the basis of the frequency with which they appear in written Chinese. What you will *not* learn here is how to pronounce any of these characters or how to combine them to form new words. Since this breaks with conventional methods for teaching characters, it is important that you understand the rationale behind the approach before setting out.

To students approaching Chinese from a mother tongue written with an alphabet, the characters represent a forbidding obstacle, one that involves the memorization of thousands of complex configurations, each of which has to be tethered to a particular sound and a particular meaning or function. Focusing for the moment just on what is involved in trying to commit the written forms to memory, imagine yourself holding a kaleidoscope up to the light as still as possible, trying to fix in memory the particular pattern that the play of light and mirrors and colored stones has created. Chances are, your mind is unaccustomed to processing such material and it will take some time to organize the pattern for retention and recall. But let us suppose that you succeed after ten or fifteen minutes. You close your eyes, trace the pattern in your head, and then check your image against the original pattern, repeating the process until you are sure you have it committed to memory.

1

Then someone passes by and jars your elbow. The pattern is lost forever and in its place a new jumble appears. Immediately your memory begins to scramble. You set the kaleidoscope aside, sit down, and try to draw what you had just memorized, but to no avail. There is simply nothing left in memory to grab hold of. The characters are like that. One can sit at one's desk and drill a number of characters for an hour or two, only to discover on the morrow that when something similar is seen, the former memory is erased or hopelessly confused by the new information. No wonder learners begin to think that they simply don't have a good memory for characters, or decide that learning to write characters is not so important anyway.

In many cases failure to retain what has been learned has much less to do with a lack of ability than with the lack of a method of learning adjusted to the circumstances of the learner. Of course we forget, and some of us forget more than others. But some of this forgetting is due to a simple misuse, even abuse, of our powers of memory, and is therefore preventable. The first step to prevention is to break with certain preconceptions about learning to write Chinese.

UPROOTING BIASES ABOUT CHARACTER LEARNING

One bias circulating among teachers and students of the Chinese language is that a character's *meaning, pronunciation, and writing need to be learned at the same time.* Chinese textbooks typically include all three bits of information for each character or compound term as it is introduced, in addition to supplying details about grammatical function and examples of usage. Of course, these things are important, but to have to learn them all at once places an unreasonable burden on memory. Little wonder that the brain slows down or grinds to a complete halt.

The Chinese themselves are not faced with this problem. As children, they are exposed first to the spoken language, learning how to associate sounds with meanings. When the time comes to learn how to read, they already have at their disposal a solid basis of words whose sounds and meanings are familiar to them; all that remains is to associate those words with written forms. Doing so opens them to printed texts, which, in turn, helps them assimilate new words and characters. Those of us who come to the language as adults can gain a similar advantage by tying each of the character forms to a particular unit of pronunciation and meaning, a "key word" in English, that we already know.

Before you dismiss the idea of affixing English words to Chinese characters out of hand, consider this: all the Chinese dialects, no matter how mutually unintelligible they are when spoken, use the same characters for writing. These characters convey the same meaning, no matter how they are pronounced. What is more, when the Japanese use Chinese characters, they assign them still other pronunciations. In other words, there is nothing in the nature of a character dictating that it must be verbalized one way or another. Unlike students coming to Chinese from an alphabetically written language, the Japanese already know the meaning and writing of a great many of the characters. By the time you finish this course, you will be in a position similar to theirs. Of course, you will eventually need to learn Chinese pronunciations, just as Japanese students do. But adding difficult and unfamiliar sounds to a solid knowledge of character forms is a much more manageable task than trying to memorize meaning, pronunciation, and writing all at the same time.

If some separation of learning tasks seems reasonable, then why not acquire a sizable vocabulary of Chinese pronunciations and meanings first—as the Chinese children do—and then pick up writing later? After all, oral language is the older, more universal, and more ordinary means of communication. Hence the bias that *if anything is to be postponed, it should be the introduction of the writing system.* The truth is, written characters bring a high degree of clarity to the multiplicity of meanings carried by homophones in the spoken language. For example, even an ordinary pocket dictionary of Mandarin lists some 60 characters that are pronounced *yi* in one or another of its tonal variants, with at least 30 distinct characters in the fourth tone alone. Each of these characters carries its own meaning or meanings, which the simple syllable *yi* of itself cannot communicate. Beginning with characters and their meanings greatly reduces this ambiguity.

The idea that writing should come after speaking is bolstered by another, more pervasive bias: *the writing of characters is the most complex part of the language to learn.* In fact, it is a far simpler task than is often supposed, as these books hope to demonstrate. In addition, beginning with the writing leaves the student with solid units of form and meaning to which Chinese pronunciations can then be attached. Even more important, completing what is usually perceived to be the most challenging task first, and in a relatively short period of time, rather than leaving it for later, cannot help but motivate one to carry on with the language. Given high attrition rates among students of Chinese in the West, the role of such positive reinforcement is not to be discounted.

Yet another bias that needs uprooting is the idea that *characters can only be mastered through constant drill and repetition.* Traditional methods for approaching the Chinese writing system have been the same as those for learning alphabets: practice writing the characters one by one, over and over again, for as long as it takes. Whatever ascetic value there is in such an exercise, it is hardly the most efficient way to approach character study. The reason this bias has such a strong hold on students of Chinese is that persons completely ignorant of the Chinese writing system naturally rely on teachers who have learned characters from childhood. Surely a pedagogy with many centuries of history behind it and over a billion users demands our respect. Here again, the prevailing wisdom is deceptive.

Native speakers of Chinese are clearly in a position to teach a good many things about their language, but they are not necessarily qualified to answer questions from non-native speakers about how best to learn the characters, for the simple reason that they themselves have never been in the situation of having to ask such a question. Having begun their study as children, in whom the powers of abstraction were not yet developed and for whom rote memory was the only option, they cannot be expected to fully grasp the learning potential an adult brings to the study of the characters. As children, we were all good *imitators*, with few habits to get in the way of our absorption of new skills. But we did not become good *learners* until we had the ability to classify, categorize, and organize discreet bits of information into larger blocks. This is precisely what young children cannot do with character forms and why they have no choice but to rely on imitation and repetition. Whatever educational and social advantages there may be to having an entire school population study Chinese characters by writing them again and again from an early age, for the adult approaching the language from the outside it amounts to little more than a gigantic waste of time. A touch of irreverence towards current pedagogical conventions, along with a little rethinking of the way the characters are studied and the order in which they are learned, can produce far better results than simple reliance on methods designed for the teaching of children.

The approach followed in these pages incorporates important elements of all three broad areas into which cognitive learning strategies are thought to fall—organization, elaboration, and rehearsal—and entails a strong reliance on memory techniques or "mnemonics." The very word is sure to tap into predispositions against the use of mnemonics in general, and for the learning of Chinese characters in particular. Here, too, the biases run deep, and we can do little more in these introductory remarks than try to identify them and offer a brief response.[1]

For some, reservations about mnemonics are grounded in the image of disreputable charlatans who hype expensive memory-training courses as the key to a better job and a better life. It is true that exaggerated claims have been

1. For more developed arguments making a case for mnemonics, see K. L. Higbee, *Your Memory: How it Works and How to Improve it* (New York: Prentice-Hall, 1988); see also T. W. Richardson, "Chinese Character Memorization and Literacy: Theoretical and Empirical Perspectives on a Sophisticated Version of an Old Strategy," in Andreas Guder, Jiang Xin, and Wan Yexin, eds., 对外汉字的认知与教学 [The cognition, learning, and teaching of Chinese characters] (Beijing: Beijing Language and Culture University Press, 2007).

made, but empirical studies over the last several decades have clearly demonstrated that well-conceived mnemonic devices can be very useful for certain memory tasks. This has lead many scholars to recommend them as legitimate learning strategies.

These scholarly developments also help address another concern: *mnemonics are simply too bizarre or too silly to use.* Actually, they can be quite sophisticated and elegant. Surely the more important question is whether they work or not. The whole range of possibilities, from the silly to the sophisticated, leaves ample room for personal taste or preference in determining what best facilitates learning.

Still another apprehension some may have is that *mnemonic devices clutter the mind and separate the learner from the matter to be learned.* On the contrary, insofar as such devices provide meaning and organization that would not otherwise exist, they actually unclutter the mind. Besides, once recall for a particular item has become automatic, the mnemonic initially used to fix that item in memory usually falls away of its own accord.

The dominant bias against the use of mnemonics for learning Chinese characters is that *it is inappropriate to overstep the boundaries of current etymological knowledge, even more so when these liberties are taken without drawing attention to the fact. To do so is not to communicate the "truth" about the characters.* This complaint speaks directly to what you will meet in these pages. On one hand, much of the course is grounded in scholarly consensus on the history of the characters. On the other, we have not hesitated to ignore established etymologies whenever doing so seemed pedagogically useful. In fact, the course relies heavily on fictions of our own invention. At least two reasons support this choice. For one thing, even the most comprehensive account of how particular characters were formed may be far from the whole "truth" concerning them. Much remains speculative or unknown. For another, however reliable the etymological information may be, for most learners of Chinese it is not as crucial as finding relief for memory—which is what we have tried to provide here. Should a student later turn to etymological studies, the procedure we have followed will become more transparent, and the fact that we did not indicate each departure from an established etymology should not cause any obstacle to learning. With this, we lay the question of mnemonics to rest.

Two final and related biases require brief comment: (1) *the learning of individual characters in isolation from compound words and grammatical patterns is mistaken;* and (2) *a single key word is often inadequate to cover a character's meaning.*

We acknowledge that effective reading requires a knowledge of compound words and grammatical patterns; however, we concur with those who stress the value of learning individual characters well in order to solidify "the network of possible morphemes upon which all dual and multi-character words are built."[2] Similarly, we are aware that one-word definitions are of limited use; however, we agree with those who see them as a solid starting point for developing a richer and more nuanced understanding. The study of individual characters, each with a distinct meaning, is only a first step towards literacy in Chinese. For the rest, only a broad and prolonged contact with the written language will suffice.

A SHORT HISTORY OF THE COURSE

When James Heisig arrived in Japan some thirty years ago, he came with no knowledge of the language. Travels through Asia had delayed his arrival at the language school where he had been pre-enrolled by his sponsors. He decided to forego classes and "catch up" on his own by working through a stack of books on grammar and structure. Through conversations with teachers and other students he soon realized that he should not postpone the study of the kanji (as the Chinese characters are called in Japanese), which, all were agreed, was the biggest chore of all. Having no idea at all how the kanji "worked" in the language, yet having found his own pace, he decided—against the advice of nearly everyone around him—to continue to study on his own rather than join one of the beginners' classes. He began studying the kanji one month after his arrival.

The first few days he spent poring over whatever he could find on the history and etymology of Japanese characters, and examining the wide variety of systems on the market for studying them. It was during those days that the basic idea underlying the method of these books came to him. The following weeks he devoted himself day and night to experimenting with the idea, which worked well enough to encourage him to carry on with it. Before the month was out he had learned the meaning and writing of some 1,900 characters and had satisfied himself that he would retain what he had memorized. It was not long before he became aware that something extraordinary had taken place.

For himself, the method he was following seemed so simple, even infantile, that it was almost an embarrassment to talk about it. And it had happened as such a matter of course that he was quite unprepared for the reaction it caused. On the one hand, some at the school accused him of having a short-term pho-

2. E. B. Hayes, "The Relationship between 'Word Length' and Memorability among Non-Native Readers of Chinese Mandarin," *Journal of the Chinese Language Teacher's Association* 25/3 (1990), 38.

tographic memory that would fade with time. On the other, there were those who pressed him to write up his "methods" for their benefit, which he did. The resulting book, originally titled *Adventures in Kanji-Land* and changed in later printings to *Remembering the Kanji*, has gone through numerous editions and been adapted for German, Spanish, French, and Portuguese.[3]

Timothy Richardson, a language teacher who had studied some Chinese at the university level, came upon a copy of *Remembering the Kanji* in the early 1990s. He quickly became interested in the possibility of adapting the work for students of Chinese. In subsequent doctoral work at the University of Texas at Austin, he focused on the method for his dissertation and subjected it to an extensive examination in terms of relevant theory and research.[4] This required careful consideration not only of the underlying cognitive processes that the method might be expected to involve but also of its reasonableness in terms of prevailing perspectives on vocabulary development and reading. His work also entailed the compilation of a new list of 1,000 high-frequency Chinese characters and their integration into a skeletal Chinese version of Heisig's original book. The results were so encouraging that Richardson sent a copy to Heisig with the suggestion that they join forces on a complete Chinese edition. Thus it was that our collaboration began.

Two immediate problems presented themselves: first, whether to opt for traditional Chinese writing or to follow the simplified forms of Mainland China; and second, how many characters to include, and which ones.

The first problem was eventually resolved with a decision to produce two parallel courses, one for each system of writing. Arguments for a learner's beginning with one or the other each have their points, and it is not our wish to take sides in the debate, even though both of us began with traditional characters. That said, the student should know that certain overlaps in the books would only cause confusion if the two versions are studied simultaneously. If your aim is to achieve fluency in writing both systems, then it is preferable to

3. *Adventures in Kanji-Land* (1978), subsequently reissued as *Remembering the Kanji* (Honolulu: University of Hawai'i Press, 2007, 5th edition, 22nd printing). Other language editions include *Kanji para recordar 1: Curso mnemotécnico para el aprendizaje de la escritura y el significado de los caracteres japoneses,* with Marc Bernabé and Verònica Calafell (Barcelona: Editorial Herder, 2005, 3rd printing); *Die Kanji lernen und behalten 1. Bedeutung und Schreibweise der japanischen Schriftzeichen,* with Robert Rauther (Frankfurt-am-Main: Vittorio Klostermann Verlag, 2006, 2nd printing); *Les Kanji dans la tête: Apprendre à ne pas oublier le sens et l'écriture des caractères japonais,* Yves Maniette (2005, 2nd printing); *Kanji: Imaginar para aprender,* with Rafael Shoji (São Paulo: JBC Editora, 2007).

4. T. W. Richardson, *James W. Heisig's System for Remembering Kanji: An Examination of Relevant Theory and Research, and a 1,000-Character Adaptation for Chinese.* Doctoral dissertation, The University of Texas at Austin, 1998.

begin with the traditional. If you are sure you will be content with recognizing the traditional and writing the simplified, then begin with the latter.

The first step to resolving our second problem was to settle on introducing a total of 3,000 most frequently used characters. This number may fall below the 3,500 to 4,500 characters that are generally thought necessary for full proficiency, but it also happens to represent about 99.5% of the characters found in running Chinese texts, as large-scale frequency counts show. What is more, students who have learned to write these 3,000 characters will be equipped with the tools for learning to write additional characters as the need arises. Next, since the top 1,000 entries in our complete frequency list account for approximately 90% of characters in running texts,[5] we decided to include all of them in the first book of both the traditional and simplified sets.

Frequency questions aside, the figure of 3,000 characters also makes available certain "economies of scale" that are possible with the method, which fewer characters would not. In the business world, economies of scale are said to arise when an increase in the scale of production leads to a decline in costs per unit. If we are producing widgets, the production cost per widget goes down as more are produced, because the initial investment in machinery has already been made. Similarly, using the method laid out in these pages to learn 3,000 characters, rather than 1,000, for instance, results in a decrease in learning cost per character, because an investment in basic mental "machinery" is largely made early on. In other words, the return on time and effort expended at the outset yields much better returns as more characters are learned.

When it came to deciding just which characters to include and on what grounds, the challenge proved far greater than we had counted on. Frequency lists compiled by specialists do indeed exist. Some of them list only traditional characters and others only simplified; some of them are more formal and others less so; some of them are more technical and some less so; and so forth. What we wanted, however, was a general-use list of 3,000 characters that would apply to the whole of the Chinese-speaking world. In a strict sense, such a list is not possible. If you were to set two pages of identical Chinese text side by

5. Based on three lists we consulted that include such data, the 3,000 most frequently used characters comprise 99.56%, 99.18%, and 99.43% of the total number of characters in their respective databases, while the top 1,000 characters comprise 90.3%, 89.14%, and 91.12% respectively. The three sources, in order, are: 新聞語料字頻統計表——語料庫爲本研究系列之一 [Corpus-based frequency count of characters in Journal Chinese: Corpus based research series no. 1]. Technical Report no. 93-01 (Taipei: Academia Sinica Institute of Information Science, 1993); J. Da, "Modern Chinese Character Frequency List 现代语单字频率列表," Chinese text computing. <http://lingua.mtsu.edu/chinese-computing> (2004); and C. H. Tsai, "Frequency of Usage and Number of Strokes of Chinese Characters." <http://technology.cht-sai.org/charfreq/> (1996).

side, one in simplified characters, the other in traditional, about two-thirds of the characters would have exactly the same form on both sides. In other words, about one-third of characters in common use differ in form from one set to the other. Sometimes the discrepancies are slight, sometimes significant. Occasionally, two or more frequently used traditional characters are reduced to a single simplified character. Taking these and other considerations into account, we assembled a core list that was then adjusted to arrive at 3,000 characters for each of the two courses.

Sparing the reader a full account of the actual mechanics of completing the task, not to mention the many detours and dead-ends encountered along the way, the steps we took were basically these: We compared four major frequency lists, two traditional and two simplified,[6] and supplemented our findings with yet another frequency list.[7] All characters that were included among the top 3,050 on at least three of the four major lists—including those of exactly the same form and those of differing form but equivalent meaning across the traditional/simplified divide—were moved to a master list. Some 2,860 traditional characters, and just under 2,800 of their equivalents on the simplified side, met these criteria, the great majority of them appearing among the top 3,050 on all four lists.

In order to select the additional characters needed to bring this common master list up to 3,000 characters, a variety of other factors had to be juggled. Some characters, for example, clearly met the criteria on two lists and fell just outside of them on the two others, while others qualified on two of the four major lists and yet were given a high ranking on the supplemental list mentioned above. In some cases, items falling just outside of frequency criteria are important as components of other characters or often show up in beginning Chinese textbooks. (The character 餃/饺, which figures as the first half of the compound for "Chinese dumplings," is a clear example of this and has been included in Book 2 of each of the courses.) Taking all these factors into account, we added more than 100 new characters to the master list. Another 14 characters representing useful nouns that did not quite meet the frequency criteria brought the total to 3,000 characters on the traditional side. Completing the simplified list required some 75 characters more to compensate for character amalgamations resulting from the simplification process.

6. In addition to the three lists mentioned in footnote 5, see also 现代汉语频率词典 [Modern Chinese frequency dictionary] (Beijing: Beijing Language Institute, 1986), as cited in J. E. Dew, *6000 Chinese Words: A Vocabulary Frequency Handbook for Chinese Language Teachers and Students* (Taipei: SMC Publishing Inc., 1999).

7. 國家言文字工作委 [National Working Committee on the Written Language], 现代汉语 常用字表 [Modern Chinese frequently-used characters list] (Beijing: Yuwen Press, 1988).

The next step was to extract a selection of 1,000 characters that would serve as a foundation for the Book 1 of each of the courses. As part of the research for his dissertation, Richardson had found 580 characters that figured among the top 1,000 characters in five different sources.[8] This was the starting point. Another 199 were included by taking characters that were in the top 1,000 in four of those sources and similarly ranked on either of two frequency lists that had not been consulted in the original research.[9] Another 74 were included by taking characters that occurred in the top 1,000 in three of the original sources and similarly ranked on *both* of the new lists, bringing the total up to 853. An additional 74 characters that had appeared among the top 1,000 items on at least three of the four major lists gave us 927.

At each step of the way, an attempt was made to avoid arbitrariness, but the challenge was to relax frequency criteria only enough to include the number of characters we needed and no more. In selecting the remaining 73 characters of the total 1,000, we felt that pedagogical concerns and personal judgments should be given greater weight, because using frequency criteria alone had generated some anomalies that needed to be addressed. For example, frequency dictated the inclusion of the characters for "winter" and "spring," but not for "summer" and "fall"; for "mama," but not for "papa." We therefore consulted a list of the 969 characters taught in the first four grades of elementary school in the Republic of China (ROC).[10] Of these, 810 were exactly the same as the 927 we had selected based on frequency alone. The remaining 73 characters were drawn from the ROC list, always with an eye on the basic frequency lists. As an added check on the simplified side, we compared our list against one of the original sources, a list of the 1,000 characters most frequently used in textbooks in elementary and high schools in the People's Republic of China (PRC).[11] The two lists had 904 characters in common, confirming the pedagogical value of the final list. Of course, all of the items on both the ROC and PRC lists that did not make it onto our list of the 1,000

---

8. *Corpus-Based Frequency Count of Characters in Journal Chinese*; M. K. M. Chan and B. Z. He, "A Study of the 1,000 Most Frequently Used Chinese Characters and their Simplification," *Journal of the Chinese Language Teachers Association* 23/3 (1988), 49–68; R. M.-W. Choy, *Read and Write Chinese* (San Francisco, California: China West Book, 1990); *Chinese Vocabulary Cards* (New Haven: Far Eastern Publications, Yale University, n.d.); Tsai, "Frequency of Usage and Number of Strokes of Chinese Characters." Note that Choy's frequency data seem to have been taken from a 1928 study by Chen Hegin.

9. See *Modern Chinese Frequency Dictionary*; Da, "Modern Chinese Character Frequency List."

10. "Target Characters by School Grade: Taiwan," as listed by J. Lau at 黃橋 [Yellow-Bridge] <http://www.yellowbridge.com/language/fc-options.php?deck=tw>.

11. See Chan and He, "A Study of the 1,000 Most Frequently Used Chinese Characters."

most frequently used characters were included elsewhere in the master list of 3,000, many of them appearing among the 500 supplemental characters found in Book 1 of both the simplified and traditional courses.

THE BASICS OF THE METHOD

There is no better way to understand the method followed in these pages than to start using it. Still, readers have a right to know what they are getting into, so a brief explanation seems in order.

To begin with, all the characters are made up of pieces, or "primitive elements" as we shall call them here. These are the basic building blocks out of which all characters are constructed. Over 200 of these have been singled out as "radicals," which are used in the organization of character dictionaries, but there are many others. Individual characters can also serve as primitive elements in other more complicated characters. If one is really determined to learn to write Chinese, and not just memorize a small number of characters to meet course requirements, it makes sense to take full advantage of these component parts by arranging the characters in the order best suited to memory.

This course begins, therefore, with a handful of uncomplicated primitive elements and combines them to make as many characters as possible. More elements are then thrown into the mix, a few at a time, allowing new characters to be learned—and so on, until the entire list has been exhausted. This process has a number of important advantages, not the least of which is that learning new elements and characters also invariably reinforces what has already been learned.

Because we are dividing the course into two books of 1,500 characters each and including the most important 1,000 characters in the first volume, not all of the characters that could be learned at a given point are actually introduced in their logical sequence; some of them are saved for later. In the long run, there is no real reduction in efficiency here. It was just a matter of relegating less frequently used characters to Book 2.

Each primitive element is assigned its own concrete image, after which the images are arranged into a composite picture associated with a definition, a unique "key word," given for each character. The key word is meant to capture a character's principal meaning, or at least one of its more important meanings. It is often concrete and visually suggestive, but it can also be conceptual and abstract. In any event, it is the key word, or its use in a familiar English phrase, that sets the stage for the composition of the elements into a single "story." As you will see, the stories are meant to stretch your imagination and get you close enough to the characters to befriend them, let them surprise you, inspire you, enlighten you, resist you, and seduce you; to make you smile or shudder or otherwise react emotionally in such a way as to fix the imagery in memory.

The whole process employs what we may call *imaginative memory*, by which we mean the faculty to recall images created purely in the mind, with no actual or remembered visual stimuli behind them. We are used to hills and roads, to the faces of people and the skylines of cities, to flowers, animals, and the phenomena of nature associated with *visual memory*. And while only a fraction of what we see is readily recalled, we are confident that, given proper attention, anything we choose to remember, we can. That confidence is lacking in the world of the characters, which generally show a remarkable lack of connection to the normal visual patterns with which we are comfortable. It is possible, however, to harness the powers of imagination to give meaning to character elements that visual memory is admittedly ill adapted for remembering. In fact, most students of the Chinese writing system do this from time to time on their own, devising their own imaginative aids, but without ever developing an organized approach to their use.

The stories and plots you will meet in these pages are all drawn with words; there are no pictures or cartoons to control or limit the way your imagination handles the information provided. There is no correct way of imagining; the sole criterion is that it work for you (though we will make frequent suggestions). The only thing you will be asked to draw are the characters themselves. But what you *see* when you make your drawing will be all yours, and most assuredly different from what scholars and historians see when they analyze the characters. A whole imaginary world will come to life for you out of the primitive elements. The more vividly you can visualize the things that inhabit this world, the less need there will be to review what you have learned. Many, if not most, of the characters can be remembered at first encounter, with no need to drill them later other than through the normal reinforcement of actually using them.

As you come to write more and more of the characters in practice, you will find that they all but write themselves once you have set pen to paper, much the same as the alphabet already does for you. In time you will find, as previously suggested, that most of the imagery and key-word meanings will have served their purpose and recede from active memory. Some, we should warn you, will stay with you forever.

THE DESIGN OF THIS BOOK

You will be guided at every step of the way, but a few things about the design of this book need to be clarified at the outset. Clusters of characters have been arranged into lessons of varying length. Many, but not all, focus on a particular class of primitive elements. Nothing more is intended by this than a way to break up the monotony and give you a sense of your overall progress. Each individual character is given its own frame, as in the example below:

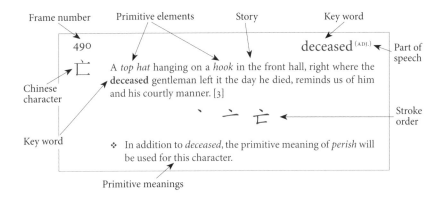

Since the goal is not simply to remember a certain number of characters, but to learn *how* to remember them (and others not included in the course), this book has been divided into three parts. The first, *Stories*, provides a full associative story for each character. By directing the student's attention, at least for the length of time it takes to read the explanation and relate it to the written form of the character, we do most of the work, even as the student acquires a feeling for the method. In the next part, *Plots*, only skeletal outlines of stories are presented, leaving it to the student to work out the details by drawing on personal memory and fantasy. The final part, *Elements*, comprises the major portion of the book, and provides only the key word and the primitive meanings, leaving the remainder of the process to the student.

The stroke order is given in a hand-drawn font. You will notice variations from time to time between the printed form and the hand-drawn form of the same character. This is due to the fact that historical variants of some characters are in common use, especially on the traditional side, and to the fact that there has been no strict standardization of character forms. A given element will occasionally appear in different variations within the same Chinese font. Rather than draw attention to each instance of this, and in order to spare the user unnecessary frustration, we have brought consistency of form to all the characters, except where general usage suggests otherwise. It is best to be aware of these character and font inconsistencies from the start, since sooner or later you will run into them in print and will need to know how to process them. In any case, we recommend that you stick with the hand-drawn forms as a model for writing.

There are five indexes included at the end of each volume; those in Book 2 are cumulative for the whole course. Index I shows all the characters in their hand-drawn form, in the order in which they are introduced in this book. Since discrepancies with the printed form do occur, the student would do well to consult this index in case of doubt. Beneath each character in Index I is its pronunciation, provided here for reference purposes. The list of elements singled out as primitives proper and brought together in Index II is restricted to basic elements that are not themselves characters, or at least not treated as such in this course. Index III organizes the characters first by number of strokes, and then by initial stroke. Index IV arranges the characters according to their pronunciation and is intended to facilitate the search for particular characters. Finally, Index V contains all the key-word and primitive meanings.

CONCLUDING COMMENTS

Before you start out on the course plotted in the following pages, your attention should be drawn to a few final points. First, you must be warned about setting out too quickly. It should not be assumed that, because the first characters are so elementary, they can be skipped over hastily. The method presented here needs to be learned step by step, lest you find yourself forced later to retreat to the first stages and start over. Some 20 or 25 characters per day would not be excessive for someone who has only a couple of hours to give to study. If you were to study them full time, there is no reason why all 1,500 characters in Book 1 could not be learned successfully in four to five weeks. Such a claim is bound to raise more eyebrows than hopes among experienced teachers, but Heisig's own experience with Japanese kanji, and reports from students around the world, bear that estimate out. In any case, by the time the first 200 characters have been studied, you should have discovered a rate of progress suitable to the time available.

Second, the repeated advice given to study the characters with pad and pencil should be taken seriously. While simply remembering the characters does not, you will discover, demand that they be written, there is really no better way to improve the aesthetic appearance of your writing and acquire a "natural feel" for the flow of the characters than by writing them. The method of this course will spare you the toil of writing the same character over and over in order to learn it, but it will not supply the fluency at writing that comes only with constant practice. If pen and paper are inconvenient, you can always make do with the palm of the hand, as the Chinese themselves do. It provides a convenient square space for tracing characters with your index finger when riding in a bus or walking down the street.

Third, the characters are best reviewed by beginning with the key word, progressing to the respective story, and then writing the character itself. Once you have been able to perform these steps, reversing the order follows as a matter of course. More will be said about this later in the book.

Fourth, it is important to note that the best order for *learning* the characters is by no means the best order for *remembering* them. They need to be recalled when and where they are met, not in the sequence in which they are presented here. For that purpose, recommendations are given in Lesson 5 for designing flash cards for random review.

Finally, perhaps only one who has seen the method through to the end can appreciate both how truly uncomplicated and obvious it is, and how accessible to any average student willing to invest time and effort. But while the method is *simple* and does eliminate a great deal of inefficiency, the task is still not an *easy* one. It requires as much stamina, concentration, and imagination as one can bring to it. Of that, too, we are convinced.

ACKNOWLEDGMENTS

We would like to express our gratitude to Robert Roche for the generous assistance he provided that enabled us to complete these books, as well as for the constant stimulus and many useful suggestions he has given us these past several years. A special word of thanks also to the staff and fellows of the Nanzan Institute for Religion and Culture, who provided the facilities and the environment to make a difficult task easier, and to Brigham Young University Hawaii for facilitating our collaborative work at Nanzan during the winter semester of 2007. Among those who lent their expertise to this project, Tsu-Pin Huang and Dr. Yifen Beus were especially helpful and generous with their time. Finally, we wish to acknowledge the support and interest in the project shown by Pat Crosby, Keith Leber, and the editorial team at the University of Hawai'i Press.

Nagoya, Japan
9 August 2007

Stories

LESSON 1

LET US BEGIN with a group of 15 characters, all of which you probably knew before you ever cracked the covers of this book. Each character has been provided with a *key word*—a simple word or phrase—to represent the basic meaning. Some of these characters will also serve later as *primitive elements* to help form other characters, often taking a different meaning, sometimes a purely fanciful invention, in the process. A remark preceded by a special symbol (❖) has been appended to alert you to the change in meaning.

The *number of strokes* of each character is given in square brackets at the end of each explanation, followed by the stroke-by-stroke *order of writing*. It cannot be stressed enough how important it is to learn to write the strokes of each character in proper order. As easy as these first characters may seem, study them all with a pad and pencil to get into the habit from the very start.

Finally, note that each key word has been carefully chosen and should not be tampered with in any way if you want to avoid confusion later on.

1	one

一

In Chinese characters, the number **one** is laid on its side, unlike the Roman numeral I which stands upright. As you would expect, it is written from left to right. [1]

一

❖ When this character is used as a primitive element, the keyword meaning is often discarded, since it is too abstract to be of much help. Instead, the single horizontal stroke takes on the meaning of *floor* or *ceiling*, depending on its position: if it stands above another primitive, it means *ceiling*; if below, *floor*.

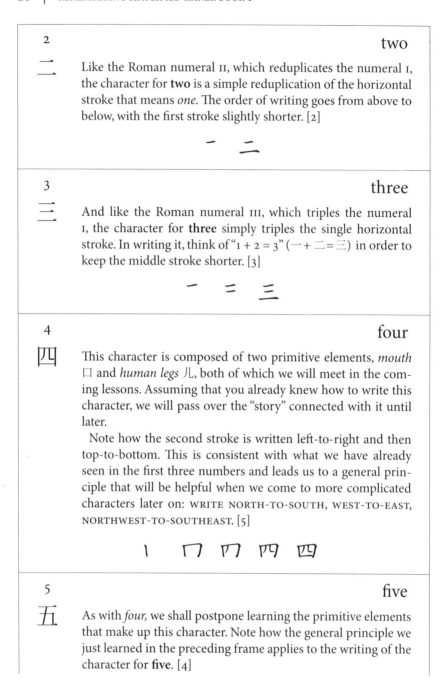

2   **two**

二

Like the Roman numeral II, which reduplicates the numeral I, the character for **two** is a simple reduplication of the horizontal stroke that means *one*. The order of writing goes from above to below, with the first stroke slightly shorter. [2]

3   **three**

三

And like the Roman numeral III, which triples the numeral I, the character for **three** simply triples the single horizontal stroke. In writing it, think of "1 + 2 = 3" ($-+ \equiv = \equiv$) in order to keep the middle stroke shorter. [3]

4   **four**

四

This character is composed of two primitive elements, *mouth* □ and *human legs* 儿, both of which we will meet in the coming lessons. Assuming that you already knew how to write this character, we will pass over the "story" connected with it until later.

Note how the second stroke is written left-to-right and then top-to-bottom. This is consistent with what we have already seen in the first three numbers and leads us to a general principle that will be helpful when we come to more complicated characters later on: WRITE NORTH-TO-SOUTH, WEST-TO-EAST, NORTHWEST-TO-SOUTHEAST. [5]

5   **five**

五

As with *four*, we shall postpone learning the primitive elements that make up this character. Note how the general principle we just learned in the preceding frame applies to the writing of the character for **five**. [4]

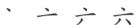

| 6 | six |

六 The primitives here are *top hat* and *animal legs*. Once again, we glide over them until later. [4]

| 7 | seven |

七 Note that the first stroke "cuts" clearly through the second. This distinguishes **seven** from the character for *spoon* 匕 (FRAME 453), in which the horizontal stroke either stops short or, depending on the font, extends just slightly beyond the vertical stroke. [2]

❖ As a primitive, this form takes on the meaning of *diced,* i.e., "cut" into little pieces, consistent both with the way the character is written and with its association with the character for *cut* 切 to be learned in a later lesson (FRAME 85).

| 8 | eight |

八 Just as the Arabic numeral "8" is composed of a small circle followed by a larger one, so the character for **eight** is composed of a short line followed by a longer line that leans towards it without touching it. And just as the "lazy 8" ∞ is the mathematical symbol for "infinity," so the expanse opened up below these two strokes sometimes carries the sense in Chinese of something "all-encompassing."

Note how the printed character on the left and the hand-drawn character below differ somewhat in form. Be sure to imitate the hand-drawn form when you practice writing. [2]

9	nine

九

If you take care to remember the stroke order of this character, you will not have trouble later keeping it distinct from the character for *power* 力 (FRAME 732). [2]

丿 九

❖ When this character is used as a primitive, we shall take it to refer to the game of *baseball*, the meaning being derived from the *nine* players who make up a team.

10	ten

十

Turn this character 45° either way and you have the x used for the Roman numeral **ten**. [2]

一 十

❖ As a primitive, this character sometimes keeps its meaning of *ten* and sometimes signifies *needle*, this latter derived from the character for *needle* 针 (FRAME 283). Since the primitive is used in the character itself, there is no need to worry about confusing the two. In fact, we shall be following this procedure regularly.

11	mouth

口

Like several of the first characters we shall learn, the character for **mouth** is a clear pictograph. Since there are no circular shapes in the characters, the square must be used to depict the circle. [3]

丨 冂 口

❖ As a primitive, this form also means *mouth*. Any of the range of possible images that the word suggests—an opening or entrance to a cave, a river, a bottle, or even the largest hole in your head—can be used for the primitive meaning.

12

日

day

This character is intended to be a pictograph of the sun. Recalling what we said in the previous frame about round forms, it is easy to detect the circle and the big smile that characterize our simplest drawings of the sun—like those yellow badges with the words, "Have a nice **day**!" [4]

丨 冂 月 日

❖ Used as a primitive, this character can mean *sun* or *day* or a *tongue wagging in the mouth*. This latter meaning, incidentally, derives from an old character meaning something like "sayeth" (see FRAME 1499) and written almost exactly the same, except that the latter is more square in shape (曰) than *sun* (日). In any case, as a primitive element the shape will alter according to its position in the full character and this distinction will become irrelevant.

13

月

month

This character is actually a picture of the moon, with the two horizontal lines representing the left eye and mouth of the mythical "man in the moon." (Actually, the Chinese see a hare in the moon, but it is a little farfetched to find one in the character.) And one **month**, of course, is one cycle of the moon. [4]

丿 几 月 月

❖ As a primitive element, this character can take on the sense of *moon, flesh,* or *part of the body.* The reasons for the latter two meanings will be explained in a later chapter.

14

田

rice field

Another pictograph, this character looks like a bird's-eye view of a **rice field** divided into four plots. Take care in writing this character to get the order of the strokes correct. You will find that it follows perfectly the principle stated in FRAME 4. [5]

丨 冂 冂 田 田

❖ When used as a primitive element, this character's most common meaning is *rice field*, but now and again it will take the meaning of *brains* from the fact that it looks a bit like that tangle of gray matter nestled under our skulls.

15

eye

目

Here again, if we round out the corners of this character and curve the two middle strokes into the shape of an iris, we get something resembling an **eye**. [5]

丨　冂　冂　月　目

❖ As a primitive, the character keeps its sense of *eye,* or to be more specific, an *eyeball.* When placed in the surroundings of a complex character, the primitive can be turned on its side (ᵐ) and take on the additional meaning of a *net.*

Although only 10 of the 15 characters treated in this lesson are formally listed as primitives—the elements that join together to make up other characters—some of the others may also take on that function from time to time, only not with enough frequency to merit learning them as separate primitive elements and attaching special meanings to them. In other words, whenever one of the characters already learned is used in another character, it will retain its key-word meaning unless we have assigned it a special primitive meaning. Even in these cases, however, the original key-word meaning can be used.

LESSON 2

IN THIS LESSON we learn what a "primitive element" is by using the first 15 characters as pieces that can be fitted together to form new characters—17 of them to be exact. Whenever the primitive meaning differs from the key-word meaning, you may want to go back to the original frame to refresh your memory. From now on, though, you should learn *both* the key-word and the primitive meaning of new characters as they appear. Index 2 contains a complete list of all the primitive elements in the book.

16	ancient

古 The primitive elements that compose this character are *ten* and *mouth,* but you may find it easier to remember it as a pictograph of a tombstone with a cross on top. Just think back to one of those graveyards you have visited, or better still, used to play in as a child, with **ancient** inscriptions on the tombstones.

This departure from the primitive elements in favor of a pictograph will take place now and again at these early stages, and almost never after that. So you need not worry about cluttering up your memory with too many character "drawings." [5]

❖ Used as a primitive element, this character keeps its key-word sense of *ancient,* but care should be taken to make that abstract notion as graphic as possible.

17	recklessly

胡 Everyone knows what a new *moon* is: the first phase when the *moon* is illuminated 0%. So, presumably, an *ancient moon,* like the one in this character, is lit up at 100% wattage. And we all know what that means: people tend to get a little "loony" and start acting **recklessly.** [9]

古　胡

18   leaf

叶

The Chinese are famous for taking a **leaf** and turning it into medicine. In this character, there are no less than *ten* different types of **leaves** that go into the concoction that the herbal doctor is stuffing into your mouth. The problem is, she didn't take the trouble to grind them up with her mortar and pestle, but is shoveling them into your *mouth* just as they came off the tree. Look at the character and you can see how the *ten* **leaves** are way too much for the one small *mouth* to handle. [5]

口   叶

19   I (literary)

吾

There are a number of characters for the word **I**, but this one is restricted to literary use in Chinese. We need a sufficiently stuffy connotation for the key word, for which the sense of a "perceiving subject" should do just fine. Now the one place in our bodies that all *five* senses are concentrated in is the head, which has no less than *five mouths*: 2 nostrils, 2 ears, and 1 mouth. Hence, *five mouths* = **I**. [7]

一   丁   开   五   五   吾   吾

20   companion

朋

The first **companion** that God made, as the Bible story goes, was Eve. Upon seeing her, Adam exclaimed, "*Flesh* of my *flesh!*" And that is precisely what this character says in so many strokes. [8]

月   朋

21   bright

明

Among nature's **bright** lights, there are two that the biblical story of creation has God set in the sky: the *sun* to rule over the day and the *moon* to rule the night. Each of them has come to represent one of the common connotations of this key word: the *sun*, the **bright** insight of the clear thinker, and the *moon*, the **bright** intuition of the poet and the seer. [8]

日　明

22　sing

唱

This one is easy! You have one *mouth* making no noise (the choirmaster) and two *mouths with wagging tongues* (the minimum for a chorus). So when you hear the key word **sing**, think of the Vienna Boys' Choir or the Mormon Tabernacle Choir and the character is yours forever. [11]

口　口日　唱

23　sparkling

晶

What else can the word **sparkling** suggest if not a diamond? And if you've ever held a diamond up to the light, you will have noticed how every facet of it becomes like a miniature *sun*. This character is a picture of a tiny *sun* in three places (that is, "everywhere"), to give the sense of something **sparkling** all over the place. Just like a diamond. In writing the primitive elements three times, note again how the rule for writing given in FRAME 4 holds true not only for the strokes in each individual element but also for the disposition of the elements in the character as a whole. [12]

日　日　晶

24　goods

品

As in the character for *sparkling*, the triplication of a single element in this character indicates "everywhere" or "heaps of." When we think of **goods** in modern industrial society, we think of what has been mass-produced—that is to say, produced for the "masses" of open *mouths* waiting like fledglings in a nest to "consume" whatever comes their way. [9]

口　口　品

| 25 | prosperous |

昌

What we mentioned in the previous two frames about three of something meaning "everywhere" or "heaps of" was not meant to be taken lightly. In this character we see two *suns*, one atop the other, which, if we are not careful, is easily confused in memory with the three *suns* of *sparkling*. Focus on the number this way: since we speak of **prosperous** times as *sunny*, what could be more **prosperous** than a sky with two *suns* in it? Just be sure to actually SEE them there. [8]

日　昌

| 26 | early |

早

This character is actually a picture of the first flower of the day, which we shall, in defiance of botanical science, call the *sun-flower*, since it begins with the element for *sun* and is held up on a stem with leaves (the pictographic representation of the final two strokes). This time, however, we shall ignore the pictograph and imagine *sun*flowers with *needles* for stems, which can be plucked and used to darn your socks.

The sense of **early** is easily remembered if one thinks of the *sun*flower as the **early** riser in the garden, because the *sun*, showing favoritism towards its namesake, shines on it before all the others (see FRAME 10). [6]

日　旦　早

❖ As a primitive element, this character takes the meaning of *sunflower*, which was used to make the abstract key word *early* more graphic.

| 27 | rising sun |

旭

The key word here immediately suggests the islands located to the east of China, which would make it, from China's point of view, the Land of the **Rising Sun**, a name easily associated with Japan's national flag. If you can picture two seams running down that great red *sun*, and then imagine it sitting on a *base-ball* bat for a flagpole, you have a slightly irreverent—but not altogether inaccurate—picture of how the sport has caught on in the Land of the **Rising Sun**. [6]

丿 九 九 旭 旭 旭

---

28 generation

世

We generally consider one **generation** as a period of thirty (or *ten* plus *ten* plus *ten*) years. If you look at this character in its completed form—not in its stroke order—you will see three *tens*. When writing it, think of the lower horizontal lines as "addition" lines written under numbers to add them up. Thus: *ten* "plus" *ten* "plus" *ten* = thirty. Actually, it's a lot easier doing it with a pencil than reading it in a book. [5]

一 十 卅 卅 世

---

29 stomach

胃

You will need to refer back to FRAMES 13 and 14 here for the special meaning of the two primitive elements that make up this character: *brain* and *flesh (part of the body)*. What the character says, if you look at it, is that the *part of the body* that keeps the *brain* in working order is the **stomach**. To keep the elements in proper order, when you write this character think of the *brain* as being "held up" by the *flesh*. [9]

田 胃

---

30 daybreak

旦

The obvious sign of **daybreak** is the *sun* peeking out over the horizon, which is pretty much what this character depicts. If you can imagine the *sun* poking its head out through a hole in your *floor*, however, you will have an easier time remembering this character. [5]

日 旦

We end this lesson with two final pictographic characters that happen to be among the easiest to recognize for their form, but among the most difficult to write. We introduce them here to run an early test on whether or not you have been paying close attention to the stroke order of the characters you have been learning.

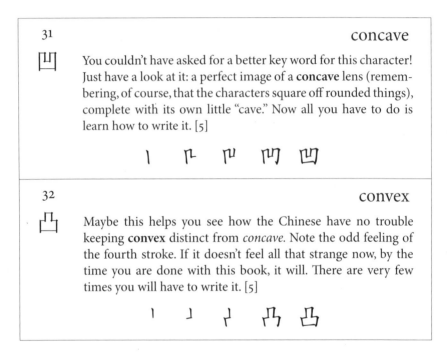

31	concave

You couldn't have asked for a better key word for this character! Just have a look at it: a perfect image of a **concave** lens (remembering, of course, that the characters square off rounded things), complete with its own little "cave." Now all you have to do is learn how to write it. [5]

32	convex

Maybe this helps you see how the Chinese have no trouble keeping **convex** distinct from *concave*. Note the odd feeling of the fourth stroke. If it doesn't feel all that strange now, by the time you are done with this book, it will. There are very few times you will have to write it. [5]

LESSON 3

AFTER LESSON 2, you should now have some idea of how an apparently complex and difficult character can be broken down into simple elements that make remembering it a great deal easier. After completing this lesson you should have a clearer idea of how the course is laid out. We merely add a couple of primitive elements to the characters we already know and see how many new characters we can form—in this case, 18 in all—and when we run out, add more primitives. And so on, until there are no characters left.

In Lesson 3 you will also be introduced to primitive elements that are not themselves characters but only used to construct other characters. These are marked with a special symbol [❖] instead of a number. There is no need to make a special effort to memorize them. The sheer frequency with which most of them show up should make remembering them automatic.

❖	a drop of

\

The meaning of this primitive is obvious from the first moment you look at it, though just what it will be **a drop of** will differ from case to case. The important thing is not to think of it as something insignificant like a "drop in the bucket" but as something so important that it can change the whole picture—like **a drop of** arsenic in your mother-in-law's coffee. [1]

, ＼

❖ In the first examples that follow, this primitive is written from right to left, but there are times when it can be slanted left to right. In addition, as we will see, the handwritten form used here will sometimes be at odds with the printed form. Finally, the *drop* will occasionally be stretched out a bit. (In cases where you have trouble remembering this, it may help to think of it as an *eyedropper* dripping drops of something or other.) If you follow the hand-drawn forms given here, you will never go wrong. Examples will follow in this lesson.

walking stick

This primitive element is a picture of just what it looks like: a cane or **walking stick**. It carries with it the connotations of lameness and whatever else one associates with the use of a cane. Rarely—but very rarely—it will be laid on its side. Whenever this occurs, it will ALWAYS be driven through the middle of some other primitive element. In this way, you need not worry about confusing it with the primitive meanings of *one*. [1]

33

oneself

You can think of this character as a stylized pictograph of the nose, that little *drop* that Mother Nature set between your *eyes*. The Chinese often refer to themselves by pointing a finger at their nose—giving us an easy way to remember the character for **oneself**. [6]

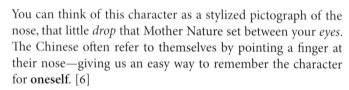

* ❖ The same meaning of *oneself* can be kept when this character is used as a primitive element, but you will generally find it better to give it the meaning of *nose* or *nostrils*, both because it accords with the story above and because it is the first part of the character for *nose* (FRAME 617).

34

white

The color **white** is a mixture of all the primary colors, both for pigments and for light, as we see when a prism breaks up the rays of the *sun*. Hence, a single *drop* of *sun* spells **white**. [5]

′　ⸯ　冂　白　白

* ❖ As a primitive, this character can either retain its meaning of *white* or take the more graphic meaning of a *white bird* or *dove*. This stems from the fact that it appears at the top of the character for *bird*, which we shall get to later (FRAME 1438).

35 百 hundred

When the Japanese borrowed the Chinese characters, they often played with their shapes to find interesting connections. For example, they came to refer to a person's 99th birthday as the start of the "*white* year" because *white* is the character you are left with if you subtract *one* from a **hundred**. [6]

一 丆 丆 万 百 百

36 皂 soap

Whatever the color of the **soap** that this character refers to, it does the same trick of *cutting* the grease and grime to make things *white*. That's a bit too abstract and reasonable, though, so you may want to imagine looking at the **soap** under a microscope and seeing little whirling blades *dicing* the blotches of dirt one by one until everything turns *white*. [7]

白 白 皂

37 旧 old

Like many of us, when *days* get **old**, they, too, need a *walking stick* to get around. Think of the phrase "the good **old** *days*," and the *walking stick* should take care of itself. [5]

丨 旧

38 中 middle (N./ADJ.)

The elements here are a *walking stick* and a *mouth*. The particular connotation we will associate with the key word **middle** is that period of life known as **middle** age, so called because it is the time in your life when you have trouble with your expanding "**middle.**" More often than not, the expansion has to do with eating more and moving around less. This character has the grotesque image of a person with a *walking stick* jammed into his *mouth*, the more easily to shovel food in without the interference of the tedious exercise of opening and closing it. [4]

Note the indicator that the character for **middle** can be used as either a noun or an adjective. Where no part of speech is indicated for a key word, assume the most common. In the case of the former frame, for example, *soap* might be taken as a verb, but one's first thought goes to the noun, which is a good place to start for that character. Be aware, though, that even where one part of speech is indicated for a character, other possibilities may exist.

39   thousand

This character is almost too simple to pull apart, but for the sake of practice, have a look at the *eyedropper* above and the *ten* below. Now put the elements together by thinking of squeezing two more zeros out of an *eyedropper* alongside the number *ten* to make it a **thousand**. [3]

40   tongue

The characters for *mouth* and *thousand* naturally form the idea of **tongue** if one thinks of a *thousand mouths* able to speak the same language, or as we say, "sharing a common **tongue**." It is easy to see the connection between the idiom and the character if you take its image literally: a single **tongue** being passed around from *mouth* to *mouth*. [6]

千 舌

41   liter

Think of a one-**liter** carafe (the kind you might serve drinks in) filled not with milk or wine but with a *thousand* sharp *needles*. You may well wonder what they are doing there, but the answer is simple: it's a kind of sports drink for a robot. [4]

´ 二 千 升

<table>
<tr><td>42</td><td>pill</td></tr>
</table>

One of the scourges of sports like modern *baseball* has been the use of performance-enhancing drugs, those tiny little **pills** that have helped turn honest competition into cut-throat business. Now look at the character and picture it as a bottle of **pills** hanging on the thigh of a *baseball* player like a PEZ dispenser, ready for the popping as the need arises. [3]

❖ As a primitive, this element takes the meaning of a *bottle of pills.*

We have already seen one example of how to form primitives from other primitives, when we formed the *daybreak* out of *sun* and *floor* (FRAME 30). Let us take two more examples of this procedure right away, so that we can do so from now on without having to draw any particular attention to the fact.

<table>
<tr><td>43</td><td>divination</td></tr>
</table>

This is a picture of a divining rod, composed of *a walking stick* and a *drop*, but easy enough to remember as a pictograph. Alternately, you can think of it as a *magic wand*. In either case, it should suggest images of **divination** or magic. [2]

$$| \quad \uparrow$$

❖ When using this character as a primitive, we will stick with the meaning of a *divining rod* or a *magic wand*.

<table>
<tr><td>44</td><td>tell fortunes</td></tr>
</table>

This is one of those characters that is a real joy of simplicity: a *divining rod* with a *mouth*—which are the two ingredients needed to **tell fortunes.**

Note how the movement from top to bottom (the movement in which the characters are written) is also the order of the elements which make up our story and of the key word itself: first *divining rod,* then *mouth.* This will not always be possible, but where it is, memory has almost no work at all to do. [5]

卜　占

---

45 above

上

The two directions, **above** and below, are usually pointed at with the finger. But the characters do not follow that custom, so we have to choose something else, easily remembered. The primitives show a *magic wand* standing **above** a *floor*—"magically," you might say. Anyway, go right on to the next frame, since the two belong together and are best remembered as a unit, just as the words **above** and *below* suggest each other. [3]

丨　卜　上

---

46 below

下

Here we see our famous *magic wand* hanging, all on its own, **below** the *ceiling*, as you probably already guessed would happen. In addition to giving us two new characters, the two shapes in this and the preceding frame also serve to illustrate the difference between the primitive meanings for *ceiling* and *floor*: it all depends on whether the single horizontal line stands above or **below** the primitive element to which it is related. [3]

一　丁　下

---

47 card

卡

The key word **card** can stand for all sorts of things, but let's settle on a credit **card** for our image. Perhaps the first thing that comes to mind is the picture of a shopkeeper sliding your credit **card** up and down (from *above* to *below* and back again) in the reading machine to record your transaction. Now imagine her doing it fast and furiously, again and again, with increasing impatience until your poor **card** is whittled away to a small strip of plastic. [5]

48	eminent

卓　The word **eminent** suggests a famous or well-known person. So all you need to do—given the primitives of a *magic wand* and a *sunflower*—is to think of the world's most **eminent** magician as one who uses a *sunflower* for a *magic wand* (like a flower-child who goes around turning the world into peace and love). [8]

The final two characters of this lesson are a good example of how a primitive element can be used to form a new character, which in turn becomes a new primitive for another character. This will happen often, so it is good to pay attention to it from the start.

❖	mist

卓　Here is the first of many examples of primitives composed of other primitives but not treated as characters themselves. At the bottom is the primitive (also a character) for *early* or *sunflower*. At the top, a *needle*. Conveniently, **mist** falls *early* in the morning, like little *needles* of rain, to assure that the *sunflower* blooms *early* as we have learned it should. [8]

十　卓

49	dynasty

朝　It is easy to imagine one of the great **dynasties** of China in all its glory. Now all we have to figure out is what the elements *moon* and *mist* have to do with it.

Picture a great palace with a powerful emperor seated on a throne in its innermost court. To keep the Wizard-of-Oz illusion that this power is beyond question and beyond the understanding of the masses, the whole complex is kept permanently shrouded in *mist*. How do they do it, you ask. On one side of the throne is a servant pulling on a cord to wave a gigantic fan back and forth. On the other, a servant with a long cord hooked on a corner of the quarter *moon*. When he pulls on it, the *moon* tilts over and spills out a month's supply of *mist* that keeps the myth of the **dynasty** alive. [12]

| 50 | ridicule ^(v.) |

If you read off the elements in the character, you have something like "*mouthing* off at the *dynasty*." When we think of what we commonly **ridicule** in civilized society, one of the oldest and most universal targets is the ruling elite. Who better to deride than one's leaders? Again, the explanation is too rational, so turn it into a story that has you **ridiculing** a particular *dynasty's* court with particular buffoonery. [15]

LESSON 4

AT THE RISK OF going a little bit too fast, we are now going to introduce three new primitive elements, all of which are very easy to remember either because of their frequency or because of their shape. But remember: there is no reason to study the primitives by themselves. They are being presented systematically to make their learning automatic.

❖   animal legs

Like the two that follow it, this primitive is not a character in its own right, though it is said to be derived from 八, the character we learned earlier for *eight*. It USUALLY comes at the bottom of the primitive to which it is related. It can mean the **legs** of any kind of **animal**: from the massive legs of an elephant to an octopus's tentacles to the spindle shanks of a spider. (The one animal not allowed is our friend homo sapiens, whose legs will appear in FRAME 56.) Even where the term "legs" will apply metaphorically to the legs of pieces of furniture, it is best to keep the association with **animal legs**. [2]

❖   bound up

The element meaning **bound up** is an "enclosure" that can wrap itself around other elements or be compressed when there is nothing to enclose. When this latter happens—usually because there is not enough room—and it is set on top, the little hook at the end is dropped off, like this: ⼍.

The sense of **bound up** is that of being "tied and gagged" or wrapped up tightly. If you have trouble remembering when it serves as an enclosure (with the hook) and when not (without the hook), you might think of the former as a **chain** and the latter as a **rope**. [2]

horns

This primitive element USUALLY appears at the top of the element to which it is related, and is usually attached, or almost attached, to the first horizontal line to come under it. The **horns** can never simply be left hanging in the air. When there is no line available, an extra horizontal stroke (like a *one*) is added. The final character of this lesson gives an example.

The meaning of this element is wide enough to embrace the **animal horns** of bulls, rams, billy goats, and moose, but not the family of musical instruments. As with other elements with such "open" meanings, it is best to settle on one that you find most vivid and stick with that image consistently. [2]

51

only

When we run across abstract key words like this one, the best way to get an image is to recall some common but suggestive phrase in which the word appears. For instance, we can think of the expression "it's the **only** one of its kind." Then we imagine a barker at a side-show advertising some strange pac-man like creature he has inside his tent, with **only** a gigantic *mouth* and two wee *animal legs*. [5]

52

贝

shellfish

When we learned the character (and primitive element) for *eye* back in FRAME 15, we suggested arching the two middle strokes to get the image of an iris. The simplified primitive element for *eye* does the same thing, just with a more contemporary touch: the three horizontal strokes are replaced with a single vertical stroke running through the *eye*. Note how this line "doubles up" with the first stroke of the element for *animal legs*, the second of the two elements that make up this character. In fact, there are only two cases where this is going to happen, here and in FRAME 58.

To put this all together, imagine a freakish **shellfish** with a single, gigantic *eye* roaming the beaches on its slender little *legs,* scaring the wits out of the sunbathers. [4]

丨　冂　冂　贝

❖ When this character is used as a primitive, in addition to *shellfish,* the meanings *shells, oysters,* and *clams* will often come in handy.

53

paste (v.)

贴

Think here of brushing on an adhesive, as when you **paste** something on a billboard. Here we have an *oyster* **pasting** a poster on his back to advertise his services in the dubious occupation of one who *tells fortunes.* Try to imagine the problem he would have reaching his back with the brush to **paste,** and then see him strutting around and calling out, "Fortunes to tell! Fortunes to tell!" [9]

贝　贴

54

chaste

贞

You have heard of Diogenes running around with his lamp looking for an honest man. Here we have an image of the famous *shellfish,* Oysterogenes, running around with his *divining rod* looking for a **chaste** man. We leave it to you to decide which one has the better luck in his quest. [6]

卜　贞

55

employee

员

How do we get a *mouth* over a *shellfish* to mean an **employee?** Simple. Just remember the advice new **employees** get about keeping their *mouths* shut and doing their jobs, and then make that more graphic by picturing an office building full of white-collar workers scurrying around with *clams* pinched to their *mouths.* [7]

口　员

| 56 | youngster |

儿

Imagine these two strokes as the long—really l-o-n-g—legs of a **youngster** who is growing out of his clothes faster than his parents can buy them. In the case of this character, he is literally "all legs." [2]

丿　儿

❖ As a primitive element, this form will mean *human legs*.

| 57 | how many? |

几

In addition to the primary meaning of **how many**, this character can take the secondary meaning of a "small table." For etymological reasons too involved to go into here, it can also mean *wind*, whether in the same shape as above or with the final stroke more shortly "hooked" (几). We will meet the full character for *wind* only in FRAME 1170.

To associate the character with the primary meaning, think of the verses to "Blowin' in the Wind," Bob Dylan's anti-war song of the 1960s: "**How many** roads must a man walk down…? **How many** times must the cannonballs fly…?" [2]

丿　几

❖ As a primitive, we will stick with the meaning of *wind* and, at least once, *small table*.

| 58 | see |

见

The elements that compose the character for **see** are the *eye* firmly fixed to a pair of *human legs*. As we saw in the element for *shellfish* a few frames ago, the iris of the *eye* is drawn with a single vertical stroke, here doubled up with the first stroke of *human legs*.

Now surely, somewhere in your experience, there is a vivid image just waiting to be dragged up to help you remember this character…. [4]

丨　冂　冃　见

59 元   beginning

"In the **beginning**..." starts that marvelous shelf of books we call the Bible. It talks about how all things were made, and tells us that when it came to humanity the Creator made *two* of them, man and woman. While we presume *two* were made of every other creature as well, we are not told as much. Hence we need only *two* and a pair of *human legs* to come to the character that means **beginning**. [4]

60 页   page

What we have to do here is turn a *shellfish* into a **page** of a book. The *one* at the top tells us that we only get a rather short book, in fact a book of only *one* **page**. Imagine a title printed on the shell of an *oyster,* let us say "Pearl of Wisdom," and then open the quaint book to its *one* and only **page**, on which you find a single, radiant *drop of* wisdom, one of the masterpiece poems of nature. [6]

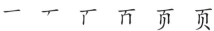

❖ As a primitive, this character will often take the unrelated meaning of a *head* (preferably one detached from its body).

61 顽   stubborn

This character refers to a block*head,* a persistently **stubborn** person who sticks to an idea or a plan just the way it was at the *beginning,* no matter what comes up along the way. The explanation makes "sense," but is hard to remember because the word *"beginning"* is too abstract. Back up to the image we used two frames ago—Adam and Eve in their Eden—and try again: The root of all this goes back to the *beginning,* with two brothers each defending his own way of life and asking their God to bless it favorably. Abel stuck to agriculture, Cain to animal-raising. Picture these two seeking the favors of heaven, one of them with an unusually **stubborn** grimace on his face. No wonder something unfortunate happened! [10]

兀   顽

---

62   ordinary

凡

While we refer to something insignificant as a "*drop* in the bucket," the character for **ordinary** shows us a "*drop* in the *wind*." To make the image stick as clearly as water dropping into a bucket, stop and think of something really **ordinary** and then say, "It's just a *drop* in the *wind*"—and imagine what that might actually look like. [3]

丿   几   凡

---

63   muscle

肌

One of the more common ways of testing the strength of one's **muscles** is to lock hands with a local hulk on a *small table* top and arm wrestle. This is the image here, depicted by the elements for *part of the body* and *small table*. The **muscle** is, therefore, the *part of the body* you test by literally bringing it to the *small table*. [6]

月   肌

---

64   defeated (ADJ.)

负

Above we have the condensed form of *bound up*, and below, the familiar *shellfish*. Now imagine two *oysters* engaged in *shell*-to-*shell* combat, the one who is **defeated** being *bound and gagged* with seaweed, the victor towering triumphantly over it. The *bound shellfish* thus becomes the symbol for anyone or anything that has been **defeated**. [6]

---

65   ten thousand

万

Chinese count higher numbers in units of **ten thousand**, unlike the West, which advances according to units of one thousand. (Thus, for instance, 50,000 would be read "five **ten-thousands**" by a Chinese, as if it were written 5,0000.) Given that the comma is used in larger numbers to *bind up* a numerical unit of four digits, the elements for *one* and *bound up* naturally come to form **ten thousand**. [3]

一 丁 万

---

66   uniform (ADJ.)

匀

The two primitives *bound up* and *two* (clearer in the hand-drawn form) combine to give the meaning of **uniform**. One of the real challenges for primary school teachers is to keep students from scattering in every which direction. If you think of the final touch to a school outfit, the shoes, and then recall the childhood jingle, "One, two, buckle my shoe," the solution is near at hand. Instead of having children buckle their shoes, they can be taught to tie their shoelaces together by changing the lyrics to read "One, two, *bind up* my shoes." This keeps them from straying very far from the group and helps teachers provide a **uniform** education. [4]

勹 匀

---

67   sentence (N.)

句

By combining the two primitives *bound up* and *mouth*, it is easy to see how this character can have the meaning of a **sentence**. The *mouth* suggests it is a spoken **sentence**. To be more precise, it is a cluster of words *bound up* tightly and neatly so that they will fit in your *mouth*. [5]

勹 句

---

68   decameron

旬

There simply is not a good phrase in English for the block of ten days which this character represents. So we resurrect the classical term **decameron**, whose connotations the tales of Boccaccio have done much to enrich. Actually, it refers to a journey of ten *days* taken by a band of people—that is, a group of people *bound together* for the *days* of the **decameron**. [6]

勹 旬

69 勺	**ladle**

If you want to *bind up drops* of anything—water, soup, lemonade—you use something to scoop these *drops* up, which is what we call a **ladle**. See the last *drop* left inside the **ladle**? [3]

勹 勺

70 的	**bull's eye**

The elements *white bird* and *ladle* easily suggest the image of a **bull's eye** if you imagine a rusty old *ladle* with a **bull's eye** painted on it in the form of a tiny *white bird*, who lets out a little "peep" every time you hit the target.

This is the most frequently used character in Chinese, serving a number of common grammatical functions. But—it ALSO means **bull's eye**. [8]

白 的

71 首	**heads**

Reading this character from the top down, we have: *horns . . . nose*. Together they bring to mind the picture of a moose-head hanging on the den wall, with its great *horns* and long *nose*. The plural form is used to stress the frequent metaphorical use of the term to refer to various kinds of **heads**, including **heads** of state. It might help to see a number of the latter lined up on the den wall alongside the moose, each fitted out with *antlers* and a whopper of a *nose*.

Here we get a good look at what we mentioned when we first introduced the element for *horns*: that they can never be left floating free and require an extra horizontal stroke to prevent that from happening, as is the case here. [9]

LESSON 5

THAT IS ABOUT all we can do with the pieces we have accumulated so far, but as we add each new primitive element to those we already know, the number of characters we will be able to form will increase by leaps and bounds.

If we were not separating into two volumes the 3,000 characters to be treated in this course, there are any number of other characters that we could learn at this time. Just to give you an idea of some of the possibilities (though you should not bother to learn them now), here are a few, with their meanings: 吋 *(English inch),* 罩 *(envelop),* 咒 *(curse),* 咱 *(we, inclusive),* and 囂 *(hubbub).* While many of the stories you have learned in the previous lessons are actually more complex than the majority you will learn in the later chapters, they are the *first* stories you have learned, and for that reason are not likely to cause you much difficulty. By now, however, you may be wondering just how to go about reviewing what you have learned. Obviously, it won't do simply to flip through the pages you have already studied, because the ordering of the characters provides too many hints. The best method for many people is to design a set of flash cards that can be added to along the way.

If you have not already started doing this on your own, you might try it this way: Buy heavy paper (about twice the thickness of normal index cards), unlined and with a semigloss finish. Cut it into cards of about 9 cm. long and 6 cm. wide. On one side, make a large ball-pen drawing of one character in the top two-thirds of the card. (Writing done with fountain pens and felt-tip pens tends to smear with the sweat that comes from holding them in your hands for a long time.) In the bottom right-hand corner, put the number of the frame in which the character appeared. On the back side, in the upper left-hand corner, write the key-word meaning of the character. Then draw a line across the middle of the card and another line about 2 cm. below it. The space between these two lines can be used for any notes you may need later to remind you of the primitive elements or stories you used to remember the character. *Only fill this in when you need to, but make a card for every character* as soon as you have learned it.

46

BELOW

wand BELOW
floor with magic

The rest of the space on the card you will not need now; but later, when you study the pronunciation of the characters, you might use the space above the double lines. The bottom part of the card, on both sides, can be left free for inserting character compounds (front side) and their readings and meanings (back side).

A final note about reviewing. You have probably gotten into the habit of writing a character several times when memorizing it, whether you need to or not; and then writing it MORE times for characters that you have trouble remembering. There is really no need to write a character more than once, unless you have trouble with the stroke order and want to get a better "feel" for it. If a character causes you trouble, spend time clarifying the imagery of its story. Simply rewriting the character will reinforce any latent suspicions you still have that the "tried and true method" of learning by repeating is the only reliable one—the very bias we are trying to uproot. Also, when you review, REVIEW ONLY FROM THE KEY WORD TO THE CHARACTER, NOT THE OTHER WAY AROUND. The reasons for this, along with further notes on reviewing, will come later.

We are now ready to return to work, adding a few new primitives one by one, and seeing what new characters they allow us to form. We shall cover 23 new characters in this lesson.

---

72   **straight**

直

Think of the first two elements, *ten eyes*, as referring to a group of five scientists working together on a top-secret, million-dollar project to draw a **straight** line on the *floor* without the aid of special equipment. In the end, all *ten eyes* verify that it is **straight**, leaving no doubt that the use of government funds was fully justified. Time to apply for another grant.

Note how the first two strokes of the element for *eye* are made a little longer so that they can touch the final stroke. The same thing will happen in the following three characters, and later on as well, so pay particular attention to the stroke order below. [8]

一 十 广 市 市 直 直 直

---

73   **set up**

置

Think of having to **set up** the *net* for a badminton or volleyball game. One of the main problems is how to keep the *net* in a *straight* line so that it doesn't sag in the middle. Which is just what this character shows us. [13]

＼　　　門　　　門　　　門　　　四　　　置

❖　　　　　　　　　　　　　　　　　　　　　　　　**tool**

Although this primitive is not very common, it is useful to know, as the following examples will show. It is usually drawn at the very bottom of any character in which it figures. The first stroke, the horizontal one, is necessary to distinguish **tool** from *animal legs*.

The sense of the element is a carpenter's **tool**, which comes from its pictographic representation of a small bench with legs (make them *animal legs* if you need a more graphic image), so that any element lying on top of it will come to be viewed as a **tool** in the hands of a carpenter. [3]

一　　　丆　　　六

74　　　　　　　　　　　　　　　　　　　　　　　　**tool**

具

Here is the full character on which the primitive of the last frame is based. If you can think of a table full of carpenter's **tools** of all sorts, each equipped with its own *eye* so that it can keep a watch over what you are doing with it, you won't have trouble later keeping the primitive and the character apart. [8]

｜　　П　　А　　日　　目　　且　　貝　　具

75　　　　　　　　　　　　　　　　　　　　　　　　**true**

真

Here is an example of how there can be different ways of identifying the primitive elements that make up a character. The most obvious is *straight* and *animal legs*, but the character could as well be analyzed into *ten* and *tool*. Let's choose the latter.

How do you know if something is **true** or not? What if there were a kit of *ten tools* you could count on to run a test? Well, at least when it comes to asking whether people are really **true** to themselves, the *ten* commandments are a good start. [10]

十 真

❖

厂

by one's side

This primitive has the look of *ten*, except that the left stroke is bent down toward the left. It indicates where one's hands (all *ten* fingers) fall when the arms are relaxed: **by one's side**. [2]

一 厂

76

工

work (N.)

The pictograph of an I-beam, like the kind that is used in heavy construction **work** on buildings and bridges, gives us the character for **work**. [3]

一 丁 工

❖ Since the key word can be too abstract when used as a primitive element, we will often revert to the clearer image of an *I-beam*.

77

左

left (N./ADJ.)

By combining the last two frames and reading the results, we get: *by one's side . . . work*. Conveniently, the **left** has traditionally been considered the "sinister" side, where dark and occult *works* are cultivated and carried out. [5]

一 厂 左

78

右

right (N./ADJ.)

When thinking of the key word **right**, in order to avoid confusion with the previous frame, take advantage of the double meaning here. Imagine a little *mouth* hanging down *by one's side*—one's **right** side, of course—like a little voice of conscience telling one the "right" thing to do. [5]

厂 右

79 possess

有

The picture here is a slab of *flesh* dangling *by one's side*, perhaps from a belt or rope tied around the waist. While we normally think of things that we have and **possess**, we also know that there are things that can have and **possess** us. Such cases might be likened to an evil spirit **possessing** one's soul. This character suggests a way to exorcize it: hang a slab of fresh *flesh by one's side* until it begins to putrefy and stink so bad that the demon departs. Take careful note of the stroke order. [6]

ナ 才 冇 有 有

80 bribe (N.)

贿

To the left we have the primitive for *shells*, and to the right, the character we just learned for *possess*. Keep the connotation of the last frame for the word *possess*, and now expand your image of *shells* to include the ancient value they had as money (a usage that will come in very helpful later on). Now people who are *possessed* by *shells* are likely to abandon any higher principles to acquire more and more wealth. These are the easiest ones to persuade with a **bribe** of a few extra *shells*. [10]

贝 贿

81 tribute

贡

A **tribute** has a kind of double meaning in English: honor paid freely and money (*shells*) collected by coercion. Simply because a ruler bestows a noble name on a deed is hardly any consolation to the masses who must part with their hard-earned *shells*. Little wonder that this ancient *work* of gathering money by calling it a **tribute** has given way to a name closer to how it feels to those who pay it: a tax. [7]

 工 贡

82 item

 项

To the right we see a *page* and to the left an element for *I-beam*. The **item** referred to here is not some specific object but an entry on an "itemized" list. Each **item** in the list you have to imagine here is preceded by a little *I-beam*—not a drawing, but an actual iron *I-beam*. Imagine lugging a list like that around the grocery store! [9]

工　项

83　　　　　　　　　　　　　　　　　sword

刀　Although this character no longer looks very much like a **sword**, it does have some resemblance to the handle of the **sword**. As it turns out, this is to our advantage, in that it helps us make a distinction between two primitive elements based on this character. [2]

丁　刀

❖ In the form of the character, this primitive means a *dagger*. When it appears to the right of another element, it is commonly stretched out like this 刂, and like this 刂 when to the left of another element. In these cases, it will take the sense of a great and flashing *saber*, a meaning it gets from a character to be introduced in Book 2.

84　　　　　　　　　　　　　　　　　blade

刃　Think of using a *dagger* as a razor **blade**, and it shouldn't be hard to imagine cutting yourself. See the little *drop of* blood dripping off the **blade**? [3]

丁　刀　刃

85　　　　　　　　　　　　　　　　　cut (v.)

切　To the right we see the *dagger* and next to it the number *seven*, whose primitive meaning we decided would be *diced* (FRAME 7). It is hard to **cut** meat or vegetables with a knife without imagining one of those skillful Japanese chefs. Only let us say that he has had too much saké to drink at a party, grabs a *dagger* lying on the mantelpiece and starts *dicing* up everything in sight, starting with the hors d'oeuvres and going on to **cut** up the furniture and carpets…. [4]

一 十 切

86　　　　　　　　　　　　　　　　　summon

召 A *sword* or *dagger* poised over a *mouth* is how the character used to **summon** a person is written. Note the immediate—how shall we put it politely?—Freudian implications of the character. (Observe, too, if you will, that it is not at all clear whether the long slender object is **summoning** the small round one or vice versa.) [5]

刀　　刀

❖ The primitive meaning remains the same. Just be sure to associate it with a very concrete image, such as a prosecutor at your door with a document that *summons* you to appear in court.

87　　　　　　　　　　　　　　　　　　evident

昭 Nothing quite works to make something **evident** like "evidence" that backs it up. Here we see a lawyer who *summons* the *sun* down from the noonday sky to stand as a witness and make the facts as **evident** as can be. [9]

日　　昭

88　　　　　　　　　　　　　　　　　rule (N.)

則 The character depicts a *clam* alongside a great and flashing *saber*. Think of digging for *clams* in an area where there are gaming **rules** governing how large a find has to be before you can keep it. So you take your trusty *saber*, which you have carefully notched like a yardstick, crack open a *clam* and then measure the poor little beastie to see if it is as long as the **rules** say it has to be. [6]

貝　　則

❖   wealth

畐 To prepare for the following frame, we introduce here a somewhat rare primitive meaning **wealth**. It takes its meaning from
the common image of the overwealthy as also being overfed.
More specifically, the character shows us *one* single *mouth*
devouring all the harvest of the *fields*, presumably while those
who labor in them go hungry. Think of the phrase exactly as it
is written when you draw the character, and the disposition of
the elements is easy. [9]

---

89   vice-

副 The key word **vice-** has the sense of someone second-in-com-
mand. The great and flashing *saber* to the right (its usual location, so you need not worry about where to put it from now
on) and the *wealth* on the left combine to create an image of
dividing one's property to give a share to one's **vice-***wealth-
holder*. [11]

---

90   fourth

丁 This character is **fourth** in a system of enumeration from first
to tenth based on the ancient lunar calendar and referred to
as "the celestial stems." What it shows us is someone waiting
fourth in line, using a giant metal spike as a makeshift chair. [2]

❖ When used as a primitive, the character changes its meaning to *nail* or *spike*. When it is written with a single stroke
(⁊) it will mean a *thumbtack*.

---

91   sting (v.)

叮 You know how a bee **stings**, right? It drives the little barbed
spike in its bottom into your skin and then pulls away. Of course,

as we noted way back in FRAME 11, the primitive element for *mouth* can refer to any kind of orifice, but imagine the damage a bee could inflict if it could **sting** with its *mouth* at the same time—a kind of bi-polar attack. [5]

口　叮

92

可

can (AUX. V.)

To begin with, you will notice that this character is composed of the very same elements as that of the former frame. Only their arrangement is different.

　Remember the story about the "Little Engine that **Could**" when you hear this key word, and the rest is simple. See the determined little locomotive huffing and puffing up the mountain—"I think I **can**, I think I **can**..."—spitting railroad *spikes* out of its *mouth* as it chews up the line to the top. [5]

丁　可

93

哥

older brother

The **older brother** is depicted here as a duplication of the character for *can*. It shouldn't take too much work to imagine him, for whatever reason, as a *can-can* brother. [10]

可　哥

94

顶

crest

The key word can refer to the summit or **crest** of a mountain, but the **crest** of the *head* works better here. The immediate image this conjures up is the *head* of a rooster with its comb or a cockatoo with its crest feathers. And from there it is but a short step to think of the punk hairstyles that imitate this look by shaping the hair into a row of brightly colored *spikes*. So a *spike-head* becomes a **crest**. [8]

丁　顶

Lesson 6

THE LAST GROUP OF primitives took us pretty far, and probably forced you to pay more attention to the workings of imagination. In this lesson we shall concentrate on primitives that have to do with people.

Remember that even those characters that are given special meanings as primitives may also retain their key-word meaning when used as primitives. Although this may sound confusing, in fact it turns out to be convenient for making stories and, in addition, helps to reinforce the original meaning of the character.

95	second (ADJ.)

乙

This character belongs to the same series of "celestial stems" as that in FRAME 90 of the last lesson. The **second** person in line is seated in what looks like a rocking chair (much better situated than the *fourth* seat). [1]

$$乙$$

❖ Since this is also a pictograph of a *hook* or *fishhook*, let us take these as primitive meanings. Its shape will rarely be quite the same as that of the character. When it appears at the bottom of another primitive, it is straightened out, almost as if the weight of the upper element had bent it out of shape: ∟. When it appears to the right of another element, the short horizontal line that gets the shape started is omitted, and the whole character is stretched out and narrowed—all for reasons of space and aesthetics: ∟.

96	fly (v.)

乩

The large *fishhook* has two wee propellers (the two *drops* on the side) attached to them for **flying**. [3]

乁　乁　乁

97 child

子

This character is a pictograph of a **child** wrapped up in one of those handy cocoons that Indian squaws fix to their backs to carry around young **children** who cannot get around by themselves. (Incidentally, this is why English has taken over the word "papoose" from the Algonquin language to refer to the device itself.) The first stroke is like a wee head popping out for air; the second shows the body and legs all wrapped up; and the final stroke shows the arms sticking out to cling to the mother's neck. [3]

❖ As a primitive, this character retains the meaning of *child*, though you might imagine a little older *child*, able to run around and get into more mischief.

98 cavity

孔

A **cavity** is really just a small hole, but the first thing we think of when we hear the word is that little pothole that shows up in a diseased tooth. The Chinese may not use the character in this sense, but what's to stop us?.

Probably the one thing most *children* fear more than anything else is the dentist's chair. Can you remember the first time as a *child* you saw your dentist hold an x-ray up to the light and pronounce the ominous word "**cavity**"? Even though you were not likely to know that the word meant that you have an extra hole in your head until you were much older, it did not take long before the sound got associated with the drill and that row of shiny *hooks* the dentist uses to torture people who are too small to fight back. [4]

子　孔

99 roar ^(v.)

吼

A *mouth* and a *cavity* combine to create the character for **roar**. It shouldn't tax your memory banks too much to think back to how you howled and **roared** the first time you had a *cavity* drilled by a doctor poking around inside your *mouth* with his weapons of dental destruction. [7]

口　吼

100　　　　　　　　　　　　　　　　　　　　　chaos

乱　When things get **chaotic**, manners are laid aside and tempers get short, even in the most courteous of circles. This character shows what happens to a *tongue* caught up in **chaos**: it gets "barbed" like a *fishhook*, and becomes sharp and biting. Be sure you see an actual *tongue* actually *hooking* people, and not rush over the metaphor with an abstract sense. [7]

舌　乱

101　　　　　　　　　　　　　　　　　　　　　(-ed)

了　This character is most frequently used as a grammatical particle. Since it can indicate completion of an action, it is here assigned the key word **-ed**. Learn this character by returning to FRAME 97 and the image given there. The only difference is that the "arms" have been left off (actually, only tuck-**ed** inside). Thus a *child* with its arms wrapp-**ed** up into the backsack is the picture of a job successfully complet-**ed**.

Incidentally, you should be aware that this grammatical particle has generated a great deal of debate among specialists. [2]

乛　了

102　　　　　　　　　　　　　　　　　　　　　woman

女　You have probably seen somewhere the form of a squatting **woman** drawn behind this character, with two legs at the bottom, two arms (the horizontal line) and the head poking out the top. A little farfetched, until you draw the character and feel the grace and flow of the three simple strokes. Remembering the character is easy; being able to write it beautifully is another thing. [3]

く　夕　女

❖ The primitive meaning is the same: *woman*. It will help if you have a particular person in mind.

103

好

good

The sense of **good** carried by this character is very broad in range. And what better image for this than a *woman* holding her *child*. [6]

夕　好

104

如

be like

Pardon us if we revert to the venerable old Dr. Freud again, but his eye for symbolism is often helpful to appreciate things that more earthy imaginations once accepted more freely but that we have learned to cover over with a veneer of etiquette. For instance, from ancient times things like the *mouth* of a cave have served as natural ritual substitutes for the opening through which a *woman* gives birth. This is just one example of the way in which one thing can **be like** another in a metaphorical sense and can help unlock the hidden meanings of ritual and symbolism. [6]

夕　如

105

母

mother

Look closely at this character and you will find the outline of the character for *woman* in it, the second stroke of which has been expanded to make space for the two breasts that help a **mother** be a **mother**. [5]

 乚　乃　乃　母　母

❖ As a primitive we shall add the meaning of *breasts* in accord with the explanation given above. Take careful note of the fact that the form is altered slightly when this character serves as a primitive, the two dots joining together to form a longer stroke: ⠔. An example follows in the next frame.

106

贯

pierce

If one is asked to think of associations for the word **pierce**, among the first to come to mind is that of **piercing** one's ears to hold earrings, a quite primitive form of self-mutilation that has survived into the twenty-first century. The character here is read, top to bottom: *mother . . . oyster*. All you need to do is imagine **piercing** an ear so that it can hold a *mother*-of-pearl you have just wrested from an *oyster*. [8]

107

兄

elder brother

The difference between "older brother" (FRAME 93) and **elder brother** is ever so slight in English, the latter sounding just a bit less colloquial. The same is the case in Chinese.

By now characters like this one should "look like" something to you even though it is more of an "ideogram" than a "pictograph." The large *mouth* on top and the *human legs* below almost jump off the page as a caricature of **elder brother**, the one with the big *mouth* (or if you prefer a kinder image, the one who "has the say" among all the children). [5]

❖ As a primitive this character will take the meaning of *teenager*, in accord with the familiar image of the big *mouth* and the gangling, clumsy *legs*.

108

克

overcome (v.)

In this frame we get a chance to use the character we just learned in its primitive meaning of *teenager*. The *needle* on top indicates one of the major problems confronting the *teenager* growing up in today's world: drugs. Many of them will fall under the shadow of the *needle* at some time during those tender years.

Only when a whole generation rises up and declares, "We Shall **Overcome**," will the *needle* cease to hang over their heads as it does in this character. [7]

LESSON 7

IN THIS LESSON we turn to primitive elements having to do with quantity. We will also introduce a form known as a "roof," a sort of overhead "enclosure" that comes in a variety of shapes. But let us begin slowly and not get ahead of ourselves, for it is only after you have mastered the simple forms that the apparently impenetrable complexities of later primitives will dissolve. The primitives we give here will immediately suggest others, on the basis of what we have already learned. Hence the somewhat haphazard order among the frames of this lesson.

109	small

小

The sense of **small** in this character is actually of three **small** *drops*, the first of which (the one in the middle) is written larger so that the character has some shape to it. The point of writing it three times is to rub the point in: **small**, **small**, nothing but **small**. [3]

丨　小　小

❖ The primitive meaning remains the same, *small*. Written above a horizontal line, its form is slightly altered, the last two strokes turning inwards like this: 丷 .

110	few

少

First we need to look at the fourth stroke, the *drop* at the bottom that has been extended into a longer diagonal stroke leaning left. This happens because a single, isolated drop will NEVER appear beneath its relative primitive in its normal size, for fear it would drop off and get lost. As for the meaning, let the *drop* indicate a further belittling of what is already *small*—thus making it a **few** of something *small*. [4]

小　少

❖ Note that when this character is used as a primitive element that is placed UNDER another element, the third stroke is

omitted, giving us 少 . We will not meet an example of this
until FRAME 380.

---

111   noisy

You might think that **noisy** should be associated with many people talking at once, but the idea in this character is much more
philosophical than that: What happens when things get **noisy**
is that people's vocabulary shrinks to a more neolithic level the
higher the volume is turned up. And so it is that **noisy** becomes
associated with the very *few* things a *mouth* can say when it
is talking loudly. Try to picture people quoting Shakespeare to
each other in a shouting match, and you will see how right this
character is. [7]

口   吵

---

112   grandchild

Ironically, the word **grandchild** suggests someone large and
grand, but the character is closer to the truth in depicting a
child that is *small*. [6]

子   孙

---

113   large

大

Here we have a simple pictograph of a person taking up the
space of an entire character and giving it the sense of **large**. It
should not be too hard to locate the two legs and outstretched
arms. [3]

一   大   大

❖ When used as a primitive, this character needs a different
meaning, since the element representing the human person
will come up later. Therefore, this shape will become a *large
dog* or, if you prefer, a *St. Bernard dog*. In FRAME 239 we will
explain why this choice was made.

---

114 tip (N.)

尖

The **tip** this character refers to is the tapered point of something like a pen or a pagoda. The composition of the elements, *small* and *large,* is perfectly suited to the image of a *small* **tip** at the end of something *larger.* [6]

小　尖

---

115 evening

夕

Just as the word **evening** adds a touch of formality or romanticism to the ordinary word "night," so the character for **evening** takes the ordinary looking *moon* in the night sky and has a cloud pass over it—partially hiding it and hence eliminating the final stroke. [3]

丿　勹　夕

---

116 many

多

"**Many** *moons* ago," begins much of Amerindian folklore—a colorful way of saying "Once upon a time" and a great deal of help for remembering this character. Here we have two *moons.* (three of them would take us back to the beginning of time, which is further than we want to go.) [6]

夕　多

---

117 enough

够

"**Enough** is **enough**." Who has not been scolded with these words in their youth by a parent or teacher who has run out of patience! If you can conjure up the memory of a particular time you used it, then imagine this short *sentence* becoming an uncontrollable obsession, as you watch yourself walk off into the sunset muttering it *many* times—over and over and over again. [11]

句　够

| 118 | outside |

外

On the left, the primitive for *evening*, and on the right, that for the *magic wand*. Now, as every magician worth his abracadabra knows, bringing your *magic wand* out into the *evening* air makes your magic much more powerful than if you were to stay indoors. Hence, *evening* and *magic wand* takes you naturally **outside**. [5]

| 119 | name (N.) |

名

Perhaps you have heard of the custom, still preserved in certain African tribes, of a father creeping into the tent or hut of his newborn child on the night of the child's birth, to whisper into its ear the **name** he has chosen for it, before making his choice public. It is an impressive "naming" custom and fits in tidily with the way this character is constructed: *evening ... mouth*. At *evening* time, a *mouth* pronounces the **name** that will accompany one throughout life. [6]

| 120 | silk gauze |

罗

Although commonly used as a family name, the character has its own meaning: **silk gauze**. True, we usually think of gauze as something to wrap a wound with, but here we have a classier sort, a **silk gauze** that is used for a hair *net*. You know, the kind you wrap your head in at *night* to keep your waves and curls in place to avoid a bad hair day tomorrow. [8]

罒 罗

| 121 | factory |

厂

The ideal **factory**, to contemporary taste, is one in which everything has been so simplified that there are no people needed to run it. Here we have a portrait of the **factory** of the future, where even the robots have been retired, leaving, well—nothing. [2]

一　厂

❖ As a primitive, the character can also mean precisely what it looks like: a steep *cliff*. You can certainly imagine someone standing at the top looking down into the abyss below.

122	hall

厅

Unlike the great **halls** this key word brings to mind, like Carnegie **Hall** or the Royal Albert, there are no concerts played in the Great **Hall** of *Nails*, which is actually the world largest *factory* for the production of paraphernalia for sideshow masochists: *nail* beds, *nail* chairs, even *nail* cribs for training the next generation. For those who don't live in the neighborhood, a "Great **Hall** of *Nails*" site is coming soon to the internet. [4]

厂　厅

123	stern

厉

The key word **stern** takes many of us back to grammar school, where we first learned the meaning of the word through first-hand experience with iron-fisted bosses masquerading as educators. The whole thing was set up like a *factory*, with students lined up in their little desks like so many automatons as one teacher after the other filled their heads with *ten thousand* tidbits of knowledge a day. Anyone at all that threatened their quota was subject to **stern** punishment—or, when all else failed, an ignominious flunk. [5]

厂　厉

124	thick

厚

When we refer to someone as **thick**-skinned or **thick**headed, we are often quick to add—even if only under our breath—something about their upbringing. Perhaps it is because deep down we cherish the belief that by nature people are basically tender and sensitive.

Be that as it may, the Chinese character for **thick** depicts a *child* abandoned out on the wild *cliffs*, exposed to the heat of the *sun,* and thus doomed to develop a head and skin as **thick** as the parent who left it there. [9]

---

125   **stone**

石

With a *mouth* under a *cliff,* what else could we have here but the entrance to a secret cavern, before which a great **stone** has been rolled so that none may enter. Perhaps it is the hiding place where Ali Baba and his band of thieves have stored their treasures, in which case that magic word known to every school child who ever delighted in the tales of the *Arabian Nights* should be enough to push the **stone** aside. But take care—the *cliff* is steep, and one slip will send you tumbling down into the ravine below.

This is the only occasion on which the second stroke in *cliff* extends to the middle of the horizontal stroke. If you think of the edge jutting outwards (as in the story above), the problem should be taken care of. [5]

❖ The *stone* is a quite common primitive element, which is not restricted to great boulders but is used for *pebbles* or *rocks* of any size or shape.

---

126   **gravel**

砂

In this character a *few stones* take on the meaning of **gravel**. Imagine ordering a wheelbarrow of *stones* from your local quarry and having them dump an entire truckload on your garden path. Imagine how annoyed you would be: "I said a *few stones,* a little **gravel** for my walkway—not a blooming mountainside!" [9]

石　砂

| 127 | wonderful |

妙

The primitive for *woman* is on the left (there and at the bottom of another primitive is where you will always find her), and to the right the element for *few*. When we refer to a *woman* as **wonderful**, we mean to praise her as the sort of person we meet but *few* of and far between. [7]

女　妙

| 128 | resemble |

肖

The word **resemble** should suggest, among other things, a son who **resembles** his father. A "chip off the old block" is the way we often put it, but the character is more simple. It speaks of a *small* bit of *flesh*. [7]

丿　丷　丷　肖

❖ When this character is used as a primitive, its meaning changes to *sparks* or *candle*.

| 129 | peel ^(v.) |

削

For want of a kitchen knife, you decide to **peel** an apple with a *saber*. You strike a warrior's pose, toss the apple into the air, and with a guttural shout, brandish your trusty *saber* in the air with lightning speed. Can you see the *sparks* flying and the peelings falling to the ground? [9]

肖　削

| 130 | ray |

光

There are really only two primitives here, *small* and *human legs*. The fourth stroke that separates them is added for reasons of aesthetics. (If that doesn't make sense, try writing the character without it and see how ugly the results look, even to your beginner's eye.)

Now if you have wondered what those little particles of "dust" are that dance around in the light **rays** that come through the window and fall on your desk, try imagining them as *small* and disembodied *human legs*, and you should have no trouble with this character. [6]

---

131 **overly**

太

All right, you are wondering, **overly** "what"? Given the legendary temperament of the *St. Bernard dog,* we may suppose that it is being **overly** affectionate. Hence the large *drop* of slobber—yuck. [4]

大　太

---

132 **economize**

省

When we decide it's time to **economize**, we take it for granted that we will need to trim back our appetites a bit. If one's *eyes* can be too big for one's stomach, they can also be too big for one's pocketbook. Or, as this character suggests, too many. Imagine yourself with *eyes* all over your head, so that in order to **economize** you will have to pluck most of them out until only a *few* remain. [9]

少　省

---

133 **strange**

奇

The elements we are given to work with here are *St. Bernard dog* and *can*. Lots of phrases pop to mind to attach these words to the key word, but they end up being too abstract because of the word *can*.

It is helpful in such cases (and there will be a number of them as we go along) to stick closely to the more basic elements, in this case, *mouth* and *nails*. Now all we need do is create a fictitious "**Strange** But True" column in the Sunday funnies, featuring a *St. Bernard dog* whose *mouth* has been sealed shut with a row of *nails* because he was hitting the brandy keg around his neck too hard. [8]

Lesson 8

FOUR BASIC ELEMENTS, it was once believed, make up the things of our universe: earth, wind, fire, and water. We have already met the element for *wind*, and now we shall introduce the others, one by one, in a somewhat longer than usual lesson.

Fortunately for our imaginative memories, these suggestive and concrete primitives play a large role in the construction of the characters, and will help us create some vivid pictures to untangle some of the complex jumbles of strokes that follow.

134	stream (N.)

川

A **stream** of water flows pretty much like the character you see in this frame. The reason there are no wavy lines is simply that the Chinese characters no longer use them. [3]

$$) \quad)\mathsf{I} \quad)\mathsf{I}|$$

❖ As a primitive, this character will denote a *stream* or a *flood*. Note, however, that there are certain small changes in the writing of the element, depending on where it appears relative to other elements:

on the left, it is written 川
on the top, it is written 巛
on the bottom, it is written 川

135	state (N.)

州

Here we see *drops of* land (little islets) rising up out of a *stream*, creating a kind of sandbar or breakwater. Ever wonder how the **state** line is drawn between **states** separated by a river? If there were little *drops of* land as in the character, there'd be nothing to it. [6]

$$' \quad) \quad 小 \quad 州 \quad 州 \quad 州$$

136   **obey**

顺

In the language of the primitives, this character would read *stream . . . head*. This turns out to be convenient for remembering its meaning of **obey**. Either one **obeys** the person who is *head* of an organization or else **obeys** by following the *stream* of opinion ("current" practice, we call it). Both these senses come together in this character. [9]

川   顺

---

137   **water** (N.)

水

This character, which looks a bit like a snowflake, is actually a pictograph of **water**—not any particular body of water or movement of water, but simply the generic name for **water**. Should you have any difficulty remembering it, simply think of a *walking stick* being dropped vertically into the **water**, sending *droplets* out in all four directions. Then all you need to learn is how to write it in proper order. [4]

亅   刁   氺   水

❖ As a primitive, this character can keep its form, or it can be written with three drops to the left of another primitive, like this: 氵. This latter, as we will see, is far more common. It can also be written stiffly, in five strokes, as 氺, in which case we will take it to mean a *snowflake*. An example will follow shortly.

---

138   **eternity**

This character also uses the full form of *water*, though its meaning seems to have nothing at all to do with it. Remember what William Blake said about seeing "infinity in a grain of sand and **eternity** in an hour"? Well, reading this character from top to bottom, we see "**eternity** in a *drop of water*."

Note how the introduction of the *drop* requires that the first stroke of *water* begin with a short horizontal "starter line." Try leaving it out and you will see how reasonable this is. [5]

` 丁 永

139

脉

blood vessels

It is estimated that if you were to lay all the **blood vessels** in the body of an average adult (about 40 billion of them) end to end, they would reach four times around the earth. Which means that when mother and father look at their newborn baby, they can take added pride in the fact that if the three of them pooled their **blood vessels**, they would reach all the way to the moon— or *flesh* from here to *eternity*. [9]

月　脉

140

求

request (v.)

Let the key word suggest a formal invitation that begins, "Mr. and Mrs. Snow **request** the honor of your presence at the wedding of their beloved daughter *Snowflake* to Drip*drop*, the son of Mr. and Mrs. Leak…." The only stroke remaining to account for is the *one* that runs between and "unites" the happy couple together until death (or sunlight) do them part. [7]

一　丁　寸　才　求　求　求

141

泉

spring (N.)

Call to mind the image of a fresh, bubbling **spring** of *water*, and you will probably notice how the top of the **spring** you are thinking of, the part where the "bubbling" goes on, is all *white*. Happily, the *white* is just where it should be, at the top, and the *water* is at the bottom. [9]

白　泉

❖ We will keep this image of a *spring* when using this character as a primitive, but not without first drawing attention to a slight change that distinguishes the primitive from the character. The final four strokes (the element for *water*) are abbreviated to the three small *drops* that we learned earlier as the character for *small*, giving us: 尿.

---

142   **flatlands**

原

♪ "The **flatlands** are alive, with the sound of muuusic...." ♪ Well, they are in this case anyway, though the setting is a rather grisly one. Watch Schwester Maria as she skips along merrily, dodging in and out of the *springs* that pop up like landmines until she comes to the edge of a *cliff* and loses her balance. Listen to her words echoing as she falls and this character should be yours forever. [10]

厂 厈 原

---

143   **swim**

泳

On the left we see again the primitive for *drops of water*. To the right, we see the character for *eternity*. Knowing how much children like to **swim**, what could be a better image of an *eternity* of bliss than an endless expanse of *water* to **swim** in without a care in the world? [8]

氵 泳

---

144   **continent**

洲

If *states* are separated by smaller bodies of *water*, **continents** are separated by great oceans. The *drops of water* to the left of *state* fill this function. [9]

氵 洲

---

145   **marsh**

沼

Unlike the *flatlands* with their cliffs, the **marsh**lands are low and near a source of *water* that feeds them until they get soggy through and through. Why certain land becomes **marsh** is probably due to the fact that it feels thirsty, and so tries its best to *summon* the *water* over to its side. But, like so many temptations, the last state of the victim is worse than the first. Hence the slushy **marsh**. [8]

氵 沼

---

146   sand (N.)

 Learn this character in connection with that for *gravel* from
FRAME 126. The difference between **sand** and gravel is one your
feet know very well from walking along the beach. The **sand**
is finer and the gravel cuts into the skin. Hence the element
for *stone* figures prominently in gravel, whereas that for *water*
(which, after all has done the work of grinding away at the stone
for centuries) shows up here in **sand**. [7]

氵 沙

---

147   Yangtze

 China's equivalent to the Mighty Mississip' is the **Yangtze**. In
fact, the character in this frame, although generically meaning
river, can be used as an abbreviation for the **Yangtze**, much the
same as the "River" of "Ole Man River" is for those who live on
the banks of the Mississippi. The elements that make it up show
water and an *I-beam*. Actually, the heavy metal *I-beam* is being
launched as a raft by some mentally challenged Huck Finn hoping to cruise on the **Yangtze**. If you see him shoving off and
imagine what happens afterwards, it could help fix the elements
in your mind. [6]

氵 江

---

148   juice (N.)

 This is not just any ordinary **juice**, but a brew of *water* and *needles*. Its distinctively sharp taste cuts your thirst by distracting it
with excruciating pain as the **juice** passes down your throat. [5]

 氵 汁

149

潮

tide

Before we get to explaining this character, take a look at it and see if you can figure out the primitive elements on your own.... On the left is the *water*—that much is easy. On the right we have only one primitive, the character for *dynasty* learned back in FRAME 49. See how an apparently complex character falls apart neatly into manageable pieces?

To get the meaning of the key word **tide**, just think of the ebb and flow of a *dynasty's* fortunes—literally. Watch as all the wealth of the empire flows into the emperor's court at high **tide**, and note how everything there empties out back into the populace when it is at low **tide**.

By the way, if you missed the question about the number of primitives, it is probably because you forgot what we said earlier about characters becoming primitives, independently of the pieces that make them up. As a rule, look for the largest character you can write and proceed from there to primitives stranded on their own. [15]

氵　潮

150

源

source

With the advice of the last frame in mind, it is easy to see *water* and *flatlands* in this character for **source**. Both in its etymology (it has a common parent with the word "surge") and in popular usage, **source** suggests the place *water* comes from. In this character, it is under the *flatlands*, where we earlier saw it breaking the surface in those bubbly little springs. [13]

氵　源

151

活

lively

When we speak of a **lively** personality or a **lively** party, we immediately think of a lot of chatter. This character depicts the idea of **lively** by having *tongues* babble and splash around like flowing *water*. [9]

氵　活

152

消

extinguish

Among the many things *water* can do is help **extinguish** fires, and that is just what we have here. First of all, take the *water* at the left as the *drops of water* that are used to depict *water* in general. In the best of all possible worlds, the most efficient way to **extinguish** a fire would be to see that each *drop of water* hits one *spark* of the conflagration. An unthinkable bit of utopian fire fighting, you say to yourself, but helpful for assigning this key word its primitives. [10]

氵　消

153

河

river

The character in this frame represents a step up from the *stream* we met in FRAME 134: it is a full-sized **river**, just like the character in FRAME 147 for *Yangtze*. The *water* to the left tells us what we are dealing with, and the *can* at the right tells us that our "little engine that *could*" has now become amphibious and is chugging down the Yellow River (which is written using this character) like a regular old riverboat. [8]

氵　河

154

鱼

fish (N.)

We have held off on this character, even though we learned its elements in earlier chapters, in order to introduce it in conjunction with the following frame.

The character shows three elements, which we list in the order of their writing: *bound up . . . rice field . . . floor.* Not much to work with at first sight. But we can join them together by thinking of a three-part story: first a **fish** is caught and *bound up* on a line with its unfortunate schoolmates; when the fisherman gets home, he cuts off the head and tosses it, with the entrails, out into the *rice fields* for fertilizer; and the rest he sets on the *floor* of his kitchen for the cat, while he tosses a package of frozen **fish** sticks into the microwave for himself. [8]

155	fishing (N.)

渔

To the story we have just made about *fish*, this character for the profession of **fishing** adds yet another element BEFORE the others: namely the *water*, where the fish was happily at home before being caught, disemboweled, and eaten. Be sure to get a clear image of the *water* when you put it all together to create a picture of **fishing**. [11]

氵 　　渔

156	lake

湖

Rather than use the character for *recklessly* from FRAME 17 as a primitive element, let us take the elements one by one: *water* . . . *ancient* . . . *flesh*. You have heard of legends of people being abandoned in the mountains when they had become too *ancient* to work. Well, here is a legend about people being set adrift in the *waters* of a stormy **lake** because their *flesh* had gotten too *ancient* to bear the burdens of life. [12]

氵 　　湖

157	fathom (V.)

测

Connoting the measurement of the depth of water, the key word **fathom** begins with the *water* primitive. To its right, we see the character for *rule* (FRAME 88) which we learned in the sense of "gaming *rules*." Now when we measure the depth of *water,* we have to follow a different set of *rules* than those we use to measure the fish we pull out of it. We **fathom** it; that is, we measure it in units of six feet. Picture yourself **fathoming** a body of *water* several hundred feet deep according to official *rules,* which stipulate that you must use a government-approved tape measure and avoid the use of electronic equipment. [9]

氵 　　测

---

158   soil ^(N.)

土

We don't like it any more than you do, but this character is not the pictograph it is trumped up to be: a mound of **soil** piled on the ground. All we can recommend is that you memorize it as it is. Anyway, it will be occurring with such frequency that you have almost no chance of forgetting it, even if you try. [3]

一　十　土

❖ When this character is used as a primitive, the sense of *soil* is extended to that of *ground* because of its connection with the character for the same (FRAME 507). From there it also takes the added meanings of *dirt* and *land*.

---

159   equal

均

The idea of making things **equal** is pictured here at its most basic: land reform. It provides *soil* in *uniform* portions to everyone. To help with the association, we may recall the famous line of Napoleon the Pig in George Orwell's *Animal Farm*: "All animals are **equal**, but some animals are more **equal** than others." Picture one of those suspicious *land* reforms going on in the barnyard and led by one group of animals (the pigs) who apportion the largest parcels to themselves and ration out among everyone else *uniform* slivers of *land* too small to live on. [7]

　均

---

160   belly

肚

Here we see a *part of the body* that looks like a mound of *soil*. What else could it be but that large compost pile that over-eaters carry around where their waistlines used to be? Happily, the key word **belly** already suggests something bell-shaped. [7]

月　肚

161	dust

尘

If this character strikes you as too logical to remember—a *small* bit of *earth* meaning **dust**—you may need to take more drastic measures. Imagine taking the *smallest* specks of **dust** you can find around the house and gathering them up into a pile of *earth* outside in your backyard, until you have enough to make a garden. It would take you forever! [6]

小　尘

162	fill in

填

When you **fill in** a form, it is expected that the information be *true*. That said, most people are less concerned with full and *true* disclosure than with protecting their privacy, whereas those who make the forms are often more interested in getting the *dirt* on them. If you can imagine **filling in** some of the blanks with shovelfuls of actual *dirt* to give them what they want, you will keep the metaphor more concrete. [13]

土　填

163	spit (v.)

吐

We have here a rather small *mouth* (it is always compressed when set on the left) next to a much larger piece of *dirt*. It is not hard to imagine what you might do if you got a *mouth* full of *dirt*. As least we know what we would do: **spit** it out as fast and far as we could! [6]

口　吐

164	pressure (N.)

压

One of the things that causes erosion on inclines is excessive **pressure** of the top*soil* on the sub*soil*. The increase in **pressure** can be caused by any number of things from heavy rainfall to heavy buildings, especially in the absence of sufficient deep-rooted vegetation to hold the layers together. Here we see a steep *cliff* without a tree in sight. The slightest **pressure** (indicated here by the tiny *drop*) will cause a landslide, which, with a little help from your imagination, you will be able to see happening in this character. [6]

一　厂　厈　压

❖ **bricks**

圭

The two characters for *soil* piled on top of one another give us the primitive element for **bricks**. Given that **bricks** are mostly made of *soil* and that they are made to be piled on top of one another, it should not take much effort to remember this element. [6]

土　圭

165 **waaah!**

哇

The shrill cries of a bawling infant can be more piercing than any noise an adult makes, which is why they are so hard to ignore. In this character, we see the sounds of that cry, **Waah!**, likened to a *mouth* spitting out *bricks* to shatter the silence of our sleep. [9]

口　哇

166 Chinese inch

寸

This character stands for a small measurement used prior to the metric system, a little less than 1⅓ English inches in length and one-tenth of a *Chinese foot* (which we will meet later, in Book 2). The character, appropriately, represents one *drop* of a *ten* (with a hook!). [3]

❖ When this character is used as a primitive, we shall use it to mean *glue* or *glued to*. There is no need to devise a story to remember this, since the primitive will appear so often you would have to struggle hard NOT to remember it.

167	seal [V.]

封

Think of the key word **seal** in connection with a letter you have written and are preparing to close. Instead of using the traditional hot wax to **seal** the document, you *glue* a *brick* on the outside—a love letter SWAB (**sealed** with a *brick*). A romantic thought, but the postage will bankrupt you. [9]

168	time [N.]

时

Time, to be measured, needs a fixed and immovable point of reference. At least in our galaxy, that role is played by the *sun.* Or, as this character has it, **time** is *glued to* the *sun.* All you need to make this memorable is to imagine a clock face actually *glued* to the face of the *sun.* [7]

169	Buddhist temple

寺

You have heard of people "attaching" themselves to a particular sect? Here is your chance to take that metaphor literally and imagine some fellow walking into a **Buddhist temple** with a fervent resolve to attach himself to the place. Since there is plenty of unused *land* around the precincts, he simply picks out a suitable patch, brushes the soles of his feet with *glue,* steps down firmly, and so joins the **Buddhist temple** as a "permanent member." [6]

170	fire [N.]

火

Just as sitting before a **fire** enlivens the imagination and lets you see almost anything you want to in the flames, this character is so simple it lets you see almost any sort of **fire** you want to see. It no longer makes a good pictograph, but we invite you to take a pencil and paper and play with the form—first writing it as shown below and then adding lines here and there—to see what you can come up with. Everything from matchbooks to cigarette lighters to volcanic eruptions to the destruction of Sodom and Gomorrah have been found here. No doubt you, too, will find something interesting to bend your memory around these four simple strokes. [4]

丶　丷　少　火

❖ Although the generic meaning of *fire* can be carried over as a primitive meaning, it is usually best to keep to the meaning of *flames* or *fireplace*. Another primitive element for *fire*, based on this one, is written ⺊⺌ and will mean *cooking fire*.

171　　destroy

灭

What we see here is a *fire*— a large *fire* with a menacing, wicked grin—raising its eyes to the *ceiling* with intent to **destroy** the very room you find yourself in as you read these lines. [5]

一　灭

172　　ashes

灰

The character for **ashes** naturally includes the primitive for *fire*, or more specifically, a *fireplace*. Now what do you do with that bucket of **ashes** you have just cleaned out of the *fireplace*? You strap it to your belt and walk around with it *by your side* until the wind scatters them, with distributive justice, over everyone else's property. [6]

一　ナ　灰

173　　vexed (ADJ.)

烦

When people are **vexed** about something, they often refer to themselves as "really burned" about it. In this character, the person's *head* is on *fire*, raising the metaphor to new heights. [10]

火　烦

174	inflammation

炎

A *fire* belongs IN the *fireplace*, not OVER it. When the *fire* spreads to the rest of the house, we have an **inflammation** of the house. As with any **inflammation**—including those that attack our bodies—the danger is always that it might spread if not checked. This is the sense behind the reduplication of the element for *fire*, one atop the other. [8]

火　炎

175	thin (ADJ.)

淡

You may not think there is such a thing as **thin** *water* or **thin** *fire*, but when you mix *fire* and *water,* the one does make the other **thin**. When you see this key word, think not of "slender" but of **thin** in the sense of pale, diluted, or weak. Paint **thin**ner makes paint **thin** in this way (though we do not recommend mixing it with *fire*, unless you want a REAL *inflammation*). [11]

氵　淡

176	lamp

灯

Since it is very hard to read by the *fireplace* without going blind from the flickering of the flames or burning up from the heat, our ancestors invented a way to *nail* down a bit of that *fire*, just enough to light up the text of their evening newspapers and no more. Voilà! The **lamp**. [6]

火　灯

177	spot (N.)

点

If you look into the flickering of a *cooking fire* for a long time and then turn aside, you will see **spots** before your eyes. Although nobody ever thought of such a thing before—as least as far as we know, they didn't—imagine using those **spots** as a way to *tell fortunes*. The old witch sits before a large iron cauldron hanging over a *cooking fire* and watches the **spots** that show up when she turns to look at you, and from that *tells* your *fortune*. Think of it as a kind of **spot**-check on your future. [9]

占　点

178　illuminate

昭

Although the range of possible meanings that the character for **illuminate** can have is about as rich as the connotations of the English word, we need to focus on just one of them: to make something obscure *evident*. If you glaze a pot and put it into the oven to "fire" it, you in fact **illuminate** it. Hence the character for **illuminate** makes a connection between the character for *evident* and the primitive element for *cooking fire*. [13]

昭　照

Lesson 9

Although the study of the four basic elements undertaken in the last lesson brought us a lot of new characters—45 in all—we have only scratched the surface as far as *water*, *earth*, *wind*, and *fire* are concerned. Perhaps by now it is clear why we said at the beginning of this lesson that we are lucky that they appear so frequently. The range of images they suggest is almost endless.

In this chapter our focus will be on a few new "roof" and "enclosure" primitives. But first, a character that we might have included in the last group but omitted so as not to be distracted from the four elements.

179 *li*

里

That's right—a ***li***. Don't bother looking it up in your English dictionary; it's a Chinese unit of distance. One ***li*** is about a half kilometer. The character depicts how the measure came to be used. Atop we see the *rice field*, and below the element for *land*. Think of those four sections you see in the *rice field* (and which we made mention of when first we introduced the character in FRAME 14) as blocks of *land*. Thus, a *land* division based on the size of a *rice field* would be a ***li***. [7]

❖ To get a more concrete primitive meaning for this character, we shall refer to it as a *computer*, a meaning deriving from the character for *logic*, which we will meet in Lesson 12. To remember the meaning, it might help to think of the alternative meaning of the primitive at the top: *brains*.

180 quantity

量

Think of **quantity** as having to do with measuring time and distance, and the rest is simple: you have a **quantity** of time in the new day that begins with *daybreak*, and a **quantity** of distance in the rural *li*. [12]

旦　量

| 181 | bury |

埋　When we **bury** something (or someone, for that matter), we usually mean putting it under *ground*. Only here, we are **burying** our beloved *computer* that has served us so well these past years. Behind us a choir chants the "Dies irae, dies illa" and there is much wailing and grief among the bystanders as they pass by to shovel a little *dirt* into what will be its final resting place. R.I.P. [10]

土　埋

Before going any further, we might pause a moment to look at precisely WHERE the primitive elements were placed in the character of the last frame: the *ground* to the left and the *computer* to the right. Neither of these is an absolutely fixed position. The character for *spit* 吐 (FRAME 163), for instance, puts *ground* on the right, and that for *wild* 野 (FRAME 1010) will put the *computer* on the left. While there is no reason to bother memorizing any "rules," a quick glance through a few general guidelines may help. Use them if they help; if not, simply adjust the story for a problem character in such a way as to help you remember the position of the elements relative to one another.

In any case, here are the guidelines that follow from the characters treated up to this point:

1. Many characters used regularly as primitives have a "strong" position or two from which they are able to give a basic "flavor" to the character. For example, *ground* at the left (or bottom) usually indicates something to do with earth, soil, land, and the like; *fire* at the bottom in the form of the four dots, or at the left in its compressed character form, usually tells us we have to do with heat, passion, and the like; a *mouth* at the left commonly signifies something to do with eating, coughing, spitting, snoring, screaming, and so forth. Where these elements appear elsewhere in the characters, they do not, as a rule, have the same overall impact on its meaning.

2. Some primitive elements ALWAYS have the same position in a character. We saw this earlier in the case of the primitive meaning three drops of *water* 氵 (page 71).

3. Enclosures like *cliff* 厂 (page 66) and *bound up* 勹 (page 39) are always set

above whatever it is they enclose. Others, as we shall see later, "wrap up" a character from the bottom.

4. All things being equal, the element with the fewer strokes (usually the more common element) has first rights to the "strong" position at the left or bottom. (Note that the left and bottom cannot BOTH be the dominant position in the same character. Either one or the other of them will dominate, usually the left.) The characters for *gravel* 砂 (FRAME 126) and *sing* 唱 (FRAME 22) illustrate the point.

---

182   black

黑

Three frames ago we noted that it might help to think of the top part of the primitive for *computer* as *brains*. In this character you will see why. Note how the third stroke, ordinarily written as a single horizontal line, is here broken up into a pair of *animal horns* right in the middle of the element. Think of this as a brain impaled (literally) on the *horns* of a dilemma.

That done, there is no problem with this character. Like most things electrical, a *computer*, too, can overheat, and often this happens because its *brain* is caught on the *horns* of a dilemma. Now look closely with your imaginative eye and you can see the *horns* sprouting out of the CPU and *flames* pouring out of the *computer* to char the keyboard, the monitor, and your desk a sooty **black** color. [12]

丶　冂　冂　冂　四　四　甲

里　黑

---

183   black ink

墨

Besides meaning **black ink**, this character also appears in the word for an inked string that is pulled taut and snapped to mark a surface, much the same as a carpenter doing repair work in your home might use a chalked string. Here it is used to mark the *dirt* on a baseball diamond with a long, heavy piece of string soaked in **black ink**. [15]

❖   hood

冂

In addition to the basic meaning of **hood**, this shape can be used for a **glass cover**, such as that used to serve "pheasant under glass." Note its difference from the element for *wind*: the second stroke is hooked INWARDS here. To help remember this detail, think of the wind as blowing "out" and a **glass cover** as keeping something "in." Among the related images suggested by this primitive are: a monk's **cowl**, a riding **hood**, a **helmet**, and an automobile **hood**. [2]

$$丨\quad 冂$$

---

184   risk (v.)

冒

In order not to **risk** being identified, burglars often wear a mask or something else draped over their face. If you look closely at the character and "read off" the primitive elements, you will end up with a *hood* with *two* slits for the *eyes*. It would almost be worth trying one on if becoming a burglar didn't **risk** a lot more than just being recognized.

   Even if you followed the explanation above, it bears repeating that the top four strokes are NOT the same as the primitive for *sun* or *day* or *tongue wagging in the mouth*. The difference is subtle but not to be ignored. [9]

$$冂\quad 曰\quad 冒$$

---

185   same

同

The primitives in this character show us *one* and *mouth* under a *hood*. Let us take the key word to connote the sense in which monks living in community share the **same** life, routine, food, and ideals. We might say they all have the **same** habits, including the "habit" they wear on their backs. Here we see the monk's *cowl*, drawn down over the eyes so that all you can see when you look at him is a *mouth*. But since monks also speak their prayers in common, it is but a short step to think of *one mouth* under a *hood* as the character for everything that is the **same** about monastic life. [6]

冂 冃 同

❖ When this character is used as a primitive, it will mean *monks* dressed in a common habit.

---

186   cave

洞

Early hermit-*monks* often lived in **caves** where they prayed and fasted for years on end. The one thing they could not do without was *water*. To fix this image, imagine a *monk* who has filled up his **cave** with *water* neck high, which makes it difficult to sleep but at least protects him from dehydration. [9]

氵   洞

---

187   lovely

丽

What could be more **lovely** than a happy couple! This character describes it as a pair of *helmets* hanging from the *ceiling*. Obviously, we have a pair of ex-Hell's Angels, now comfortably situated in their suburban home, with only those icons from the past to remind them of their former life. By way of exception, let the *drops* stand as pictographs of the chin straps. [7]

一   丆   丙   丽

---

188   orientation

向

This character begins with a mysterious *drop* off in the distance. Then we find a sort of transparent *helmet* with no eyes or nose, but only a prominent *mouth* under it—obviously an extraterrestrial. And what is it jabbering on about with its *mouth* open like that? It has strayed far from its spaceship (the *drop* off in the distance) whose fuel tanks are bone dry. Seeing that the poor creature is completely "disoriented," you offer a first **orientation** to life on earth by handing him a few bucks and pointing the way to the nearest gas station. [6]

---

189   echo (N.)

响

When we need *orientation* in a dark place, where we are blind as a bat, we usually grope our way around the nearest wall to navigate our way out. If we were really as blind as the bat, we could do what the bat does: let out a shrill sound from our *mouth* and use the **echo** to guide us. [9]

口   响

---

190   esteem (V.)

尚

Above we see the primitive for *small* attached to one of those *glass covers* you might use to display a family heirloom. Its being *small* is important, because what is in fact on display is the shrunken, stuffed, and mounted *mouth* of an ancestor we particularly **esteem**. We may be used to **esteeming** the words our forebears leave behind, but here we also **esteem** the very *mouth* that spoke them. We leave it to you to imagine a suitable place in your room for displaying such an unusual conversation piece. [8]

       屮   尚

❖   house

This extremely useful primitive element depicts the roof of a **house**. You can see the chimney at the top and the eaves on either side without much trouble. It is a "crown" element, which means that it is invariably set atop other things. Examples follow immediately. [3]

ˋ   ̇ ̇   宀

---

191   character

Here is the character for **character** itself. Not just Chinese characters but any written **character** from hieroglyphs to Sanskrit to our own Roman alphabet. It shows us simply a *child* in a *house*. But let us take advantage of the double meaning of the key word to note that just as a *child* born to a Chinese *house*

is given **characters** for its name, so it is also stamped with the "character" of those who raise it from infancy on. [6]

| 192 | guard ^(v.) |

守

If you want to **guard,** the best way is to post a watchman, like the royal soldiers in front of Buckingham Palace or the Pope's Swiss Guard. The whole idea of hiring people to **guard** is that they should stick like *glue* to your *house* to protect it from unwanted prowlers. So go ahead and find a watchman who is really stuck on his job and *glue* him to your *house* to **guard** it. [6]

---

193 | finish ^(v.)

完

To start a *house* we lay the foundations; to **finish** it, a roof. This character shows the "finished" product, from the *beginnings* in the foundation at the bottom, to the roof with its chimney at the top. Come to think of it, the same holds true of anything we start and **finish.** [7]

---

194 | disaster

灾

Take the key word, **disaster,** and one of the first phrases that should pop into mind is "when **disaster** strikes…." That should be all it takes, because what strikes before the **disaster** is a match in an old wooden *house*, consuming the entire structure in a great, roaring *fire.* [7]

---

195 | proclaim

宣

Think of the key word in its religious sense of a missionary preaching: "**proclaiming** the good news to all nations" and "shouting it from the *house*tops" all day, day in and day out.

The element for *daybreak* that follows below has an additional stroke at the top. Remembering what we said about the *sun* creeping up over the horizon (the *floor*) at *daybreak* (FRAME 30), the extra stroke can represent the other horizon towards which the *sun* journeys, giving us "*sun*rise, *sun*set." That should be enough to help you remember this simple character, used in fact both for traditional missionary work as well as for one of its contemporary replacements: propaganda. [9]

---

196   nighttime

宵

Unlike the "evening" (FRAME 115), **nighttime** suggests time spent at night, as in pulling an all-nighter to prepare for an exam when everyone else is fast asleep in bed. The character expresses this by picturing a *house* with a *candle* in it. The reason is obvious: whoever is living there is passing the **nighttime** "burning the *candle* at both ends." [10]

---

197   peaceful

安

To be told that the place of the *woman* is in the *house* may not sit well with modern thought, but like all cultural habits the Chinese characters bear the birthmarks of their age. So indulge yourself in a Norman Rockwell image of a **peaceful** moment: a weary *woman* of the *house* slouched asleep in the living room chair, her hair in curlers and a duster lying in her lap. [6]

---

198   banquet

宴

To carry on from the last frame, we note the entire *day* of work that comes between a *woman* and her *house* in preparing for a dinner **banquet**, pictorially "interrupting" her *peaceful* relaxation. [10]

宀　官　宴

199

mail (v.)

寄

Now there is nothing particularly *strange* about your normal mailbox, but the one depicted here is a *strange house* that you actually have to enter to drop off your letters. Think of the haunted *House* of Usher that Edgar Allen Poe immortalized, or the enchanted Gingerbread *House* that Hansel and Gretel are heading towards with an armful of letters to **mail**. [11]

200

wealthy

富

Here we have the original character on which the primitive element for *wealth* is based. In keeping with the story introduced back then, note how many **wealthy** people get that way through simple inheritance, being born into the *wealth* of their parents' *house*. [12]

201

store up

貯

This character shows a family that **stores up** its *clams* by hiding some of them under the roof of the *house* and others under the *floor*boards. [8]

貝　貯　貯

LESSON 10

Of the several primitive elements that have to do with plants and grasses, we introduce two of the most common in this lesson: *trees* and *flowers*. In most cases, as we shall see, their presence in a "strong" position (in this case, to the left and at the top, respectively) helps give a meaning to the character.

202	tree

 This is a pictograph of a **tree**, the main trunk shown in the long vertical stroke and the boughs in the long horizontal stroke and the final two strokes sweeping down in both directions. Although it may look similar at first sight to the character for *water* (FRAME 137), the order in which it is written is completely different and this affects its final appearance. [4]

❖ As a primitive, this character can mean *tree* or *wood*. When the last two strokes are detached from the trunk (朩), we shall change its meaning to *pole* or *wooden pole*.

203	woods

 Learn this frame in connection with the next one. A **woods** is a small cluster of *trees*. Hence the simple reduplication of the character for *tree* gives us a **woods**. [8]

204	forest

森 A **forest** is a large expanse of *trees*, or "*trees, trees* everywhere," to adopt the expression we used back in FRAMES 23 and 24. [12]

205   dream (N.)

梦

Here we see a *woods* in the *evening*. In your **dreams** you may often find yourself wandering into the *woods* alone, there to have fairytale adventures. All you need do is picture the *woods* hovering overhead, as in this character, luring you, in the dark of *evening*, into their enchanted, **dream**like world. [11]

林　梦

206   machine

机

Most of us, at one time or another, have dreamed of inventing a **machine** to land our creation on the pages of history alongside Elie Whitney's cotton gin and Doc Brown's flux capacitor. Here you get your chance, with a **machine** that takes whole trunks of mahogany *trees* in one end and spits out *small tables* on the other, completely crafted, varnished, and ready for market. [6]

才　机

207   plant (V.)

植

You have no doubt seen how people practicing the Japanese art of bonsai take those helpless little saplings and twist them into crippled dwarves before they have a chance to grow up as they should. The more proper way to **plant** a young *tree* and give it a fair shake in life is to set it into the earth in such a way that it can grow up *straight*. [12]

才　植

208   apricot

杏

Since **apricots** can be eaten just as they fall from the *trees*, picture this *mouth* agape at the bottom of a *tree* (just as the elements have it), waiting for **apricots** to fall into it. [7]

木　杏

| 209 | dim-witted |

呆

The **dim-witted** thimblehead in this character is seated in the topmost branches of a *tree* with his mouth agape, waiting for the fruit to fall into it, but the only thing that happens is that nothing happens. [7]

口　呆

| 210 | withered |

枯

When a *tree* is **withered** and about to die, it is probably due to a kind of arteriosclerosis that keeps its sap from flowing freely. This character shows us an *ancient* and wrinkled *tree* with poor circulation, **withered** up and whiling away its remaining days in a retirement center. [9]

才　枯

| 211 | village |

村

The character for *village* shows a circle of *trees glued* together to measure off the confines of a **village**. [7]

才　村

| 212 | one another |

相

The key word **one another** stirs up associations of people interacting. When we read off the elements, *tree . . . eye*, we are given an idea of how to keep this interaction amicable by calling to mind the scriptural proverb about first taking the *tree* trunk out of your own *eye* before helping your neighbors remove the splinters from theirs. [9]

才　相

| 213 | notebook |

本

Recalling that **notebooks** are made of paper, and paper made of *trees*, one might think of a **notebook** as a slice of a *tree*. Can you see the "cross-cut" in the trunk of the *tree*? Picture a chainsaw cutting you out a few **notebooks** to take to school. [5]

---

214   case

案

The **case** that this key word refers to is the legal kind and the image contrasts the attitudes of the parties involved. While you are in a frazzle, the lawyer answers all your phone calls with, "I'm working on your **case**," when actually she is swaying, relaxed and *peaceful*, in a hammock strung up between the *trees* in her backyard. Imagine that—people actually get paid to take it easy while you do all the worrying. [10]

---

215   not yet

未

As the key word suggests, this character has to do with something not quite over and done with. More concretely, it shows us a *tree* that is **not yet** fully grown. The extra short stroke in the upper branches shows new branches spreading out, leaving one with the feeling that the *tree* has a ways to go yet before it reaches maturity. In other words, the character conveys its meaning pictographically, playing on the earlier pictograph of the *tree*. [5]

---

216   last <small>(N./ADJ.)</small>

末

This character is best learned in connection with that of the previous frame. The first stroke shows a branch that is longer than the main branch, indicating that the tree has reached the **last** of its growth, so that its top branches stop spreading and start drooping downwards. Be sure to keep this imagery in mind, to avoid confusing this key word with synonyms that will appear later. [5]

一　末

217　　　　　　　　　　　　　　　　　　　　　　　　　　　**foam**

沫　The **foam** this character refers to is the *last* stage of *water* after it has dashed and splashed against the rocks, spraying in all directions. The **foam** is thus a wave that has run its full course and reached its *last* on the rocky seashore. If you picture it in your mind's eye, this somewhat rare (but oh-so-easy-to-learn) character is yours for good. [8]

氵　沫

218　　　　　　　　　　　　　　　　　　　　　　　　　　　**flavor** (N.)

味　When a tree has *not yet* finished growing, it produces fruit with a full **flavor**. When the official taster (the professional *mouth* to the left) determines that full **flavor** has been reached, the tree is pruned back so that it remains permanently *not yet* grown. A neat little agricultural trick and an easy way to see the sense of **flavor** hidden in this character. [8]

口　味

219　　　　　　　　　　　　　　　　　　　　　　　　　　　**younger sister**

妹　The **younger sister** in the family is the *woman* in the family who, like the newest branch in a tree, is *not yet* old enough or mature enough to do everything the older sister can do (see FRAME 1346). [8]

女　妹

220　　　　　　　　　　　　　　　　　　　　　　　　　　　**investigate**

查　To **investigate** is to get to the bottom of something or track something down, which often has you working all through the night, right to *daybreak*. In the case of this character, it is Sir Isaac Newton, who is **investigating** the laws of physics when the appearance of the sun at *daybreak* prompts the *tree* to stretch and welcome a new day. At that, an apple drops from its branches square on Sir Isaac's head, inspiring him to discover the law of universal gravitation. [9]

木　查

---

221 sediment

渣

This character has you in your scuba-diving gear *investigating* at the bottom of a reservoir to see what has made the *water* go bad. See yourself mucking around the **sediment** and finding remnants of all sorts of garbage and chemical waste. Hopefully, someone will find the "dregs" of society that put it there and bring them to justice. [12]

氵　渣

---

222 dye (v.)

染

Take a handful of ash tree seeds, plant them in your backyard, and sprinkle them with *water* mixed with your mother's hair **dye**. If you are patient enough to nurture this little orchard of ash *trees* to full size, you could carve yourself out the first-ever-in-history brunette or platinum-streaked *baseball* bat. [9]

氵　氿　染

---

223 plum

李

Little Jack Horner has left his corner and his Christmas pie to try out his fortunes with a *tree* in the garden. He sticks in his thumb and out drops a **plum**, which says, "What a weird *child* you are!" [7]

木　李

---

224 table

桌

You have to think here of a group of magicians seated around a magical **table**, which is made out of the stump of a *tree*, and has the image of a large *sun* carved into its surface. The magicians pass the *magic wand* around from hand to hand to see if any of them can make the *sun* shine. At last, one of them succeeds, and the *sun* begins to glow (burning a hole in the **table** in the process). [10]

225

杂

miscellaneous

Try to associate the key word of this character with *baseball* bats. Usually, they are numbered according to their length, but at the end of the row, there are a few marked **misc.** The reason is that they are pretty far beyond regulation size, several inches longer and thick as telephone *poles*, no doubt a result of steroids that have rubbed off on them from the batters. [6]

❖

艹

flower

We are not yet equipped with all the pieces necessary to learn the character for **flower**, so shall have to content ourselves here with the first three strokes, which represent the primitive of the same meaning. Concentrate on the actual "bloom" of the **flower**, and keep a particular flower in mind. Try a rose, a tulip, or a daisy, since none of them will have their own character. Think about it well, since once you have decided on your **flower** of choice, you will be using it in a rather large number of stories later on. [3]

一   十   艹

226

若

as if

Here we see a *flower* held in the *right* hand, calling to mind the famous story of the Buddha who held up a *flower* with his *right* hand to a small gathering of his disciples. Most of them were perplexed, but Kasyapa smiled and the Buddha handed him the *flower*, **as if** he had understood something that everyone else had missed. To this day it remains a mystery what it was that the Buddha communicated to Kasyapa, but everyone treats the story **as if** it is of pivotal importance. [8]

艹 若

227

草

grass

Perhaps you know the custom of seeding **grass** randomly or in some particular pattern with the *flower* called the crocus, which blooms for a few days each year in *early* spring. As the **grass** begins to turn green again after winter has passed, these tiny *flowers* dot up here and there. Now just look out your window at a patch of **grass** somewhere and think what a nice idea it would be to have your name spelled out in *flowers* once as a sort of *early* harbinger of spring. [9]

艹 草

228

艺

technique

The **technique** we are shown in this character is for catching the ones that keep getting away. The *fishhook* is fitted out with a bouquet of sweet-smelling *flowers*, along with a romantic note, of course. [4]

艹 艺

229

苦

suffering (N.)

The picture of **suffering** we are given here is that of a *flower* that has grown *ancient*. When a flower ages, it pales and dries up, and probably even endures a kind of botanical **suffering**. If you think that plants are incapable of such feelings, then ask yourself why so many people believe that talking to their flowers helps them bloom better. [8]

艹 苦

230

宽

wide

Let the key word suggest the sign on the back of a slow-moving rig that is slowing down traffic: WIDE LOAD. Here, as is often the case, it is a *house* that is being transported to a new location at turtle speed. As you approach, you notice that the walls and roof are all made of glass. It's a *see*-through house, not suitable for people but ideal for *flowers* that need all the sun they can get (and which are never in the habit of throwing stones). To complete this image, put yourself back in the driver's seat of the car immediately behind the rig and pop a **wide**-angle lens onto your camera for a souvenir photo. [10]

---

231   nobody

莫

A rickety old sign with the warning written on it "**Nobody,** but **Nobody** Leaves Here" dangles from a shingle over the entrance to a graveyard. But, contrary to what you expect, this is a thoroughly modern graveyard. Gone are the cobwebs and gnarled trees, the tilted headstones and dark, moonless nights that used to scare the wits out of our childhood imaginations. Instead, we see brightly colored *flowers* placed before the tombstones, the *sun* shining gloriously overhead, and a cuddly *St. Bernard dog* sitting at the gate, making sure that **nobody** tries to leave. [10]

❖ When this character is used as a primitive element, we will replace the abstract key word with the more concrete *graveyard*.

---

232   imitate

模

Ah, but haven't they made a parody of the modern *graveyard* in trying to **imitate** its classic ancestors! The flowers are plastic, the writing on the stones is unimaginative and cold, and the whole thing looks more like a marble orchard than a right and proper *graveyard*. This character continues with the modernization trend by picturing artificial *trees* in the *graveyard*. But of course, how convenient! They don't need pruning or fertilizing, their leaves don't fall, and they remain the same color all year long. But far from **imitating** the real thing, they end up a cheap "imitation." [14]

木　模

233

desert (N.)

漢

Let this key word suggest to you a mirage in a **desert**. The haze rising up from the **desert** sands creates the illusion of a body of *water* in the distance. In fact, the mirage only recedes as you crawl your way across the surface of what will soon be your *graveyard*. To fix the image, imagine yourself reaching the mirage and finding out that it is in fact a *graveyard*, in which there is a headstone with your name on it. [13]

氵　漢

234

grave

墓

The mounds of *soil* with crude wooden crosses set at their head suggests those Boot Hill **graves** near Tombstone, Arizona, that many of you will remember from cowboy lore. The only odd thing about this character is that the *soil* comes UNDER the *graveyard*, rather than to its left, where we might expect it. Just think of how it looks as you walk toward Boot Hill, with the cross and mound of *soil* in the foreground.

By the way, this is not the first time, nor will it be the last, that we learn a character whose key word is the same, or almost the same, as a primitive element based on it, but whose shape differs somewhat. There is no cause to worry. By using the primitive in a variety of other characters, as we have done here, the confusion will be averted as a matter of course. In most cases, as here, the primitive element is simply one part of the fuller original character. [13]

莫　墓

235

seedling

苗

To avoid confusion with images of real seedlings to appear later, we shall take these **seedlings** out of their agricultural setting in the *rice fields* and into the frame of Brave New World surgery, where "ideas" or "values" are being implanted into *brains* like

seedlings to insure a harmonious society. Then you need only imagine them taking root and breaking out into *flower* right through the tops of the skulls of people walking around on the streets. [8]

艹　苗

❖ When this character is used as a primitive element, we will adjust its meaning to *tomato seedling*.

236　　　　　　　　　　　　　　　　　　　　aim

瞄

In order to **aim** at something through the sights of a rifle, you fix your *eyes* on the thin crosshairs. In this case, however, the usual crosshairs have been replaced with the completely useless serrated leaves of a *tomato seedling*. And not only that, they are poking out of where the lens should be and keep tickling your *eyeball*, keeping you from **aiming** properly. Obviously the sabotage of peacemakers working in a rifle factory. [13]

目　瞄

LESSON 11

Now that we have made our way through well over 200 characters, it is time to pause and consider how you are getting on with the method introduced in this book. While this lesson will be a short one (only 21 new characters) you might want to spend some time reviewing your progress in light of the remarks that follow. In them we have tried to draw out the main principles that have been woven into the fabric of the text from frame to frame and lesson to lesson. We do so by looking at some of the typical problems that can arise:

If you can remember the key word when you see the character, but have trouble remembering the character when you have only the key word to go on...

Probably you did not take seriously the advice about studying these stories with a pad and pencil. If you try to shortcut the process by merely learning to recognize the characters for their meaning without worrying about their writing, you will find that you have missed one bird with two stones, when you could have bagged two with one. Let us repeat: study only from key word to character; the reverse will take care of itself.

If you find yourself having to go back to a character, once you have written it, to make corrections or additions...

Our guess is that you are asking your visual memory to do the work that belongs to imaginative memory. After Lesson 12, you will be given more leeway to create your own images and stories, so it is important that you nip this problem in the bud before going any further. A small step in the wrong direction on a journey of 3,000 characters will land you in deep trouble in no time. Here are the steps you should be following each time you come to a new frame:

1. Read the key word and take note of the particular connotation that has been given it. There is only one such meaning, sometimes associated with a colloquial phrase, sometimes with one of the several meanings of the word, sometimes with a well-known cultural phenomenon. Think of that connotation and repeat it to yourself. When you're sure you've got the right one, carry on.

2. Read through the particular little story that goes with the key word and let the whole picture establish itself clearly.

3. Now close your eyes, focus on those images in the story that belong to the key word and primitive elements, and let go of the controls. It may take a few seconds, sometimes as long as a minute, but the picture will

start to change on its own. The exaggerated focal points will start to take on a life of their own and enhance the image with your own particular experiences and memories. You will know your work is done when you have succeeded in creating a memorable image that is both succinct and complete, both faithful to the original story and yet your very own.

4. Open your eyes and repeat the key word and primitive elements, keeping that image in mind. This will clear away any fog, and at the same time make sure that when you let go you didn't let go of the original story, too.

5. In your mind, juxtapose the elements relative to one another in line with your image or the way they normally appear in the characters.

6. Take pencil and paper and write the character once, retelling the story as you go.

These are basically the same steps you were led through in reading the stories, even though they were not laid out so clearly before. If you think back to the characters that "worked" best for you, you will probably find that each of these steps was accomplished perfectly. And if you look back at the ones you are forgetting, you should also be able to locate which step you skipped over. In reviewing, these same steps should be followed, with the only clue to set the imagination in motion being the key word.

If you find that you are forgetting the relative position of the elements in a character...

Before all else, go back and reread the frame for that character to see if there were any helpful hints or explanatory notes. If not, return to the frame where the particular primitives were first introduced to see if there is any clue there. If this is not the problem, then, taking care not to add any new words or focal points to your story (since they might end up being elements later on), rethink the story in such a way that the image for each element actually takes the position it has in the character itself. This should not happen often, but when it does, it is worth spending a few minutes to get things sorted out.

If you are confusing one character with another...

Take a careful look at the two stories. Perhaps you have made one or the other of them so vivid that it has attracted extraneous elements to itself that make the image of one character melt into that of another. Or again, it may be that you did not pay sufficient attention to the advice about clarifying a single connotation for the key word.

Whether or not you have had all or only a few of these problems, now is the time to review the first ten lessons keeping an eye out for them. Put aside any schedule you may have set yourself until you have those lessons down perfectly, that is, until you can run through all six steps outlined above for every character, without a hitch. The most important thing in this review is not really to see whether you are remembering the characters, but to learn how to locate problems and deal with them.

One final note before you close the book and begin running your review. Everyone's imagination works differently. Each has its own gifts and its own defects. The more you pay attention to how you imagine things, the more likely you are to find out what works best for you—and more importantly, *why*. The one thing you must distrust, if the system outlined in this book is to work for you, is your ability to remember characters just as they are, without doing any work on them. Once you start making exceptions for characters you "know" or "have no trouble with" or "don't need to run through all the steps with," you are headed for a frustration that will take you a great deal of trouble to dig yourself out of. In other words, if you start using the method only as a "crutch" to help you only with the characters you have trouble with, you will quickly be limping along worse than ever. What we are offering here is not a crutch, but a different way to walk.

That said, let us pick up where we left off. In this lesson we turn from primitive elements having to do with plants to those having to do with animals, four of them in all.

---

237   **portent**

兆

Here we have a pictograph of the back of a turtle, the two sloping vertical strokes representing the central ridge and the four short strokes the pattern. Think of reading turtle shells as a way to foretell the future, and in particular things that **portend** coming evils. [6]

丿　丿　丬　氺　兆　兆

❖ When this character is used as a primitive in its full form, we keep the key-word sense of *portent*. When it appears to the left in its abbreviated form (namely, the left half only, 丬), we shall give it the sense of a *turtle* from the explanation above.

---

238   **peach**

桃

To associate the **peach** with the primitive for *portent*, recall the famous Japanese legend of Momotarō, the **Peach** Boy. It begins once upon a time with a fisherman and his wife who wanted badly to have a child, but none was born to them. Then one day the old man caught a giant **peach**, out of which jumped a healthy young lad whom they named **Peach** Boy. Though the boy was destined to perform heroic deeds, his birth foreshadowed great misfortune (how else could he become a hero?). Thus the **peach** *tree* is seen as a *portent* of coming evil. [10]

---

239   **pooch**

犬

We have already learned that the character for *large* takes on the meaning of the *St. Bernard dog* when used as a primitive. In this frame we finally see why. The *drop* added as a fourth and final stroke means that we have to do with a much smaller dog, a **pooch**, which compared to the *St. Bernard dog* is no more than a *drop* in the kennel. [4]

大 犬

    ❖   As a primitive this character can take two meanings. In the form given here it will mean a very small dog (which we shall refer to as a *chihuahua* for convenience sake). When it takes the form 犭 to the left of a character, we shall give it the meaning of *a pack of wild dogs.*

---

240   **remarkable**

We learn this next character here simply because it is the easiest place to learn it. Later it will figure as an element of other, more complex characters.

The only thing that distinguishes this character from the *pooch* is its **remarkable** *human leg.* As the story goes, the poor creature lost its leg in a car accident and hobbled around pitifully, until one day a mad scientist caught sight of it, dragged it into his castle, and fastened on it the severed leg of a local chorus girl (whose leg had mysteriously flown off her chassis in the middle of a performance, striking a French tourist on the head). So there you have it, the altogether **remarkable** Franken*pooch*. [4]

一　ナ　尢　尤

❖ As a primitive, this character will keep its meaning of the *Frankenpooch*.

241

detest

厌

There are plenty of things in modern civilization to **detest** already, but with the pet-cloning industry looming on the horizon, it's only a matter of time before we find things like *chihuahua factories* engineering made-to-order companions for lonely singles. And who is going to **detest** this more than the flourishing *chihuahua* match-making industry! [6]

厂　厌

242

state of affairs

状

Did you ever hear the legend of the *turtle* who fell madly in love with a *chihuahua* but could not have her because their two families did not like the idea of their children intermarrying? Like all classic stories of ill-fated love, this one shows how the young upset the established **state of affairs** (or "status quo") with an emotion older and more powerful than anything their elders have devised to counter it: blind love. [7]

丶　冫　丬　状

243

put on makeup

妆

The old *woman* across the aisle from you in the subway pulls out her compact to powder her nose, and you are astonished to see that the compact she is using to **put on makeup** is actually a *turtle*. Watch as she turns it over on its shell and rubs its belly with a small brush before applying it to her cheeks, giving them a kind of green blush. You watch with amusement as the *turtle* giggles with glee each time she rubs the brush across its belly. [6]

丬　妆

244	General

将

Inspired by Dr. Seuss's "Yertle the **Turtle**" and already well into his second childhood, the Five-Star **General,** shown here in formal *evening* attire, has replaced the stars on his shoulder straps with ten live baby *turtles,* five on a side. To keep them from falling off, he has *glued* them to his uniform by the shells, belly-up. Little wonder nobody at the military ball wants to waltz with him! [9]

扌　扩　将

245	seize

获

You know the Latin phrase "Carpe diem!" (literally, "Seize the day!"). The classical, and more poetic translation—which is useful to know in any case but particularly helpful for this character—is: "**Seize** the *flower* of the day!" Here we see a *chihuahua* who has **seized** a *flower* only to be chased by a *pack of wild dogs* whom the owner had let loose to retrieve her prize orchid. Not exactly what the ancients had in mind. [10]

246	silent

默

"But my words, like **silent** raindrops fell…." The famous ode to "silence" from which these words were taken begins with an enigmatic phrase that this character will clear up once and for all: "Hello, Darkness, my old friend…." It has long been assumed that Darkness referred to nighttime, but actually it was the name of a **silent** *black chihuahua* that hung around the set without ever once barking, eventually inspiring the song. [16]

247	sort of thing

然

The character in this frame is used as a suffix for certain adverbs and adjectives, and for too many other purposes to capture in a single key word. Rather arbitrarily, we have settled on "**sort of**

thing." Reverting to the time when dog was more widely eaten than it is today (see FRAME 249), we see the *flesh* of a *chihuahua* roasting over a *cooking fire*—a "hot-diggity, dog-diggity" **sort of thing.** [12]

❖   chatterbox

口口   We introduce this element here even though there is only one character we can use it in at this point, since the other examples will be scattered throughout the book. The two *mouths* naturally come to mean **chatterbox** if you recall Mark Twain's famous line: "If we were meant to talk more than listen, we would have two *mouths* and one ear." It will help here to think of a particular **chatterbox** you know, one of those people who talk so incessantly that they could keep two *mouths* busy.

Alternatively, you could use the image of a pair of those *wind-up teeth* you find in novelty shops. In any case, we will use the word **chatterbox** throughout to identify it. [6]

口　　口口

---

248   cry (v.)

哭   Here we have a *chatterbox* of a *chihuahua*. Listen to it gabbing away in its high, shrill voice and you have a pretty good idea of what you sound like when you **cry.** [10]

口口　　哭

---

249   utensil

器   The picture in this character is not a pleasant one. It shows a tiny little *chihuahua* lying on a platter all stuffed and stewed and garnished with vegetables, its paws in the air and a cherry in its mouth. At each corner of the table sits an empty but eager *mouth*, waiting for the **utensils** to arrive so the feast can begin. [16]

口　　口口　　哭　　哭　　器

250   stinking (ADJ.)

臭

This character is a bit friendlier to the animal world than the last one. Our friend the *chihuahua* is alive and well, its *nose* in the air sniffing suspiciously after something **stinking** somewhere or other. [10]

自　臭

251   dog

狗

This is the generic character for **dog**, indicated by the elements for *pack of wild dogs* and *sentence*. Think of the twenty-six letters of the alphabet as a *pack of wild dogs* that run things down in order to work them into *sentences*. Here they are chasing after your fleet-footed pet terrier. When they catch up with the poor little creature, they circle around it and form themselves into the famous *sentence* that contains all the letters of the alphabet: "The quick brown **dog** jumped over the lazy fox." [8]

犭　狗

252   COW

牛

Can you see the "doodle" of a **cow** that has just been run over by a steamroller? The small dot in the first stroke shows its head turned to one side, and the next two strokes, the four legs. [4]

丿　𠂉　⺁　牛

❖ When this character is used as a primitive, the same sense of *cow* is kept. Note only that when it is placed OVER another element, its tail is cut off, giving us 牛. In this case, and when the element appears on the left (牜), the order of the final two strokes is changed.

253   special (ADJ.)

特

We shall let the key word of this frame refer to something in a **special** class all its own—like the sacred *cows* of India that wander freely without fear of being butchered and ground into hamburger. Even though the practice is originally a Hindu one, and in any case no longer followed among the majority of Mahayana Buddhist monks, the Buddha's refusal to take the life of any sentient being makes it only fitting that *cows*, **special** as they are, should be placed on the sacred grounds of a *Buddhist temple* in this character. [10]

丿　　ﾄ　　牜　　牛　　特

---

	declare
254 告	Folklore throughout the world tells us of talking animals who show a wisdom superior to that of human beings, and that same tradition has found its way into television shows and cartoons right in our own century. This character depicts a *cow* with a large *mouth* that utters, with oracular wisdom, answers to questions posed to her. She begins each reply by opening her *mouth* wide enough to swallow you whole and stating (in a thick southern drawl), "Aah do **declare**...."

Observe that the stroke order of the *cow* element changes in the abbreviated form it takes here. [7]

丿　　ﾄ　　牛　　生　　告

---

	vast
255 浩	The word **vast** almost inevitably suggests an endless body of *water*. Only in the case of this character, it is not located in any of the known bodies of *water* but inside the large *mouth* of the oracular cow. Take a peek inside and see if you can see the waves splashing against her palate. [10]

氵　　浩

---

	before
256 先	Take this key word in its physical, not its temporal, sense (even though it refers to both). If you have a *cow* with *human legs,* as the elements show us here, it can only be because you have two people in a *cow* suit. Who would not prefer to be the one standing **before**, rather than the one that holds up the rear and becomes the "butt" of everyone's laughter! [6]

生 牛 先

257　　　　　　　　　　　　　　　　　　wash (v.)

洗

This character is so logical that one is tempted to let the elements speak for themselves: *water . . . before.* Let's see what we can do to make it more memorable.

We all know the parental insistence inflicted on children, "**Wash** your hands *before* you come to the table." At some point, your mom gets so fed up with repeating it that she calls in a plumber to fix a small *water* spigot to the edge of the table in front of each chair. Mom dutifully **washes** her own hands to drop the hint, and everyone does the same in turn. Of course, we would end up with wet laps and *water* all over the floor, but at least everyone's hands would be clean. [9]

氵　洗

Lesson 12

IN THIS THE final lesson of Stories we introduce the useful compound primitive for metal and the elements needed to form it, in addition to picking up a number of stray characters that have fallen by the wayside.

❖   **umbrella**

人 The actual character on which this primitive meaning **umbrella** is based will not show up until Book 2. Meantime, think of it as a large and brightly colored beach **umbrella**. If you compare this with FRAME 8, you will notice how the two strokes touch here, while the character for *eight* would leave a gaping leak in the top. [2]

---

258   **individual**

个 When you see the key word **individual**, think of someone who cultivates eccentricity, or to be more specific still, an idiosyncratic Englishman strutting down Piccadilly with his *umbrella* and his *walking stick*.

   Grammatically, this character is a "classifier" or "measure word," in fact the most common of all. [3]

❖   **crutches**

川 The two vertical lines of this primitive form a clear pictograph of a pair of **crutches**. In contrast to the element for *saber* introduced in FRAME 83, the lines are kept further apart. [2]

259	introduce

At this year's annual convention of the Ambulatory Apparatus Assistance Association (AAAA), the British lobby has succeeded in having the *umbrella* officially approved for membership. To do the honors, we see a pair of *crutches* step up to the podium to **introduce** an *umbrella* representative to the assembly. [4]

260	world

界

Whoever it is that decides to *introduce* the construction of more and more buildings in our cities as "development projects" should be held accountable someday for what a mess we are making of the natural **world**, not to mention the living and working conditions of those who populate them. From a bird's eye view, this glass-and-cement jungle begins to look more and more like a gigantic checkerboard (replacing the neatly partitioned *rice fields*). If you look closely at the character, you should be able to see a kind of movement taking place as still more buildings are being *introduced* into already cramped spaces. [9]

261	tea

As everyone knows, **tea** is made from **tea** leaves. But the **tea** plant itself has its own *flowers,* which can be quite beautiful and add a special flavor to the **tea,** as the Chinese found out over 4,600 years ago. With the image of a terrace of *flowering* **tea** bushes in mind, picture a number of brightly painted and very l-o-n-g *wooden poles* (FRAME 202) placed here and there in their midst, with an *umbrella* at the top of each of them to shade the delicate-tasting **tea** *flowers.* [9]

meeting

This compound primitive depicts a **meeting** as a massive gathering of people under *one umbrella*. The full character from which this derives will be introduced later in FRAME 677. The important thing here is to picture the scene just described and associate it with the word **meeting**. [3]

---

262 **fit** (v.)

The character for **fit** reads literally, top to bottom, as a *meeting* of *mouths*—which is a rather descriptive way of speaking of a romantic kiss. We all know what happens when there is no meeting of minds and when people's ideas don't **fit** with one another. But this character invites us to imagine what happened to the romance of a certain unfortunate couple whose *mouths* didn't **fit**. [6]

---

263 **ha!**

This is a "sound character" for the sound of laughter. Write it twice and it is read—what else!—**ha-ha**. Now nothing *fits* the human *mouth* better than a good laugh, one of the few things that separate us scientifically from other primates. Can it be accidental that the sound of laughter is universal across languages? Another reason to say that it *fits* the *mouth* perfectly. [9]

---

264 **pagoda**

On the left we see a mound of *dirt* and on the right, *flowers* made to *fit* together. The two combine to create a great **pagoda** made of *dirt*, with *flowers* by the tens of thousands made to *fit* together for the roofing of each of the layers. Be sure to put yourself in the scene and *fit* a few of the *flowers* in place yourself so that the image works its way into memory with full force. [12]

扌 扩 塔

---

265 king

王

See what you can do to come up with a pictograph of a **king's** scepter here that suits your own idea of what it should look like. You might even begin with the basic element for *I-beam* and then try to fit the remaining third stroke in. [4]

一 二 干 王

❖ As a primitive, this character can mean either *king* or *scepter*, but it will usually be taken to mean *jewel* or *ball* (from the characters introduced in FRAMES 266 and 268 below).

---

266 jade

玉

Note the *drop* here in the king's *scepter,* which is exactly what you would expect it to be: a gold staff with a large **jade** jewel on the handle, a symbol of his wealth and power. [5]

王 玉

❖ When this character is used as a primitive and retains its original shape, it will keep the original meaning of *jade*. When it appears on the left, however, it will be lacking the final stroke, making it the same as the character in the previous frame, 王. In such cases, its meaning will be *jewel* or *ball*.

---

267 treasure [N.]

宝

Imagine yourself living in a *house* with a hidden **treasure**, a *jade* statuette that is worth all the tea in China. Then picture yourself tearing your *house* apart (the one you are living in now), board by board on a mad **treasure** hunt. [8]

宀 宝

268	ball

球

Immediately we introduce the primitive element for *ball* and we meet the full character for **ball** on which it is based. As an aid to remembering it, think of a catcher signaling the pitcher his *request* not for a strike but for a **ball**. As if he was going to throw his glove or his hat. What else can the pitcher throw? Heaven only knows what Alexander Cartwright was smoking when he gave it that name. [11]

王　球

269	present (ADJ.)

现

Do not think of a "gift" here, but of the **present** time, as distinct from the future and the past. The character gives us a *ball* in which we see the **present** moment—obviously a crystal *ball* that enables us to *see* things going on at the **present** time in faraway places. [8]

王　现

270	play (V.)

玩

The very first game people **played** dates back to the *beginning* of creation, in the Garden of Paradise. For those who see it as a story of original sin, it went something like the game children **play** called "hot potato." You take a *ball* and pass it around as quickly as possible until someone drops the *ball*, thereby losing. In the case of Adam and Eve, it was a piece of fruit from the forbidden tree. "It's not mine, it's his." "No it's not, she had it first…." In any case, if you see an original sin in all of this, then both of them clearly dropped the *ball* for the rest of us. [8]

王　玩

271	crazy

狂

We sometimes refer to people or ideas that are **crazy** as being "looney," which literally means driven mad by the light of the moon. The most famous of the "looneys" are the legendary lycanthropes or "wolfmen." Sometimes the transformation is only a temporary phenomenon; sometimes it is permanent. In the latter case, the poor chap takes off on all fours to live with the beasts. To remember this character, imagine one of these lycanthropes going **crazy** and setting himself up as *king* of a *pack of wild dogs* that roams about and terrorizes innocent suburban communities. [7]

犭 狂

---

272 | emperor

皇

An **emperor**, as we all know, is a ruler—something like a *king* but higher in status. The *white bird* perched above the *king*, elevating him to "imperial" heights, is the messenger the **emperor** sends back and forth to the gods to request advice and special favors, something that *white birds* have long done in folklore throughout the world. [9]

白 皇

---

273 | resplendent

煌

In this character we see a *fire-emperor*, **resplendent** in his glory. He is not an *emperor* who rules over *fire*, but one made of *fire*. His speeches, his temper, his eyes—everything about him is "fiery." [13]

火 煌

---

274 | submit

呈

The trick to remembering this character lies in associating the key word **submit** with the line from the nursery rhyme about four and twenty blackbirds baked in a pie: "Wasn't this a dainty dish to set before the *king*?" If we think of **submit** as "setting before" or "presenting to," then all we have to do to complete the picture is imagine a *king* with his head thrown back and his *mouth* wide open as twenty-four blackbirds fly in one after the other. Dainty? [7]

口　呈

❖ Note that when this character is used as a primitive, in some fonts the first stroke of *king* is drawn from right to left and slanting downwards, replacing the usual horizontal stroke shown here, drawn left to right.

275　　　　　　　　　　　　　　　　　　　　　　　**whole**

全

Being **whole** suggests physical and spiritual health, "having one's act together." This character compares being **whole** to "being *king* under one's own *umbrella*," that is, giving order to one's own life. Granted it sounds terribly abstract, but what could be more abstract than the word **whole**? [6]

人　全

276　　　　　　　　　　　　　　　　　　　　　　　**logic**

理

We first referred to this character back in FRAME 179, to which you might want to return to have a peek. The image of **logic** we are given is something like a central *jewel* in a *computer,* like the *jewels* in old clocks that keep them running smoothly. Try to picture yourself making your way through all the RAMS and ROMS and approaching this shining *jewel,* a chorus of voices and a blast of trumpets in the background heralding the great seat of all-knowing **logic**. [11]

王　理

277　　　　　　　　　　　　　　　　　　　　　　　**lord**

主

"A man's home is his castle," goes the proverb from an age where it was the male who was **lord** of the household. Fundamentally, it means only that every one of us is a bit (or *drop*) of a *king* in our own environment. As for the positioning of the elements, if you take care to "read off" the primitives in this way, you won't end up putting the *drop* down below, where it turns the character into *jade*. [5]

丶 主

❖ When using this character as a primitive element, we set the key word aside entirely and take it as a pictograph of a solid brass *candlestick* (with the drop representing the flame at the top).

278

pour

注

Picture yourself trying to hold your hand steady as you **pour** *water* from a lighted *candlestick*. What could be more ridiculous, or simpler, as a way to recall this character? [8]

氵 注

279

gold

金

If this were not one of the most common characters you will ever have to write, we would apologize for having to give the explanation that follows. Anyway, we want to depict bars of **gold** bullion with an *umbrella* overhead to shade them from the heat (and perhaps to hide them as well). The bullion is made by melting down all the *scepters* of the kingdom, *drop* by *drop*, and shaping them into bars. [8]

丿 入 仝 今 全 余 余 金

❖ When this character is used as a primitive, it means not only *gold* but any *metal* at all. Note how it changes shape when it stands to the left of other elements: the last four strokes are simplified to a single line with a hook at the end: 钅.

280

bell

钟

Reading off the elements we have *metal middle*. And what has a *metal middle*? Why, a **bell**, of course. If you can imagine a clump of *metal* dangling somewhere in your own *middle*, you'd **bellow**, too. Think of it before you go on to the next frame. [9]

丿 ㄏ ㄎ 钅 钅 钟

281

铜
copper

Picture an order of *monks* serving as chaplains for the police force. Their special habit, made of protective *metal,* is distinguished by a row of **copper** buttons just like the "**cops**" they serve. [11]

钅 铜

282

钓
go fishin'

The character we learned for *fishing* (FRAME 155) refers to the professional, net-casting industry, while the key word in this frame, **go fishin'**, is related to the pastime or sport. The odd thing is that your "go-fishin'" rod is a *golden ladle* which you are using to scoop *gold*fish out of a river. [8]

钅 钓

283

针
needle [N.]

In FRAME 10 we referred ahead to this full character from which the primitive for *needle* (on the right) derives. Since we already expect that **needles** are made of *metal,* let us picture a set of solid *gold* darning **needles** to complete the character. [7]

钅 针

284

钉
nail [N.]

Here we have the full character for **nail** from which the primitive element of the same meaning derived (see page 54). As long as you picture the **nail** as made of pure *gold* and bending out of shape ever time you try to hammer it, you should have no trouble remembering it. [7]

钅 钉

| 285 | inscription |

铭

Take **inscription** in the sense of the *name* you ask the jeweler to carve on a *gold* bracelet or inside a *gold* ring to identify its owner or communicate some sentimental message. It will help if you can recall the first time you had this done and the feelings you had at the time. [11]

钅 铭

| 286 | at ease |

镇

The first lie-detector machines of the twentieth century worked by wiring pieces of *metal* to the body to measure the amount of sweat produced when questions were asked. It was discovered that nervousness produced more sweat, indicating subconscious reactions when the *true* facts of the matter were getting too close for comfort. The only way to beat the apparatus is to have complete control over yourself and remain perfectly **at ease**. Picture yourself trying to do it while the examiners ask questions guaranteed to extract buckets of sweat from you. [15]

钅 镇

With that, we come to the end of the first part of this book. Before going on to the next section, it would be a good idea to return to the Introduction and read it once again. Anything that did not make sense at first should now be clear.

By this time, too, you should be familiar with the use of all the Indexes. If not, take a few minutes to study them, since you will no doubt find them useful in the pages ahead.

Plots

LESSON 13

By this time, if you have been following along methodically frame by frame, you may find yourself growing impatient at the thought of having to read through more than 3,000 of these little stories. You probably want to move at a quicker pace and in your own way. Take heart, for that is precisely what we are going to start doing from now on. But if you happen to be one of those people who are perfectly content to have someone else do all the work for them, then brace yourself for the task that lies ahead.

We begin the weaning process by abbreviating the stories into simple plots, leaving it up to you to patch together the necessary details in a manner similar to what we did in the previous lessons. As mentioned in the Introduction, the purpose of the longer stories was to impress on you the importance of recreating a complete picture in imagination, and to insure that you did not merely try to associate words with *other words* but with *images*. The same holds true for the characters that remain.

Before setting out on our way again, a word of caution is in order. Left to its own, your imagination will automatically tend to add elements and see connections that could prove counterproductive in the long run. For example, you might think it perfectly innocent and admissible to alter the primitive meaning for *child* to *infant*, or that for *cliff* to *cave*. In fact, these changes would be confusing when you meet the characters and primitives with those meanings later on. You would return to the earlier characters and find that everything had become one great confusion.

You may have experienced this problem already when you decided to alter a story to suit your own associations. That should help you appreciate how hard it is to wipe out a story once you have learned it, particularly a vivid one. To protect yourself against this, stick faithfully to the key words as they are given, and try not to move beyond the range of primitive meanings listed. Where such confusion can be anticipated, a longer story will be presented as a protective measure, but you will have to take care of the rest.

We start our Plots with a group of 31 characters having to do with travel, and the primitives that accompany them: a *road*, a pair of *walking legs*, and a *car*.

❖

辶

road

The **road** envisioned here is a road for traffic, or a path or walk-way. The natural sweep of these three simple strokes should be easy to remember, as it appears so often. [3]

丶　　 氵　　 辶

287

道

way

The key word carries both the sense of a road or **way** for transit and a **way** or method of doing something. The primitives here read: *heads* and *road*. You've probably heard about companies cleaning house and threatening that "*heads* are going to roll." Well, here is the *road* they are rolling on. If you want, think of it as the **Way** of the Bottom Line. [12]

首　　 道

288

达

reach (v.)

Traveling down the *road* in the Swiss Alps, you are accosted by a prodigal *St. Bernard* who draws his six-shooters and orders you to "**Reach** for the sky!" as he and his band of mutts proceed to rob you of your belongings. [6]

大　　 达

289

远

distant

We usually think of something **distant** as located at the end of the *road*, but here it is pictured as **distant** in the other direction on the *road* of time—at the *beginning*. [7]

元　　 远

290

适

suitable

As an alternative punishment to the proverbial bar of soap for persons who use language not **suitable** in polite company, this character has offenders licking a stretch of *road* clean with their *tongue.* The hope is that they will come to appreciate **suitable** language as their naughty words "bite the dust" once and for all. [9]

舌　适

---

291   cross (v.)

过

Why didn't the chicken **cross** the *road*, even though the light was green? Because its feet were *glued to* the sidewalk. [6]

寸　过

---

292   stride

迈

We measure the distance we walk on a *road* with a pedometer attached to our belt. If you think of walking the recommended *ten-thousand*-steps-a-day to better health, this character takes care of itself. [6]

辶　迈

---

293   speedy

迅

This character shows a **Speedy** Gonzales wanna-be tearing down the highway in his '57 Chevy, only to be brought to an abrupt halt by the highway police who have scattered *hooks* and *needles* across the *road* to puncture his tires. [6]

乁　凡　迅

---

294   create

造

In the biblical story the Almighty **creates** the world in six days, simply by *declaring* "Let there be this! Let there be that!" Wouldn't it be a lot easier on everyone if we could invoke such divine assistance in repairing our *roads* without having to close down lanes and force detours? [10]

告　造

295 escape (v.)

逃

The thing about a *portent* is that it points to what lies ahead as inevitable, like something at the end of a one-lane, one-directional *road*. You can run, but you can't **escape** it. [9]

兆　逃

296 patrol (v.)

巡

The motorcycle police, exercising their duty to **patrol** the highways, are pictured in this character as a virtual *flood* washing down a *road*. [6]

巛　巡

297 choose

选

"Two *roads* diverged in a yellow wood," begins "The *Road* Less Travelled," the famous poem by Robert Frost that talks about having to **choose** one's path in life. The elements *before* and *road* should be more than enough to make the connections. [9]

298 modest

逊

The *grandchild* we see on the *road* here is taking grandma for a ride in his little red wagon, a rather more **modest** means of transportation than the Rolls Royce grandma is used to. [9]

299 stroll

逛

A *crazy* person decides to **stroll** down the middle of a very busy *road* during rush hour. [10]

狂　逛

300 car

车

You may keep the whole range of connotations for this key word, **car**, provided they do not interfere with the pictograph. Look for the front and back axles (the first and last horizontal strokes) and the seat in the carriage in the middle. [4]

一　二　车　车

❖ *Car, cart, wagon,* and *vehicle* may all be used as primitive meanings.

| 301 | one after another |

连

Imagine a convoy of large *vehicles* transporting heavy construction equipment. They are following **one after another** and hogging the entire *road* for miles on end. [7]

车　连

| 302 | lotus |

莲

Imagine yourself sitting on the edge of a **lotus** pond in the early morning as the pink and white **lotus** *flowers* softly pop into bloom, *one after another.* Given the subtlety of sound they make, it is no surprise that the opening of the **lotus** *flower* has served Buddhist monks for centuries as an image of the moment of spiritual enlightenment. [10]

艹　莲

| ❖ | butcher |

刖

The elements for *flesh* and *saber* here combine to create a compound element for a *butcher* and his trade. [6]

月　刖

| 303 | in front |

前

Picture a pair of *horns* (borrowed from a Texas steer) hanging **in front** of a *butcher's* shop. [9]

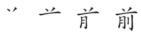

❖ Following the explanation above, when this character is used as a primitive, the meaning will be a *butcher shop.*

---

304   shears

剪

Here, weld together a pair of *daggers* to make some meat **shears** for use in the *butcher shop*. [11]

❖   slaughterhouse

俞

The first three strokes of this primitive, you will remember, are the primitive element for *meeting*. The most common *meeting* place for *butchers* is a **slaughterhouse**. [9]

亼   俞

---

305   transport

输

Usually we employ *vehicles* to **transport** refrigerated meats, but here we have an entire *slaughterhouse* that is being carried across the country on wheels. [13]

---

306   exceed

逾

The *road* to the *slaughterhouse* is a two-lane, one-way highway, crowded with animals of all sizes approaching their doomsday. To accommodate the chickens, the speed limit is set at 2 mph. A motorcycle cop drives up and down warning the buffalo and ostriches not to **exceed** the speed limit. [12]

俞   逾

---

                                 walking legs

夂

We call this element **walking legs** because it indicates "legs in motion," whether you want to think of them as jogging or walking in long strides, as the shape seems to suggest. Be careful how you write it, with the first two strokes like a stylized "7." [3]

307   strip [N.]

条

Think of the *walking legs* of an acrobat, a long balancing *pole* in hand, as he makes his way across the tightrope which, unbenownst to the spectators, is really a long **strip** of velcro that sticks firmly to his slippers. The cat is let out of the bag when he loses his balance and rolls over without falling. [7]

夂   条

308   location

处

A dowser is called in to find water. Back and forth he goes, his *walking legs* making their way over the property until his *divining rod* starts to dip downwards, telling him that he has at last found the right **location**. [5]

夂   处

309   each

各

"Suum cuique" goes the popular Latin proverb. A certain disease of the English language makes it almost impossible to translate the phrase without gender bias. In any event, here we see someone walking with his/her *mouth* between his/her *walking legs*, giving us an image of "To **each** his/her own." [6]

夂   各

❖ The sense of the proverb should help when using this character as a primitive; otherwise, reduce it to its original elements. But do NOT associate it in any way with the word "every," which we shall meet later in another context.

310   pattern

格

To *each tree* its own **pattern**. Think of the key word as referring to the **patterns** on an array of Hawaiian shirts that you are dressing up the *trees* in your garden with to give to *each* its own identity and keep them distinct from one another. Take a moment to admire the whole fashion show. [10]

才　格

311　abbreviation

略

Each field has its own **abbreviations** (chemistry, philosophy, sports, etc.). Needless to say, the "stronger" primitive—that is to say, the simpler and more often used one—takes the dominant position on the left, even though the story would read them off the other way around. [11]

田　略

312　guest

客

When you are a **guest** in a courteous town, *each house*hold has its own way of welcoming you, and *each house* becomes your home. [9]

宀　客

313　forehead

额

As Miss Manners will be the first to tell you, out of respect one does not look straight into the eyes of one's *guests* of honor, but focuses on the knots of their neckties. Here, however, you are told to look at the upper part of the *head*, to the **forehead** of your *guest*. [15]

客　额

314　summer

夏

In the **summer**, fatigued by the heat, you have devised a creative and energy-saving fan: you have hired a couple of racewalking stars in training for the **summer** Olympics, stuck their *noses* to the *ceiling*, and asked them to practice by moving their *walking legs* around quickly in mid-air, giving you a fresh breeze and enhancing their chances of picking up a medal. [10]

一　百　夏

315   L.A.

洛

The key word (the well-known abbreviation of the city of Los Angeles) represents one of the important uses of this character in Chinese, namely, as the first character in the full compound for Los Angeles. How do we get from *each drop of water* to the city of **L.A.**? Think of what happens to the moisture in the air over that city. To *each droplet of water* is added its own particle of pollutant. Hence the gray blanket of smog that hangs over that unfortunate symbol of industrial devastation. [9]

氵　洛

316   fall

落

One of the worst consequences of the smog in cities like *L. A.* is that the petals of *flowers* exposed to the open air **fall** before their time—good news for the artificial *flower* industry, but bad news for those who prefer the real thing. [12]

艹　落

317   prepare

备

Here we see Rocky Balboa as he **prepares** for a bout in southern China. Instead of running up the steps to the Philadelphia Museum of Art, his *walking legs* now have to slog their way through the thick mud of the local *rice fields*. [8]

夂　备

LESSON 14

THE NEXT group of primitives, around which this lesson is designed, have to do with lids and headgear.

❖   crown

⌐

This pictograph of a simple **crown** is distinguished from the *roof* only by the absence of the chimney (the first *drop* at the top). It can be used for all the principal connotations of the word **crown**. We will meet the full character from which this element is derived later on, in FRAME 322. [2]

ı   ⌐

---

318   superfluous

兀

A *crown* is supposed to be a sign of leadership, wisdom, and nobility. Without those virtues, it is a **superfluous** symbol, as in the case of the royal airhead depicted in this character. You can actually see the *wind* blowing between his ears. [4]

⌐   兀

---

319   profound

沉

See the philosopher lost in **profound** speculation on matters metaphysical, the *drops of water* on his forehead showing the intensity of his concentration, and the accusation of his more pragmatic neighbors that the whole thing is **profound**ly *superfluous*. [7]

氵   沉

---

320   army

军

The *crowned vehicle* depicted here is a "chariot," symbol of a Caesar's **army**. [6]

冖 军

❖ Used as a primitive this character means only *chariot*.

---

321   radiance

辉

Take advantage of the first syllable of the key word to think of the *ray* of light to the left. Now add the glittering *chariot* that is emitting those *rays* and you have **radiance**. [12]

光 辉

---

322   crown

冠

By having the **crown** pass from one age to the next, a people keeps itself *glued* to its *beginnings*. [9]

冖 冠 冠

❖

亠

                                     top hat

The broad rim and tall top of the **top hat** is pictured graphically here in these two simple strokes.

   At this point, by the way, you can revert back to FRAME 6. If you have had any trouble with that character, you now have the requisite elements to make a story: **Six** suggests the number of legs on a bug of some sort. Actually, it's a cockroach standing on its hind *animal legs* and sporting a tall silk *top hat* in a hopeless attempt to pass itself off as a gentlebug. [2]

丶 亠

❖

亢

                                  whirlwind

A formal high, silk *top hat* resting atop an eddy of *wind* represents a **whirlwind**. To keep it distinct from *wind*, try to picture the vortex, or tornado-like spinning movement, of a *whirlwind*. The next frame should help. [4]

亠 亢

323

坑

pit (N.)

A *whirlwind* begins to dig its way into the *soil* like a drill until it makes a deep **pit**. [7]

土　坑

324

亩

Chinese acre

A **Chinese acre**, whose size can change according to the region, is shown here as a *rice field* marked off at its corners with a *top hat*. A convenient marker, when you think of it, since if set on a pole it can also serve as a scarecrow. [7]

亠　亩

325

高

tall

Recalling an image from FRAME 188, first see the *mouth* under the extraterrestrial's transparent *helmet*, and then the *mouth* under the *top hat* of one of his mates who has tried on the *top hat* only to find that this strange earthlings' headgear makes him look much, much **taller** than everyone else. [10]

亠　古　亭　高

❖ As a primitive, this character keeps its sense of *tall* and its position at the top of other primitives, but its writing is abbreviated in one of two forms: when drawn with only the first five strokes (亠), it keeps the generic meaning of *tall*, but when the next two strokes are added (亯). it will mean a tall *tiara*, since the element for *hood* is compressed into the form of a *crown*.

326

享

enjoy

While the other *children* **enjoy** themselves at hopscotch and jacks, this one, a *tall child*—but a REALLY *tall child*, 11 feet 4 inches and only in second grade—**enjoys** herself at less terrestrial play: peeping into bird nests, chatting up the giraffes at the zoo, and high-jumping over the pole-vault bar. [8]

言　享

327　ripe

熟

When fruit is **ripe** and in season, we can't get enough of it. The problem is, we want to *enjoy* the taste of **ripe** peaches and mangos all year round. What we have here is a *bottle of pills* distilled from **ripe** fruit, after stewing for hours over a *cooking fire*, into "essence of peach" and "essence of mango." *Enjoy* them whenever you want. [15]

享　孰　熟

328　pavilion

亭

Think of all the **pavilions** at County Fairs or World Expos you have wandered into or seen advertised in the media, and you will no doubt see rising up among them the towering *spike* of a structure with a revolving restaurant at the top—often the only **pavilion** to survive the event. The difference here is that the restaurant is in the shape of a high, bejeweled golden *tiara*. [9]

329　shiny

亮

To restore those musty old *tiaras* in the museum back to their original **shiny** luster, it occurs to you to try an air blaster. Picture yourself with a tank of compressed air strapped to your back, protective goggles over your eyes, and nozzle in hand. As you approach the row of irreplaceable treasures, you squeeze the trigger and a hurricane-force *wind* sends the whole display flying against the far wall and landing in a heap of junk. [9]

330　capital

京

When you think of a **capital** city, think of the *tall*, domed capitol building with swarms of *small* folk gathered around its base, probably demonstrating for their government's attention. [8]

亠 京

❖ As a primitive element, this character will take the meaning of a *capitol building*.

---

331 景

scenery

Scenery is depicted as a *sun* rising over a *capitol building*, which is as close as some city dwellers get to natural **scenery** for years at a time! [12]

日 景

---

332 就

at once

The key word **at once** suggests an order to be carried out immediately. In this case, it is our little *Frankenpooch* being summoned to come **at once** to the *capitol building* to testify before a subcommittee on organized crime in the canine world. [12]

京 就

❖ 吉

lidded crock

Soil over the *mouth* of a container gives us a piece of clay pottery with its lid. Behold the **lidded crock**. [6]

土 吉

---

333 周

circumference

Look more closely at your *lidded crock* and you will see little ruler marks along its bottom edge. This is so you can use it to calculate the **circumference** of your motorcycle *helmet*: just begin at a fixed point and turn the *lidded crock* around and around, keeping it flush against the side of the *helmet*, until you come back to your starting point. If you kept track of how many turns and part-turns your *lidded crock* made, you now know the **circumference**.

You could also think of the marks on the **circumference** as indicating the days of the week, since this is another meaning attached to this character. [8]

几　周

❖ As a primitive, this character can take the added significance of a *lap*.

334

土

soldier

The shape of this character, slightly differing from that for *soil* by virtue of its shorter final stroke, hints at a broad-shouldered, slender-waisted **soldier** standing at attention. [3]

一　十　士

335

吉

lucky

Here we see a statue of the famous *Soldier* of Good Fortune, G. L. ("Good Luck") Joe, standing on a street with a gigantic open *mouth*. Every day people walk up to and stick their heads down deep inside. As the superstition goes, G. L. Joe will make this their **lucky** day. [6]

士　吉

❖ When this character is used as a primitive, we shall take this shape to mean an *aerosol can*, from the *mouth* and the very tight-fitting *lid* (note how it differs here from the *lidded crock*).

336

壮

robust

The most **robust** *turtles* are singled out to become *soldiers* in the elite amphibious assault force. [6]

丬　壮

LESSON 15

IN THIS LESSON WE consider a group of primitives associated one way or another with schooling. Be sure to give your stories enough time to come to life in imagination, because your images will need a lot more vividness than these brief "plots" allow for. You know that you are NOT giving enough time when you find yourself memorizing definitions rather than playing with images.

❖   schoolhouse

Here we see a little red **schoolhouse** with three dots on the roof. As you write it in the following frames, you should acquire a "feel" for the way the first two short strokes move left to right, and the third one right to left. Write it twice now, saying to yourself the first time as you write the first three strokes, "In the **schoolhouse** we learn our A-B-Cs," and the second time, "In the **schoolhouse** we learn our 1-2-3s." [5]

---

337   study (v.)

The *child* in the little red *schoolhouse* is there for one reason only: to **study**. Anyone who has gone through the schooling system knows well enough to **study** is one thing and to learn is quite another. [8]

---

338   senses (N.)

In addition to the five external **senses**, we often speak of a "sixth sense" that doesn't always agree with the other five. In today's, science-dominated *schoolhouses*, children are taught to trust what they can *see* with their eyes, but sooner or later they will have also to learn to trust in what they can *see* intuitively. [9]

㣺 覚

taskmaster

❖

夂

First find the long rod (the first stroke), held in the hand of someone seated (the next 3 strokes, not unlike the pictograph for *woman*, but quite different from that for *walking legs* introduced in Lesson 13). The only thing left to do is conjure up the memory of some **taskmaster** (or taskmistress) from your past whom you will "never forget." [4]

丿 乚 ケ 夂

339

攻

attack

A foreman, the *taskmaster* at a large construction site, orders his workers to pick up their *I-beams* and **attack** the house of the little old grandmother who refuses to leave the home she has lived in all of her life. [7]

工 攻

340

敌

enemy

The **enemy** suggested here is not one who stands before you with a weapon, but the *taskmaster* who stands behind you and lashes you with his *tongue*. Literally. [10]

舌 敌

341

败

fail

The *taskmaster* lays the rod to all the *clams* that **fail** to make the grade in Marine School. [8]

贝 败

342   **deliberately**

故

To do something wrong **deliberately** is to risk the ire of that most *ancient* of *taskmasters:* the law. [9]

古   故

343   rescue^(v.)

救

Usually it is the school *taskmaster* who is *requesting* something or other of us, but here you are drowning in the swimming pool and the only one around is that most dreaded of all your curricular *taskmasters*, your English poetry teacher. You carefully parse your words: "I respectfully *request* that you **rescue** me immediately." [11]

求   救

344   revere

敬

When you **revere** someone, you get self-conscious and may try to speak in *flowery sentences* out of veneration or fear. The *taskmaster* at the right is drilling you in the practice of "polite language." [12]

艹   苟   敬

345   spacious

敞

The leap from *esteem* and *taskmaster* to **spacious** seems huge, but if we associate the key word with the song "America the Beautiful," it becomes but a small step. "O beautiful for **spacious** skies..." begin the well-known lyrics that *esteem* the natural beauties with which the country has been blessed. But then, directly in the second stanza, the song enjoins the country to "Confirm thy soul in self-control," reminding us of the need to be *taskmasters* over our selfish appetites. [12]

尚   敞

346   say

言

Fearing that "what you **say** can and will be held against you," people will often play fast and loose with the truth, "talking out of *two* sides of their *mouth*." But even putting a *top hat* on their hypocrisy in a masquerade of politeness does little to hide the duplicity of what they **say**. [7]

* When this character appears as a primitive, it will often be given the meaning of *words*. Used as a primitive, to the left, this character changes its shape to 讠, following the same principles as *metal* (see FRAME 279).

347   police (N.)

警

For all the negative things some people have to say about the **police**, when they get pulled over on the highway, chances are they bite their tongues and make a special effort to *revere* the officers' *words*, hoping to get off with just a warning. [19]

敬 警

348   plan (N.)

计

Words and a *needle* combine to form the character for a **plan**. Think of the *needle* on some kind of meter or gauge, depending on what kind of **plan** you intend for your story. [4]

讠 计

349   yield

让

Think of the **yield** sign you see at an intersection. The assumption that all drivers understand what they are supposed to **yield**, and to whom, is clearly unwarranted. We therefore recommend that a cartoon bubble be placed *above* the **yield** sign to spell things out for them in plain and simple *words*. [5]

讠 让

350	prison

狱

Here we have a typical scene in a high-security **prison** for the scum of the canine world: a weak and vulnerable *chihuahua* (doing time for insider trading) surrounded on the **prison** yard by a ferocious looking *pack of wild dogs* (all long-timers and hardened criminals). The only thing the *chihuahua* has to protect himself from the pack are his shrill and frightened *words*. [9]

犭　犰　狱

351	condemn

讨

Words spoken to **condemn** us stick to us like *glue* in a way no other *words* can. [5]

讠　讨

352	instruction

训

The personalism connoted by the word **instruction**, as opposed to "teaching" or "discipline," suits the picture here of *words* guiding one's progress like the gentle flowing of a *stream*. Even the etymology of the word **instruction** suggests the sense of "pouring into". [5]

讠　训

353	knowledge

识

The character for **knowledge** suggests something that is *only words*—until, that is, they have been turned into action or internalized into wisdom. That is the plot. It's up to you to turn it into a memorable image. [7]

讠　识

354	talk (N.)

话

That the *words* of the *tongue* should form the character for **talk** is no surprise. Think of the phrase, "He's all **talk**," and a story should not be far behind. [8]

讠　话

355 　　　　　　　　　　　　　　　　　　　　　poem

诗

Since silence is treasured so highly at a *Buddhist temple*, the *words* spoken there must be well chosen. Perhaps this is why the records of the monks often read to us like **poems**. [8]

讠　诗

356 　　　　　　　　　　　　　　　　　　　language

语

Whereas the character for *say* and *talk* (FRAMES 346 and 354) focused on the actual talking, the character for **language** stresses the fact that although it is *I* (remember: the *literary I*) who use them, the *words* of a **language** are not my own. [9]

讠　语

357 　　　　　　　　　　　　　　　　　　　tune (N.)

调

A complete **tune** is composed not only of a succession of notes but also of one *lap* of the *words* that go with it. [10]

讠　调

358 　　　　　　　　　　　　　　　　　　　discuss

谈

In attempts to **discuss** an issue, the fervor of one's convictions can come to the surface and create an *inflammation* of *words* (if you will, the "cuss" in **discuss**). [10]

讠　谈

LESSON 16

IN THIS SHORT lesson of 20 characters we come to an interesting cluster of primitive elements—unique among all those we have met or will meet throughout this book—built up step by step from one element. Be sure to study this lesson as a unit in order to appreciate the similarities and differences of the various elements, which will appear frequently later on.

---

arrow

Here we see a pictograph of a long and slightly warped **arrow**. By extending the short final stroke in both directions, you should see the **arrow**head without any difficulty. The hook at the bottom represents the feathers at the butt end. When it serves as a semi-enclosure for other primitives, the first stroke is drawn longer, as we shall see in the following frames. [3]

359

式

style (N.)

Take **style** in its sense of some fashion design or model. Then let the element *arrow* and *craft* stand for the well-known **style** of shirts known as "*Arrow* shirts" because of the little *arrow* sewn on each one. [6]

一　　工　　式　　式

360

试

test

When a manufacturer produces a new *style* for the market, the first thing that is done is to run a **test** on consumers, asking them to *say* frankly what they think about the product. Never mind the anachronism (the character was there well before our capitalistic market system) if it helps you remember. [8]

361	halberd

A halberd is a kind of lance made up of a long, *arrowhead*-shaped pike with two curved blades below it. If you don't have one in your closet, you might consult a dictionary. [4]

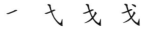

❖ When this character is used as a primitive, we will revert to a friendler meaning. Think of the third stroke as a kind of deocrative tassle fixed to the shaft of an *arrow* to indicate that it is no longer a weapon but a symbol of a *fiesta*.

362	war

There was once a very wise leader who consulted a clairvoyant to *tell his fortune* as he was about to go to **war**. The picture she painted of death and destruction was so grim that right then and there he ordered that all preparations for **war** be halted and threw a grand *fiesta* for the troops instead. [9]

363	scratch ^(v.)

Here we see a contest taking place at a local *fiesta*, with two *saber*-wielding combatants. The first to **scratch** his opponent is the winner. Serious wounds are prohibited; just the slightest **scratch** or nick is enough to claim victory. See them prancing about each other like ballerinas, ever so gently moving their weapons so as not to inflict any real harm. [6]

364	or

Unless you were one of those saintly children who always did what they were told, you should have no trouble associating the key word in this frame with the stern warning of a parent or teacher to do something—"**or** else!" Here we see a rather grim depiction of the **or** else: you are lying down with your *mouth* on the *floor* (an inventive substitute to wearing a dunce-cap and sitting in the corner) while everyone else is out enjoying the *fiesta*.

Just as the phrase "**or** else" does not necessarily imply dire consequences but can be used as a simple indication of an alternative, so, too, this character is a simple conjunction. Pay special attention to the stroke order. [8]

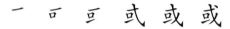

---

365   burglar

贼

From a **burglar's** point of view, a *fiesta* is an occasion to take out the old lockpicking *needle* and break into the unattended safe filled with the family *shells* (the old form of money, as we saw in FRAME 80). [10]

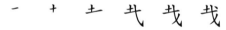

❖   Thanksgiving

To make this primitive more concrete, we choose the word **Thanksgiving**. The term, as the primitives make clear, refers to a *"land fiesta"* or harvest feast. [6]

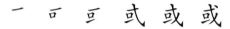

---

366   laden

载

It is not hard to think of the folks from the Little House on the Prairie riding a *cart* **laden** to overflowing with all the trimmings of a great *Thanksgiving* feast. [10]

❖   parade

Note first the order of the writing. The second stroke, which has been added to *fiesta*, gives us a full-fledged enclosure, because of which we should always think of this as a **parade** OF something or other, namely whatever is inside the enclosure. [5]

一 厂 戊

367

茂

lush

The sense of the key word **lush** is that of something growing luxuriously, though not necessarily in excess—in this case a whole *parade* of weeds (outcast *flowers*). By way of exception, the *flowers* take their normal place OVER the enclosure. [8]

艹 茂

368

成

turn into

Let the phrase "**turn into**" suggest some sort of a magical change. What happens here is that the *parade* marching down main street **turns into** a *dagger*-throwing bout between competing bands. Note how only one stroke has to be added to make the change. [6]

一 厂 厅 成

369

城

city

In this frame, we see a mound of *dirt* that is being *turned into* the walls of a **city** (the way you may have built a sand castle as a child playing on the beach). [9]

土 城

370

诚

sincere

The sure test of how **sincere** you are is whether or not your *words* are being *turned into* deeds. [8]

讠 诚

❖

戌

march

As distinct from the *parade*, the **march** points to a formal demonstration, whose emotions are generally a far cry from the happy spirit of the *parade*. The inclusion of the *one* gives a sense of the singlemindedness and unity of the group joined in the **march**. As was the case with *parade*, the primitive inside the enclosure indicates who or what is **marching**. [6]

一　厂　厂　戌　戌　戌

371

might ^(N.)

威

Here we see a *march* of *women* demonstrating on behalf of equal rights, a show of **might** not always welcome to the male chauvinist population. [9]

厂　反　威

372

salty

咸

This character describes an unfinished and little-known album by an even less known rock band entitled "**Salty** Peppers Lonely Hearts Club Band." The *mouths*, of course, belong to the band members who have been given their *marching* orders—right out of the recording studio—to make room for a group of four long-haired Liverpudlean lads. [9]

厂　咸　咸

❖

float

戋

The **floats** that are such an important part of a *fiesta* are shown here by the addition of the extra horizontal stroke, which you may take as a quasi-pictographic representation of the platform structure of a **float**. [5]

一　二　弐　戋　戋

373

coin ^(N.)

钱

Those special *gold*-colored tokens minted each year for the Mardi Gras and thrown into the crowds by people on the *floats* give us the character for **coins**. [10]

钅　钱

374	shallow
浅	An entourage of *floats* going from one town to the next must always seek a **shallow** place to cross the *water*. Try to picture what happens if they don't. [8]

氵 浅

375	cheap
贱	When the town tightwad agrees to enter a *float* in the annual parade, he first calculates how many *clams* it is going to set him back and then starts pinching pennies to make it as **cheap** as possible. [9]

376	Yao
尧	This character, used as a family name, is best associated with the legendary sage king **Yao**, who lived around 2300 BCE and became a model for rulers in ancient China. One fact about this king is that he is said to have invented the board game of Go as a way to sharpen the brain of his dim-witted son. Another little-known fact, unsupported by any respectable historian of China or any evidence whatever that we know of, is that King **Yao** modified the head of his son's *halberd* (the missing final stroke) so that it could be thrown like a javelin. The invention, intended originally for **Yao** Junior's physical development, was later passed on to the Greeks, who painted it on their vases and introduced it into the first Olympic Games. The horizontal stroke is, of course, the foul line beyond which the *human legs* of the javelin thrower must not cross. [6]

❖ When this character is used as a primitive, it will take the meaning of a *javelin thrower* from the story above.

377	fever
烧	**Fevers** come from devilish supernaturals who cast down *fire* on unsuspecting mortals the way the Nordic God of thunder, Thor, casts down his thunderbolts. Here we see a *javelin thrower*

heaving *fire* at his victims and causing their body temperatures to surge to 103°F (in the shade). [10]

火　烧

378

dawn

晓

Unlike Homer's "rosy-fingered **dawn**," which gently rouses one from slumber, this character depicts a kind of "slap-in-the-face **dawn**" intended for incorrigible sluggards on earth: the first rays of morning light **are** hurled down from the *sun* by a merciless *javelin thrower* of a deity. [10]

日　晓

LESSON 17

BECAUSE OF THE rather special nature of that last group of primitives, it might be a good idea not to rush too quickly into this lesson until you are sure you have them all learned and fitted out with good images. Now we will take up another set of primitives built up from a common base, though fewer in number and lacking the similarity of meaning we saw in the last lesson.

379	stop [(v.)]

止

The character for **stop** is easiest to learn as a pictograph, though you have to take a moment to see it. Take it as a rather crude drawing of a footprint, the track that is left when your foot has **stopped** long enough to make an impression. The first three strokes represent the front of the foot and the last one, the heel. The big toe (the second stroke sticking out to the right) indicates that this is a left foot. [4]

$$| \quad \vdash \quad 止 \quad 止$$

❖ Although the meaning of *stop* will be retained, we will return often to the pictographic meaning of *footprint*. When the last two strokes are moved to look like this 止, it means a whole *trail of footprints,* as you might find on the beach. We will not see an example of this until FRAME 1050.

380	footstep

步

Footprints that follow one another a *few* at a time indicate **footsteps.** Don't forget what we mentioned back in FRAME 110 about the abbreviation of the element for *few* when it appears under another element. [7]

$$止 \quad 牛 \quad 牛 \quad 步$$

381	ford [(v.)]

涉

One way to **ford** a body of *water* is to wade across it on foot. You need to take your *footsteps* one after the other, but unlike a stroll on dry land, you have to be careful to keep your balance and not end up in the *water*. Remember what is feels like to walk gingerly on the slippery bottom of a shallow stream, calculating your every *footstep* as you go. [10]

氵 涉

382

repeatedly

频

The image of something occurring **repeatedly**, over and over again, is of having one's *head* walked on, a succession of *footsteps* trampling on your cranium. [13]

步 频

383

agree

肯

Seeing *footprints* on someone's *flesh* indicates a rather brutal way of having persuaded that person to **agree**. [8]

止 肯

384

look forward to

企

Who doesn't **look forward to** *stopping* under a large beach *umbrella* for a day of relaxation and "dolce far niente"? [6]

人 企

385

military (ADJ.)

武

Think of the 24-hour clock, also known as "**military** time," as a watch face whose numbers actually go from 1 to 24, but which has only the hour hand on it (the elements for *one* and *arrow*), due to cutbacks in **military** expenditure. Now all you have to do is find a way to introduce the element that can mean either *stop* or *footprint*. Be sure to retain a **military** flavor in your image. [8]

一 二 正 武 武

386	levy (N.)
赋	A **levy** can be imposed for any number of reasons, but here it is pictured as a certain number of *clams* (money) collected by the powers that be to offset current *military* expenses—presumably so they can get back the minute hand for watches like the one in the last frame. [12]

贝　赋

387	correct (V./ADJ.)
正	"A journey of a thousand miles begins with a single step," says the Chinese proverb. Here we see *one footprint*, complementing that proverb with the sound advice that if the first step is not **correct**, the rest of the journey will be off track. This is the ideal that teachers are supposed to have in **correcting** their students, and parents in **correcting** their children. [5]

一　正

388	evidence
证	*Words* that establish facts as being *correct* are classified as **evidence**. [7]

讠　证

389	politics
政	To the many definitions for **politics** that already exist, this character offers yet another: *correct taskmastering*. When those in **politics** twist this ideal and start maneuvering people to their own advantage, it is time to elect a *correct taskmaster*. [9]

正　政

疋	mending
	This primitive differs from the character for *correct* only by the movement added to the last two strokes, the "-ing" of **mending**

if you will. But take a more concrete sense, like **mending** holes in socks. [5]

390

定

settle on

To **settle on**, in the sense of deciding on a certain course of action, is likened here to *mending* one's *house*. [8]

宀　定

391

走

walk

To **walk**, we are told here, has the effect of *mending* the *soil*. If you consider what driving an automobile over the *soil* does to it, taking more time off to **walk** might not be a bad idea.

Note that the final stroke of *soil* doubles up with the first stroke of *mending*. Of course, you could also use *soil* and *trail of footprints* as the primitive elements, but if you do, you're on your own. [7]

土　走

392

超

transcend

Things that are beneath us tempt us to be satisfied with less than we are capable of. It is the things that **transcend** us that *summon* us to *walk* the path to a higher state.

Note in this and the following frame how the element for *walk* can embrace other elements from below, much the same way as the element for *road* does. In order to do this, the final stroke needs to be lengthened. [12]

393

越

surpass

Here we see two *parades* in competition, each trying to **surpass** the other by *walking* at breakneck pace from one town to the next. Note the little "hook" at the end of the first stroke of the element for *parade*. This is the ONLY time it appears like this in the characters treated in these books. [12]

走　走　赱　越

394	be
是	

"To **be**, or not to be: that is the question." Hamlet's soliloquy is a prime example of how memorizing a little Shakespeare can *mend* a *tongue wagging in the mouth*, transforming the broken speech of everyday English into a few minutes of golden eloquence. Like Hamlet, we, too, are riddled with doubt. "To Shakespeare or not to Shakespeare: that **be** the question." [9]

日　是

395	topic
題	

The **topic** of your term paper appears at the top of the first *page*. That *be* what your paper's about, dude. [15]

是　題

❖	stretch
爻	

The primitive meaning to **stretch** might at first seem similar to that for *road*. Take a moment to study it more carefully and you will see the difference. Like *road*, this character holds other primitives above its sweeping final stroke. [2]

㇋　爻

396	prolong
延	

To **prolong** something enjoyable, like a vacation, is to *stretch* it out for as long as you can. If you look closely, you can see a stopper (the long *drop*) halting the progress of the *footprints* of time. Note that the third and fourth strokes of the element for *footprints* merge into one in this and the following frame. [6]

㇒　千　正　延

| 397 | nativity |

诞

The key word, of course, calls to mind the feast of Christmas. As the famous poem at the start of St. John's gospel tells us, the **nativity** we celebrate at Christmas had its origins at the very start of time and governs all of human history. Celebrating the **nativity** *prolongs* the memory of the eternal *Word* in time and space. [8]

| ❖ | brush |

聿

We introduce this primitive element, not itself a character, in order to learn one more character with the *stretch* primitive. It is a pictograph of a writing **brush**. Let the first three strokes represent the hairs at the tip of the **brush**, and the following two strokes the thumb and forefinger that guide it when you write. Note how the long vertical stroke, cutting through everything, is drawn last. This is standard procedure when you have such a stroke running the length of a character. However, as we saw in the case of *cow*, when this primitive appears on top of another primitive, its "tail" is cut off, giving us . [6]

| 398 | build |

建

To **build** something complex, you first need to draw a set of plans (the writing *brush*) and then s-t-r-e-t-c-h your drawing out to scale in reality. [8]

| ❖ | zoo |

To avoid confusion with the animals that will be showing up, this primitive will signify a **zoo**. Except for the downward hook at the end of the first stroke, this element is indistinguishable from *mending*. Perhaps by now you have developed a quick eye for such details. If not, you will before long. [5]

一　丁　下　疋　疋

399   clear (ADJ.)

楚　If you build a *zoo* in the *woods*, the animals might feel comfortable, but the visitors wouldn't get a **clear** view of anything but
the trees. [13]

林　　楚

LESSON 18

THE THREE GROUPS of characters brought together in this rather long lesson are clustered around three sets of primitives dealing respectively with cloth and clothing, weather, and postures.

400	clothing

 At the top we see the *top hat*, and at the bottom a pictographic representation of the folds of a piece of clothing. If you break the four folds into two sets of two strokes, you will find it easier to remember the character for **clothing**. [6]

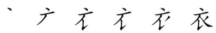

❖ When this character is used as a primitive element, particular attention has to be paid to the changes in shape that it can undergo. In fact, it is the most volatile of all the characters we shall treat, and for that reason we will assign distinct meanings to each of the variant shapes.

When it appears to the left, it looks like this: 衤, and we shall generally take it to mean *cloak*. At the bottom, when attached to the stroke immediately above it, the first two strokes (the *top hat*) are omitted, giving us: 𧘇, which we shall take to mean a *scarf*.

On rare occasions, the final four strokes are drawn with the first two strokes slightly repositioned to give us 𧘇. We will refer to this element as a *bandana*. An example will not show up until FRAME 661.

Occasionally the element can be torn right across the middle, with the first two strokes appearing at the top and the last four at the bottom of another primitive or cluster of primitives: 𧘇, in which cases we shall speak of a *top hat and scarf*.

And finally, of course, the element can keep its original character shape, along with its original meaning of *clothing* in general.

---

401   tailor ^(v.)

裁

You might think here of *clothing* that has been specially **tailored** for a *Thanksgiving* reenactment. [12]

土 表 裁

---

402   attire ^(N.)

装

The **attire** we have in mind here is military **attire**, to be specific, the camouflage *clothing* worn by the *turtle soldiers* we met back in FRAME 336. [12]

壮 装

---

403   grief

哀

A drunken sot in a tattered *top hat and* soiled silk *scarf* with a giant *mouth* guzzling something or other gives **grief** to family and friends alike. It sounds like a role W. C. Fields might have played with relish. [9]

亠 㐅 哀

---

404   Yuan

袁

It is used today as a family name, well illustrated by **Yuan** Shikai (1859–1916). As President of the Republic of China and successor to Sun Yatsen, he remains a very controversial figure. The *lidded crock* and *scarf* should be easy enough to associate with a suspicious politician. [10]

吉 袁

---

405   elementary

初

The primitives here take care of themselves: *cloak* and *dagger*. And to whom might those terms apply? "**Elementary**, my dear Watson." [7]

丶 ㇀ 礻 衤 初

---

406   patch [v.]

补

It's a lot simpler to **patch** an article of *clothing* if you have a *magic wand* like Cinderella's Fairy Godmother to help. Salicadoola, Menchicaboola, Bippity Boppity Boo! [7]

衤 补

---

407   inner garments

衬

The important thing about **inner garments** is that they keep on the inside. This character suggests a way to insure just that: *glue* them to the inside of your outer *clothing*. [8]

衤 衬

---

408   agriculture

农

This character combines a *crown* and a *scarf*. For instance, if you associate the key word with a harvest festival celebrating the joys of **agriculture,** you can imagine a young woman shivering in the open air of late October, wearing her *crown* and the coveted woolen *scarf* awarded to the harvest queen and inscribed with the words "Miss Stubble Mulch." [6]

丶 冖 ⺈ 农 农 农

---

409   concentrated

浓

Think of a healthy drink made of **concentrated** vegetables, squeeze-dried into bottles right in the field where they are picked. All you need is to add *water* to have a bit of **concentrated** *agriculture* in a bottle.[9]

氵 浓

---

410   towel

巾

The basic meaning of this character is a **towel**. Its shape suggests a super-thin fashion model who has just stepped out of the bath and thrown a **towel** over her shoulders. [3]

丿　冂　巾

411　　　　　　　　　　　　　　　　　　　commander

帅

The **commander** is shown here wiping off his *saber* with a *towel*. We leave it to you to decide what he is wiping off it. [5]

丿　帅

412　　　　　　　　　　　　　　　　　　　teacher

师

The only thing that distinguishes a **teacher** from a *commander* is the element for *ceiling*. The *commander's* battlefield is outdoors and the **teacher's** indoors. [6]

丿　丿￢　师

413　　　　　　　　　　　　　　　　　　　lion

狮

The **lion** here is obviously an old retired **lion** king, who has been exiled from the pride and taken up serving as a *teacher* for a *pack of wild dogs* in order to earn a living. [9]

犭　狮

414　　　　　　　　　　　　　　　　　　　cloth

布

Think of a bolt of terry **cloth** that the maid drags along *by her side*, cutting out new *towels* as they are needed and saving herself the trouble of doing the extra laundry. [5]

一　𠂇　布

415　　　　　　　　　　　　　　　　　　　streamer

帜

Instead of a **streamer** shaped like a carp, as is common in Japan, here we have a piece of colored *towel with a large mouth* on one end and a pair of *animal legs* behind it. (You could also use the key-word meaning of the element on the right and think of the **streamer** as the *only* one of its kind). [8]

巾 帜

---

416   hat

帽

Because of some *risk* or other (you decide on the details), you tie up a makeshift **hat** out of a dirty old *towel*. [12]

巾 帽

---

417   curtain

幕

Instead of the usual gates, this *graveyard* has a **curtain** at its entrance sewn together from *towels* that the occupants had stolen from hotels around the world, come back to haunt them after death. So next time you think of slipping that beautifully imprinted *towel* with the logo of a hotel into your suitcase, remember that one day it will be **curtains** for both of you. [13]

莫 幕

❖   white towel

帛

This primitive element is simple to remember. All you need do is read off the elements that make it up: *white towel*. [8]

白 帛

---

418   cotton

棉

Cotton usually grows on bushes, but here we see it growing on a rather large *tree*. The clumps of **cotton** are big, in fact, the size of large *white towels*. When you get tired of picking, you take one of them and use it to wipe your brow. [12]

木 棉

| 419 | market ^(N.) |

市

Dressed in nothing but a bath *towel* and *top hat*, one sets off to the **market** in search of a bargain or two. [5]

一　市

420　lungs

肺

One is surprised, strolling through the *market*, to find amidst the *flesh* hung out for sale a slab marked: **lungs**. [9]

月　肺

❖　apron

帀

The *towel* that has edges trimmed with little *crowns* is the cook's **apron**. [5]

宀　帀

421　sash

带

The part of the *apron* where one finds the buckle (represented pictorially by the first four strokes, and drawn like a *one* followed by something like *small*) is on the **sash**. It may help if you think of one of those giant flashy buckles on the title belts that professional wrestlers compete for. [9]

一　十　卄　卅　卅　带

422　stagnant

滞

People who have been "*sashed*" to something (whether their mother's apron strings or a particular job) for too long are like *water* that has stopped moving: they become **stagnant**. [12]

氵　滞

❖

belt

巾

This primitive, clearly derived from that for *towel*, is always hung on another vertical stroke, and takes the meaning of a **belt**. [2]

丿　冂

❖

thorn

束

Here we see a *belt of* **thorns** wrapping itself around a *tree* and choking the life out of it. [6]

一　厂　冂　市　束　束

423

thorn

刺

The full character for **thorn** differs only by the addition of the *saber* to the right, presumably to indicate how the poor tree feels as it is being cut into by the heartless *thorns*. [8]

一　厂　冂　市　束　束　刺

424

system

制

This character shows a unique **system** for leading a *cow* to the slaughterer's *saber*: one ties a *belt* about its waist and fixes that *belt* to an overhead cable, pulling the *cow* up into the air where it hangs suspended, helpless against the fate that awaits it. [8]

丿　丿　乍　午　告　牜　制

425

rain

雨

This character, also a primitive, is one of the clearest instances we have of a complex pictograph. The top line is the sky, the next three strokes a pair of clouds, and the final four dots the **rain** collected there and waiting to fall. [8]

一　厂　冂　市　币　雨　雨　雨

❖ As a primitive it can mean either *rain* or *weather* in general. Because it takes so much space, it usually has to be contracted into a crown by shortening the second and third strokes into a *crown* like this: 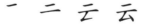. Note how the four dots are straightened out here, something that often occurs in printed forms.

---

426   thunder [N.]

雷

The full rumble and roar and terror of **thunder** is best felt not with your head tucked under your pillow safe in bed, but out in an open *rice field* where you can get the real feel of the *weather*. [13]

雷　雷

---

427   frost

霜

Think of **frost** as a venture in which the malevolent forces of *weather* cooperate with *one another*. See them sitting around a conference table and finally deciding to allow a small amount of moisture to fall just before a short and sudden freeze. [17]

霜　霜

---

428   cloud

云

This primitive is meant to depict in graphic fashion a **cloud** of something **rising** upwards, like vapor or smoke or dust. [4]

一　二　云　云

❖ When used as a primitive element, this character will take the meaning of a *rising cloud* of something or other.

---

429   carry

运

Think of the sweet chariot that the spiritual sings about, comin' for to **carry** you home. It swings low to pick you up as you're strolling along the *road* of life, and then **carries** you off in a *rising cloud*. [7]

云 运

❖

冫   **ice**

The condensation of the three drops we have been using to mean *water* into two drops signals the solidifying of *water* into **ice**. Note that when this primitive appears to the left, it is written like the first and the last strokes of the element for *water* to give us 冫. However, when it appears under another primitive, it looks more like the first two strokes of the *water* primitive: ⌐. [2]

`   ⟩

430

冰   **ice**

This is the full character for **ice** from which we derived the primitive element in the previous frame. The presence of the primitive for *water* in its full form tells us that we have something to do with *water* here, and the primitive for *ice* tells us what kind of water. [6]

冫   冰

431

况   **situation**

Given the deteriorating **situation** in today's high schools, the cryogenic solution is to put all *teenagers* on *ice* for five years and thaw them out when they're ready for college. [7]

冫   况

432

冲   **collide**

The key word easily suggests what happens when two nuclear particles **collide**—namely a nuclear reaction. If this process spins out of control it can destroy the atmosphere and create a nuclear winter. This gives us a graphic image for this character: in the *middle*, the **colliding** particles; and all around, everything turned to *ice*. [6]

冫 冲

433 reduce

减

To reduce winter *ice* on the roads, local municipalities often spread salt over them. But when it comes to your own driveway, anything *salty* will do: your old soy sauce, stale saltines, or—the pièce de résistance—your mother-in-law's tuna casserole. [11]

冫 减

434 cool

凉

To keep **cool** in the heat of summer, a cadre of pork-barrelling legislators decide to drape the entire *capitol building* in *ice*. [10]

冫 凉

435 winter

冬

Walking legs slipping on the *ice* are a sure sign of **winter**. [5]

夂 冬

436 heavens

天

This character is meant to be a pictograph of a great man, said to represent the Lord of the **Heavens**. (You may, of course, use the elements *ceiling* and *St. Bernard dog* instead.) [4]

一 二 チ 天

❖ The primitive can mean either the *heaven* of eternal bliss or the general term for sky, the *heavens*.

437 Wu

吴

This character, used chiefly for a family name, is pronounced **Wu**. Think of dapper young Master **Wu** wooing his woman with a portion of that famous Italian dessert, Tiramisu (or "lift me up")—more romantically known as *Heaven* in your *Mouth*. [7]

口 吴

❖ In line with the explanation above, the primitive meaning will remain *Heaven in your Mouth*.

---

438   **amusement**

娱

Here we see *Wu's* woman. What she is doing for **amusement** is, of course, scarfing down another plate of *Heaven in your Mouth.* [10]

女 娱

---

439   **error**

误

Often an **error** will go undetected because it is couched in beautiful *words.* What seems like *Heaven in your Mouth* may be hell for your waist. [9]

讠 误

---

440   **die young**

夭

If you've ever wondered where the *St. Bernard dog* got its name, this character suggests a plausible answer. The first of these friendly Alpine canines, originally known simply as "Bernard dogs," **died young** in a sudden avalanche. Being blameless, she was wafted right up to her heavenly reward and fitted out with a halo one size too big for her hallowed head (the extended *drop* of the first stroke, written right to left). Centuries later she was "caninized" and came to be known as *St. Bernardette,* which later chauvinist theologians altered to *St. Bernard.* [4]

 夭

---

441   **pretend**

乔

A student who sprained her ankle and is seeking sympathy from her classmates, **pretends** that it is a mortal wound. See her hobbling around on *crutches* with the long, sad face of one who is about to *die young.* [6]

天　乔

❖ When used as a primitive, this character will take the meaning of an *angel* (on crutches for all eternity, if you think our young student deserves it for such a bad performance).

---

442 | bridge

桥

The **bridge** shown here is made of *trees* in their natural form, except that the trunks have been carved into the forms of *angels*, a sort of "Ponte degli Angeli." [10]

木　桥

---

443 | attractive

娇

Associating a particularly **attractive** *woman* you know with an *angel* should be no problem. [9]

女　娇

---

444 | standing up (ADJ.)

立

The general posture of anything **standing up** is represented here by the pictograph of a vase **standing up**. [5]

丶　二　亠　亣　立

❖ When used as a primitive, this character can also mean *vase*. When taking its character meaning, it is best to think of something *standing up* that is normally lying down, or something *standing* in an unusual way.

---

445 | weep

泣

One **weeps** and **weeps** until one is *standing up* knee-deep in *water* (or until one has **wept** a large *vase*-full of *water*). [8]

氵　泣

---

446   station (N.)

站   Picture someone *telling fortunes* on a large Ming *vase* outside the **station** at which you most often catch your trains. [10]

立   站

---

447   chapter

章   Imagine a large *sunflower* that grows miniature cloisonnée *vases* instead of seeds. The wee *vases* are just the right size for a keychain or bracelet. Your challenge is to associate this with the **chapter** of a book. [11]

立   章

---

448   compete

竞   A *teenager* is seen here holding a *vase* overhead—actually, a trophy he just won in the annual flower arranging festival, in which he **competes** every year. [10]

立   竞

---

449   sovereign (N.)

帝   An uncommon, but not altogether unlikely picture of a reigning **sovereign** has him *standing up* in his *apron*, presumably at the behest of HIS **sovereign** (she who is to be obeyed), who needs help with washing the dishes.

     Note how the last stroke of *standing up* doubles up as the first stroke of *apron*. [9]

亠   立   帝

---

450   juvenile (N.)

童   This frame shows up the image of a **juvenile** *standing* on top of a *computer,* or rather jumping up and down on it, because it refused to come up with the right answer. [12]

---

451   salesman

立

See the peddler *standing* atop his motorcycle *helmet* as if it were a soapbox, hawking his wares to passersby. Make the *animal legs* and *mouth* represent the tools of the **salesman's** trade any way you can. [11]

❖   antique

商

The primitive meaning **antique**, not itself a character, depicts a *vase* kept under a *glass hood* because it is *ancient*. As the character is drawn, the *vase* is out on display, but it will soon return to safer quarters. When you write it, think *vase . . . glass hood . . . ancient* and you won't have any trouble. [11]

---

452   drip (v.)

滴

During the night *water* **drips** on what you thought were precious *antiques*. In the morning you are shocked to discover that the artificial aging painted on them is running! [14]

---

453   spoon

匕

This character, a pictograph of a **spoon**, is easy enough to remember, provided you keep it distinct from that for *seven*, where the first stroke is written left to right (the opposite of here) and cuts noticeably across the second. [2]

ノ 匕

❖ As a primitive, this character can take on the additional meaning of *someone sitting on the ground*, of which it can also be considered a pictograph.

---

454   north

北

The cold air from the **north** is so strong that we see *two people sitting on the ground* back to back, their arms interlocked so they don't blow away. (Pay special attention to the drawing of the first three strokes.) [5]

丨　⺬　丬　北

---

455   back (N.)

背

The *part of the body* you turn to shield you from the cold wind from the *north* is your **back** [9]

北　背

---

456   compare

比

With *two spoons*, one in each hand, you **compare** your mother's cooking with your mother-in-law's.

Be careful here: the first stroke of the first *spoon* is drawn left to right, and the first stroke of the second *spoon*, from right to left. [4]

一　ト　比

---

457   descendants

昆

Like most proverbs, "There is nothing new under the *sun*" is not true all of the time. This character has us *comparing* family **descendants** under the *sun*. The resemblances are obvious, but it's also true that each generation brings something new to the family. [8]

日　昆

---

458   mix (v.)

混

Marriages that **mix** peoples and cultures traditionally kept apart from one another, this character suggests, *water* down the quality of one's *descendants*—the oldest racial nonsense in the world! [11]

氵 混

459 all

皆

Think of the housewives in those TV commercials *comparing* how *white* their laundry turned out. The clear winner is the one who used the popular detergent known as **All**. (If you don't know the brand, surely you've heard the phrases "**all**-purpose detergent" or "**all**-temperature detergent.") [9]

比 皆

460 this (literary)

此

To create an image of this most abstract of all the key words, picture a literary work whose opening sentence begins with the word **This**, the initial "T" of which is embellished in medieval style to fill up half the page. Look closely at the drawing and you will see the hundreds of little *footprints* and silver *spoons* that make it up. [6]

止 此

461 somewhat

些

The sense of the key word **somewhat** is that of "slightly" or "to some small degree." Then recall the minutely embellished "T" from the story for *this (literary)* and contrast it with the smaller and only **somewhat** fancy "T" that appeared in Volume *Two* of the work. [8]

此 些

462 it

它

In the children's game of tag, there is usually a designated place that renders one safe from being tagged and becoming "**it**." Here it is a little play*house* in the back yard, in which there is already *someone sitting on the ground.* [5]

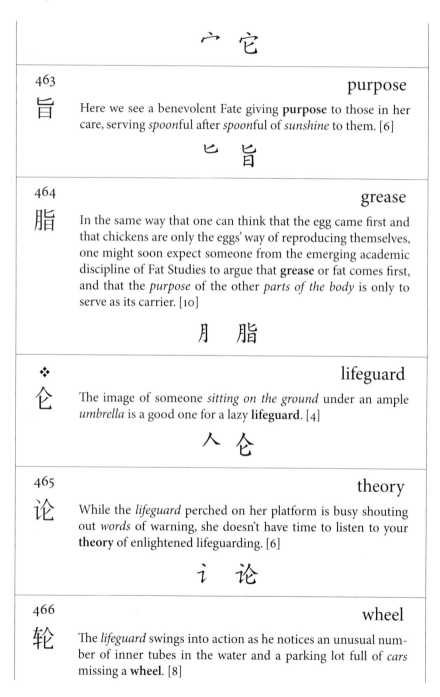

宀 它

463 purpose

旨

Here we see a benevolent Fate giving **purpose** to those in her care, serving *spoon*ful after *spoon*ful of *sunshine* to them. [6]

匕 旨

464 grease

脂

In the same way that one can think that the egg came first and that chickens are only the eggs' way of reproducing themselves, one might soon expect someone from the emerging academic discipline of Fat Studies to argue that **grease** or fat comes first, and that the *purpose* of the other *parts of the body* is only to serve as its carrier. [10]

月 脂

❖ lifeguard

仓

The image of someone *sitting on the ground* under an ample *umbrella* is a good one for a lazy **lifeguard**. [4]

人 仓

465 theory

论

While the *lifeguard* perched on her platform is busy shouting out *words* of warning, she doesn't have time to listen to your **theory** of enlightened lifeguarding. [6]

讠 论

466 wheel

轮

The *lifeguard* swings into action as he notices an unusual number of inner tubes in the water and a parking lot full of *cars* missing a **wheel**. [8]

车 轮

❖
厂

reclining

The picture is obvious: the first stroke represents the head, and the second the body of someone **reclining**. You may also use the synonyms *lying* or *lying down*. [2]

丿 厂

467
每

every

"Behind **every** successful person *lies* a woman…," who usually turns out to be one's *mother*! [7]

厂 每

468
梅

small plum

Behind *every* Jack Horner, there's a pie maker, and behind every pie maker, a *tree* full of **small plums** just the right size for little Jack's thumb. [11]

木 梅

469
海

sea

Behind *every* **sea**, the countless *drops of water* from which it originated. [10]

氵 海

470
乞

beg

See someone *lying down* in a public place with a *hook* in place of a hand and forced to **beg** a morsel of rice or a few pence. [3]

厂 乞

471   eat

吃

"**Eat** to live, not live to **eat**," goes the advice from *Poor Richard's Almanac*. Measured by that standard, those who have to open the *mouths* to *beg* for enough food to keep them alive are better off than those who stuff their *mouths,* every chance they get, with as much as they can **eat**. [6]

口　　　吃

472   duplicate (v.)

复

As moderns, we easily think of a photocopy machine when we hear the word **duplicate**. If you ever wondered what it is doing at night when the staff has gone home, the answer is simple: it's *reclining*. After a full *day* of running back and forth across page after page of material (did you know that that green light actually has tiny *walking legs* on it?), we see it *reclining* for some well-deserved rest. [9]

厂　　　𦥑　　　复

❖ As a primitive, this character will take the meaning of *double back*, in the sense of turning around and heading back during one's travels.

473   abdomen

腹

The secret to a picture-perfect **abdomen** is a little-known technique developed by circus acrobats. No need to fork out your hard-earned cash for some overpriced gym contraption. Just double the top half of your body forward till your nose touches your knees, then straighten up and **double back** until the back of your head hits your calfs. Forty times in a row and you've got **abs** to die for. [13]

月　　　腹

474

欠

lack [v.]

The pictograph hidden in this character is of someone yawning. The first stroke shows the head thrown back; the second, the arm bent at the elbow as the hand reaches up to cover the mouth; and the last two, the legs. Yawning is a sign that there is something you **lack**: psychologically, interest; physiologically, sleep. [4]

丿 ᄼ 欠

❖ Used as a primitive, this character can mean either *yawn* or *lack*.

475

吹

blow [v.]

To **blow** is really no more than a deliberate effort to make one's *mouth lack* all the air that is in it. [7]

口 吹

476

歌

song

The **song** in this character is being sung by a chorus line of *can-can* girls. Why should the whole audience be *yawning* then?

Of course, you can always try the primitive for *older brother* on the audience instead of the *can-can* girls. [14]

哥 歌

477

软

soft

If the cushions of one's *car* are too **soft**, one may begin to *yawn* at the wheel. [8]

车 软

478

次

next

This key word connotes the "**next** in line" of a succession of people or things. Put yourself in a line of people who *lack ice* on

the hottest day of summer, waiting impatiently for the distribu-
tor to call out "**Next!**" [6]

㇇　次

❖ As a primitive, this character can either retain its key word
meaning of *next* or the related meaning of *secondary*.

| 479 | assets |

资

The first *shells* (money) you earn, you use to pay your debts. The
next shells you accumulate become your **assets**. [10]

次　资

| 480 | looks (N.) |

姿

This character depicts a *woman's* **looks** as a sort of *secondary
self*. [9]

次　姿

| 481 | consult with |

咨

To seek advice from a *secondary mouth* is to **consult with** someone about something. [9]

次　咨

LESSON 19

WE CONCLUDE our Plots by picking up most of the remaining primitives that can be built up from elements already at our disposal, and learning the characters that are based on them. When you have completed this section, you might want to run through all the frames from Lesson 13 on, jotting down notes at any point you think helpful. That way, even if you have not made any notations on your review cards, you will at least have some record of the images you used.

❖

音

muzzle

The element for **muzzle** shows a *vase* fixed over a *mouth*, perhaps with a rubber band running around the back of the head to keep it in place. [8]

立　音

482

赔

compensate

Picture a *clam* used as a *muzzle* to quiet the complaints of a fisherman's widow asking the Channel 7 weatherman to **compensate** her for the husband she lost at sea. [12]

贝　赔

483

培

cultivate

The barrel hoops used by some enterprising farmers to stretch clear plastic over rows of vegetables in a garden patch can be thought of as a way to *muzzle* the *soil*, creating a controlled environment that allows them to **cultivate** bigger and bigger vegetables. [11]

土　培

---

484 — sound

音

The character for **sound** depicts something *standing* in the air over a *tongue wagging in a mouth*, much the same as a **sound** does for the briefest of moments before disappearing. [9]

立　音

❖ Used as a primitive, this character retains its meaning of a *sound*.

---

485 — dark

暗

Think of the **dark** emptiness of outer space, in which there is not only no *sun* but no *sound* either. [13]

日　暗

---

486 — rhyme (N.)

韵

Poetry that uses **rhyme** is forced to find words of the same *sound* in order to make the ending of lines *uniform*. [13]

音　韵

---

487 — unexpectedly

竟

This character gets its meaning from the following frame. It shows a queen *standing* in front of a mirror and asking who is the fairest of them all. **Unexpectedly,** the mirror sprouts a pair of *human legs* and begins to run around the room. A giant *tongue wagging in the mouth* appears on its surface, announcing that the mirror itself is fairer by far than the queen and all the maidens of the kingdom put together. [11]

❖ The primitive meaning for this character will be a *mirror*.

---

488   **mirror**

镜

After lakes but before glass, polished *metal* was used for **mirrors**. These *metal mirrors* are recalled in this character for a **mirror**. [16]

钅 镜

---

489   **boundary**

境

Imagine the **boundary** of a plot of *land* marked with gigantic *mirrors* enabling the landowner to keep trespassers in sight at all times. [14]

土 境

---

490   **deceased** (ADJ.)

亡

A *top hat* hanging on a *hook* in the front hall, right where the **deceased** gentleman left it the day he died, reminds us of him and his courtly manner. [3]

丶 亠 亡

❖ In addition to *deceased*, the primitive meaning of *perish* will be used for this character.

---

491   **blind** (ADJ.)

盲

If one's *eyes perish* before death, one remains **blind** for the rest of life. [8]

盲 盲

---

492   **absurd** (ADJ.)

妄

It is **absurd** to waste time daydreaming about the "ideal *woman*," who can never be more than a delusion. Hence, *perish* the thought of her. [6]

亡 妄

493   expect

望

As the *king* walks amid the remains of his fallen army, *perishing flesh* all around him, he **expects** the worst for his kingdom. [11]

亡   朢   望

494   direction

方

Spinning a *dagger* about on its hilt on the top of a *top hat*—waiting to see in which **direction** it points when it comes to rest—one leaves to fate where one is going next. Take care in writing this character. [4]

亠   方   方

❖ As a primitive, this character will take the sense of a *compass*, the instrument used to determine *direction*.

495   hinder

妨

Imagine a romantic *compass* that is disturbed every time a *woman* passes by: the mere smell of perfume **hinders** its ability to function, sending the needle spinning madly round and round. [7]

女   妨

496   release ^(v.)

放

The *taskmaster* **releases** an unruly servant into the wilderness, giving him no more than a quick glance at the *compass* and a boot from behind. [8]

方   放

497   excite

激

Some cosmic *taskmaster* hovering overhead **excites** the waves to make them dash violently against the shore. In the *white* foam that covers the *water* we see a broken *compass* floating, all that remains of a shipwreck. That ought to **excite** the unfortunate investors. [16]

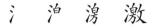

| 498 | side [N.] |

产

Think of the key word **side** in connection with the image of a **side**kick, an assistant or companion so named because he is always along**side** you. He, or she, is the one who carries the *compass*, the *crown*, and the *vase*. All you have to do is find a way to relate these three elements to the kinds of adventures the two of you are used to getting into. [10]

| 499 | convert [V.] |

兑

The key word should be understood in the sense of changing one thing into another, as when we **convert** currency. The character shows a *teenager* with a devil's *horns*, which most parents with adolescents will have no difficulty sympathizing with, as their *teenagers* systematically and continually **convert** their parents' hard-earned wages into feed for the vultures at the shopping mall. [7]

ソ 兑

❖ The primitive meaning for this character will be *devil*, in line with the explanation above.

| 500 | undress |

脱

To **undress** is to expose the *flesh* and bring out the *devil* in one's onlookers. Ignore the moral if you want, but not the *devil*. [11]

月 脱

501　　　　　　　　　　　　　　　speak

说

"Sticks and stones may break my bones, but *words* will never hurt me." Yea, sure. Just think of all the ways that the *words one* **speaks** can bruise and wound and sting; they can be barbed and sharp, cruel and inflammatory. Let there be no doubt about it: there can be a *devil* in the *words* we **speak**. [9]

ì　　说

502　　　　　　　　　　　　　　　formerly

曾

For the key word, think of individuals who **formerly** held office as administrators or heads of state. The character is composed of a pair of *horns* growing out of a *brain* impaled on the *horns* of a dilemma—with a *tongue wagging in the mouth* beneath. The dilemma of **formerly** prominent public figures is how to stay in the public eye even after retirement. The *wagging tongue* shows how so many of them do it, namely, by advertising their opinions on public policy. The *horns* growing out of the top show what a devilish nuisance they often make of themselves in the process. [12]

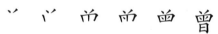

❖ The primitive meaning of this character, *increase,* comes from the next frame. Always think of something multiplying wildly as you watch.

503　　　　　　　　　　　　　　increase ^(v.)

增

In this character we see the *soil* **increase**, multiplying so fast that it literally buries everything in its path. [15]

　增

504　　　　　　　　　　　make a present of

赠

In today's world, there are fewer and fewer ways of **making a present of** something without seeing it as an investment awaiting its just return in time. And not only in today's world. How often unscrupulous colonizers in different parts of the world **made a present of** a handful of trinkets or *clams* (money) to unsuspecting locals as an investment that ended up *increasing* a million times over as they expropriated land, precious metals, and natural resources. Do not confuse this key word with the temporal word "present" (FRAME 269). [16]

贝　赠

Elements

WE COME NOW to the third major step in our study of the characters: the invention of plots from primitive elements. From now on, the ordering of the remaining characters according to their primitives will be taken care of, but the reader will be required to do most of the work. Particularly difficult characters will be supplied with supplementary hints, plots, or even whole stories.

You should now have a feel for the way details can be worked into a character story so as to create a more vivid ambience for the primitive elements to interact. What may be more difficult is experimenting with plots and discarding them until the simplest one is fixed on, and then embellished and nuanced. You may find it helpful occasionally to study some of the earlier stories that you found especially impressive, in order to discover precisely why they struck you, and then to imitate their vitality in the stories you will now be inventing. Equally helpful will be any attention you give to those characters whose stories you have found it difficult to remember, or have easily confused with those of other characters. As you progress through this final section, you may even wish to return and amend some of those earlier stories. But do it with the knowledge that once a story has been learned, it is generally better to review it and perhaps repair it slightly than to discard it entirely and start over.

LESSON 20

IF YOU HAVE found some of the characters in the last brief lesson difficult to work with, we can only assure you that it will get easier with time, beginning with this long lesson. Remember, however, that as it *does* get easier you should not skip over the stories too quickly, trusting only in the most superficial of images. If you spend up to five minutes on each character focusing the composition of the primitives into a tidy plot, and then filling out the details of a little story, you will not be wasting time, but saving yourself the time it takes to relearn it later.

---

505 也   **also**

This character is a pictograph of the scorpion, the first two strokes representing its head and pincers, the last stroke its barbed tail, in which you may recognize the *fishhook*.

To associate this image with the key word, think of the two terms that the word "**also**" links in a sentence and place a scorpion there, its head biting on one word, its tail stinging the other. [3]

⁊ 𠃊 也

❖ The primitive meaning will remain *scorpion*, in line with the above explanation.

---

506 她   **she**

Woman . . . scorpion. Note to male readers: to avoid any complications with the **she** in your life, you might want to adjust the second primitive to its character meaning, *also*. [6]

女 她

---

507 地   **ground** (N.)

Soil and a *scorpion* (an "earth animal"). This is, of course, the full character from which the primitive for **ground** derives. [6]

土 地

---

508 池   **pond**

Water . . . scorpion. It would be easy to slip into a "lazy image" in cases like this one, picturing, let us say, a *scorpion* near the *water*. But if you picture a *scorpion* letting its venom out *drop by drop* until it has made a whole **pond** of the stuff, the image is more likely to remain fixed. [6]

509	insect

虫

Work with this character as you wish, to create the image of an **insect**. [6]

口　中　虫　虫

❖ Used as a primitive, it will appear in characters for all sorts of worms and bugs and other creepy, crawling things.

510	shrimp

虾

Think of the **shrimp** as a crustacean on the top (the head, antennae, and shell) and an *insect* (the legs) *below*—a kind of chimera of the sea. [9]

虫　虾

511	alone

独

A *pack of wild dogs*, starved and rabid, surrounds a poor little *insect* for a sad image of what it means to feel **alone**. [9]

犭　独

512	although

虽

A *mouth* full of *insects*. [9]

口　虽

513	serpent

蛇

Insect . . . it. [11]

虫　蛇

514	egg

蛋

Zoo . . . insect. [11]

疋 蛋

515

己

self

This character carries the abstract sense of the **self**, the deep-down inner structure of the human person that mythology has often depicted as a *snake*—of which it is a pictograph. Be sure to keep it distinct from the similar key words, *oneself* (FRAME 33) and *I* (FRAME 588). [3]

フ　コ　己

❖ As a primitive element, this character will take the meaning of a *snake,* along with any of the various concrete symbolic meanings the *snake* has in myth and fable.

516

起

begin

Walk . . . snake. [10]

走　起

517

改

alter

Snake . . . taskmaster. If you can find your way to working the key word **alter** into the story, you might think of Ireland's most famous reformer, St. Patrick, who, legend has it, drove away the *snakes* from the land. [7]

己　改

518

记

remember

Words . . . snake. [5]

讠　记

519	**already**

已

The *snake* with its mouth half closed (depicted in the slight extension of the final stroke) suggests that it is **already** dead and gone, ready to be stripped of its skin to become a belt or handbag. [3]

コ　コ　已

❖ When this character is used as a primitive, it changes shape to close the gap between the first and last strokes: 巳. Its meaning will be a *snakeskin*.

520	**wrap** (v.)

包

Bind up . . . snakeskin. [5]

勹　包

521	**bubbles**

泡

Water . . . wrap. [8]

氵　泡

522	**guide** (v.)

导

Snakeskin . . . glue. [6]

巳　导

523	**look back**

顾

Cliff . . . snakeskin . . . head. Note how the cramped space forces the second stroke of *snakeskin* to bend upwards. [10]

厂　戶　顾

❖ SOW ^(N.)

豕 Let this primitive represent a fat **sow**. Easier than pulling it apart into smaller elements is remembering its shape as a highly styl-ized pictograph. Practice its seven strokes a few times before going on to examples of its use in the next few frames. [7]

一 丆 丆 丆 豸 豸 豕

524 pursue

逐 *Sows ... road.* [10]

豕 逐

525 house ^(N.)

家 This is the full character whose primitive form we learned already. To help a little, this character recalls the times when the "domestic" animals were, as the word itself suggests, really kept in the **house**. Hence: *house ... sow.* [10]

宀 家

❖ piglets

勿 This abbreviation of the full primitive for a *sow*, quite naturally, means **piglets**. [3]

勹 勽 勿

526 site

场 *Soil ... piglets.* [6]

土 场

527 soup

汤 *Water ... piglets.* [6]

氵 汤

528 **sheep**

羊 This pictograph shows the animal *horns* at the top attached to the head (third stroke), the front and back legs (strokes four and five), and body (final stroke). [6]

丶 丷 䒑 兰 兰 羊

❖ The primitive meaning remains *sheep*. As we saw with the *cow*, the "tail" is cut off when it is set immediately over another element: ⺷. Note the change in stroke order, as exemplified in the following frame.

529 **beautiful**

美 Try to think of what the Chinese were on to when they associated **beautiful** with a *large sheep*. [9]

丶 丷 䒑 兰 𢆉 ⺷ 美

530 **ocean**

洋 *Water . . . sheep*. Be sure to keep the stories and key word of this character distinct from those for *sea*. (FRAME 469). [9]

氵 洋

531 **fresh**

鲜 *Fish . . . sheep*. [14]

鱼 鲜

532 **appearance**

样 *Tree . . . sheep*. [10]

木 样

---

533   orchid

兰

This character is drawn exactly the same as that for *sheep* except that the final stroke is omitted. Think of taking a *sheep* by the tail and pulling it out, with your two feet pushing hard against the back end of the poor creature. At last, it jerks free and you fall back on the ground, with a beautiful **orchid** in your hand —the famous "ram's head **orchid**" hidden in the *sheep*. [5]

丷　兰

---

534   spoiled

烂

Fire . . . orchid. [9]

火　烂

❖
羊

                                             wool

This rather uncommon primitive is made by pulling the tail of the *sheep* to one side to create a semi-enclosure. The meaning of **wool** is derived from the fact that the shearer is holding the *sheep* by the tail in order to trim its **wool**. [6]

兰　羊

---

535   fall short of

差

Wool . . . I-beam. [9]

羊　差

---

536   -ing

着

We cannot resist help-**ing** you with this character for ongo-**ing** action, since it nicely illustrates "pull-**ing** the *wool* over one's eyes." [11]

羊　着

| 537 | raise ^(v.) |

养

The key word is used in connection with **raising** animals, family, flowers, and so forth. Note how the final stroke of *wool* and the first stroke of *introduce* double up here. If you want to **raise** sheep to be more than just sheep, you should *introduce* them to *wool* merchants from an early age. Of course, like the celebrated Black Sheep, they would have to be sent to school to learn how to say things like, "Yes sir, yes sir, three bags full." [9]

羊 养

| ❖ | turkey |

隹

This primitive is best remembered as an old **turkey**, complete with pipe and horn-rimmed glasses. Its writing is somewhat peculiar, so take note of the order of the strokes. Let the first four strokes stand for the *turkey's* head, neck, and drooping chin. The remainder can then be pictographic of the plumage. [8]

丿 亻 亻 仁 仨 仨 佳 隹

| 538 | gather |

集

Turkeys . . . atop a tree. [12]

隹 集

| 539 | standard ^(N.) |

准

Think of a **standard** of measure or quality. *Ice . . . turkey.* [10]

冫 准

| 540 | who? |

谁

Words . . . turkey. It might help if you think of the Cheshire Cat from the Disney production of "Alice in Wonderland" as a Cheshire *Turkey* asking passers-by "W-h-o aaaare you?" [10]

讠 谁

541

售

vend

Let the key word suggest **street** peddlers who **vend** their wares. *Turkey . . . mouth.* [11]

佳　售

542

午

noon

With a bit of stretching, you might see a horse's head pointing leftward in this character. That gives the primary meaning of the Chinese zodiacal sign of the horse, which corresponds to the hour of **noon**. Note how this character differs from that for *cow* (FRAME 252). [4]

ノ　⺊　⺘　午

❖ As a primitive, this character gets the meaning of a *stick horse.*

543

许

permit (v.)

Words . . . stick horse. [6]

讠　许

544

羽

feathers

From the pictograph of two bird wings, we get **feathers**. [6]

⺆　⺆　⺚　羽

❖ The related image of *wings* can be added as a primitive meaning.

545

习

learn

Here we have the pictograph of a single *wing*, indicating novices who still have a lot to **learn** before they earn their other *wing*. [3]

丁　刁　习

546　　　　　　　　　　　　　　　　　　soar

翔　　*Sheep . . . feathers.* [12]

羊　　翔

LESSON 21

THIS IS A GOOD TIME TO stop for a moment and have a look at how primitive elements get contracted and distorted by reason of their position within a character. Reference has been made to the fact here and there in passing, but now that you have attained greater fluency in writing, we may address the phenomenon more systematically.

1. At the left, a primitive will generally be squeezed in from the sides and slanted upwards. For instance, *gold* 金 comes to be written 金 when it functions as the primitive for *metal*. Or again, *tree* has its character form 木 flattened into 木 when it comes to the left.

2. Long strokes ending in a hook, which would normally flow out gracefully, are squeezed into angular form when made part of a primitive at the left. We see this in the way the character for *ray* 光 gets altered to 光 in the character for *radiance* 輝. In like manner, the *spoon* that is spread out on the right side of *compare* 比 is compressed on the left. Certain characters are pressed down and widened when weighted down by other elements from above. Such is the case, for example, with *woman,* which is flattened into 女 when it appears in the lowest position of *banquet* 宴.

3. A long vertical stroke cutting through a series of horizontal lines is often cut off below the lowest horizontal line. We saw this in changing the *cow* 牛 to fit into *declare* 告, the *sheep* 羊 to fit into *beautiful* 美, and the *brush* 聿 that appeared in the character for *book* 書.

4. The long downward swooping stroke that we see in *fire* is an example of another group of distortions. Crowded in by something to its right, it is compressed into 火. Hence *fire* 火 and *vexed* 煩.

5. Again, we have seen how horizontal lines can double up as the bottom of an upper primitive and the top of a lower primitive, for instance, when *stand* 立 comes in the character for *salesman* 商.

6. Finally, there are situations in which an entire character is changed to assume a considerably altered primitive form. *Water* 水, *fire* 火, and *heart* 心 can thus become 氵, ⺣, and 忄 in other characters. Because the full forms are ALSO used as primitives, we have often altered the meaning or given distinctions in meaning in order to be sure that the story in each case dictates precisely how the character is to be written.

From this chapter on, the stroke order will not be given unless it is entirely new, departs from the procedures we have learned so far, or might otherwise cause confusion. All hand-drawn characters, you will remember, are indicated by frame number in Index 1. Should you have any trouble with the writing of a particular primitive, you can refer to Index 11, which will direct you to the page where that primitive was first introduced.

With that, we carry on.

❖	pent in
口	This primitive depicts a corral or pen surrounding something, which is thus **pent in**. Note that this primitive is much larger than a mouth, in fact large enough to include a mouth inside of it in FRAME 554. [3]
	｜　冂　口

547	trapped
困	*Pent in . . . trees.* [7]
	冂　困　困

548	solid
固	*Pent in . . . ancient.* Leave people out of your story to avoid complications later when we add the element for "person," which will also appear with the primitive for *pent in* (FRAME 793). [8]

549	country
国	*Pent in . . . jade.* [8]

550	round
圆	*Pent in . . . employee .* [10]

551	cause [N.]
因	*Pent in . . . St. Bernard dog.* [6]

552	smoke^(N.)
烟	*Fire... cause.* [10]

553	park^(N.)
园	*Pent in ... beginning.* [7]

554	return^(V.)
回	The elements are *pent in* and *mouth*, but you may find it more helpful to forget the primitives and think of one circle revolving inside of another. [6]

冂　回　回

555	picture^(N.)
图	*Pent in ... winter.* [8]

556	extensive
广	This primitive combines the *cliff* (the last two strokes) with the first dot we use on the roof of the *house*. Together they offer the picture of a "cliff house" or cave. All you have to do is picture it located on the side of the Grand Canyon, giving the ideal description of an **extensive** view to the person who is living in it. [3]

丶　丷　广

❖ As a primitive, we will stick with the concrete meaning of a *cave* from the explanation above. When so used, the element "encloses" other primitives beneath it and to the right.

557	store^(N.)
店	*Cave ... tell fortunes.* [8]

广　店

558	warehouse
库	*Cave . . . car.* [7]

559	trousers
裤	*Cloak/clothing . . . warehouse.* [12]

560	bed
床	*Cave . . . tree.* [7]

561	hemp
麻	*Cave . . . woods.* If it helps, this is the **hemp** marijuana comes from. [11]

562	hamlet
庄	*Cave . . . soil.* [6]

563	heart
心	This character, a pictographic representation of the **heart**, is among the most widely used primitives we shall meet. [4]

丶　心　心　心

❖ As a primitive, it can take three forms, to which we shall assign three distinct meanings.

In its character form, it appears BENEATH or to the RIGHT of its relative primitive and means the physical organ of the *heart*.

To the LEFT, it is abbreviated to three strokes, 忄, and means a wildly emotional *state of mind*.

And finally, at the very BOTTOM, it can take the form ⺗, in which case we give it the meaning of a *valentine*. Examples will not appear until Book 2.

564	forget
忘	*Perish . . . heart.* [7]

亡　忘

565	endure
忍	*Blade . . . heart.* We give the drawing here to remind you that the third stroke is drawn somewhat differently than the printed form. [7]

刃　忍

566	general (ADJ.)
总	*Animal horns . . . mouth . . . heart.* [9]

567	attitude
态	*Overly . . . heart.* [8]

568	aspiration
志	*Soldier . . . heart.* [7]

569	consider
思	*Brains . . . heart.* [9]

570	kindness
恩	*Cause . . . heart.* [10]

571	wish (N.)
愿	*Flatlands . . . heart.* [14]

572	idea
意	*Sound . . . heart.* [13]

573	think
想	*One another . . . heart.* [13]

574 息	*Nose . . . heart.* [10]	breath

575 恐	*Work . . . ordinary . . . heart.* [10]	fear (v.)

576 感	*Salty . . . heart.* [13]	feel (v.)

577 憾	*State of mind . . . feel.* [16]	regret (N.)

丨　丨　忄　憾　憾

578 忧	*State of mind . . . Frankenpooch.* [7]	worried

579 惊	*State of mind . . . capitol building.* [11]	startled

580 怕	*State of mind . . . dove.* [8]	dread (v.)

581 忙	*State of mind . . . perish.* [6]	busy (ADJ.)

582 惯	*State of mind . . . pierce.* [11]	accustomed to

583 必	First note the stroke order of this character, which did not really evolve from the *heart* even though we take it that way. If one takes it as a pictograph "dividing" the *heart* in two, then one has	certainly

arrived at a "certitude" about human anatomy: that each *heart* is **certainly** divided into two halves. [5]

丶　心　心　心　必

LESSON 22

IN THIS LENGTHY lesson we focus on elements having to do with hands and arms. As always, the one protection you have against confusing the elements is to form clear and distinct images the first time you meet them. If you make it through this chapter smoothly, the worst will be behind you, and you should have nothing more to fear the rest of the way.

584 手	**hand** Any way you count them, there are either too many or too few fingers to see a good pictograph of a **hand** in this character. But that it is, and so you must. [4] 一　二　三　手 ❖ Keep to the etymology when using this character as a primitive: a single *hand* all by itself.
585 看	**look at** *Hand . . . eyes.* [9] <div align="center">手　看</div>
586 摩	**rub** *Hemp . . . hand.* [15] <div align="center">麻　摩</div>
587 拿	**hold** (v.) *Fit . . . hand.* [10]
588 我	**I** *Hand . . . fiesta.* Note how the second stroke of the *hand* is stretched across to double up as the first stroke of the tasseled

arrow we use for *fiesta*. Be sure keep the meaning of this key word distinct from those in FRAMES 19, 33, and 515. [7]

′   ⼆   于   手   ⺀   我   我

❖

fingers

扌

This alternate form of the primitive for *hand* we shall use to represent *finger* or *fingers*. It always appears at the left. [3]

‒   十   扌

589

embrace (v.)

抱

Fingers . . . wrap. [8]

‒   十   扌   抱

590

combat (v.)

抗

Fingers . . . whirlwind. [7]

591

criticize

批

Finger . . . compare. [7]

592

beckon

招

Finger . . . summon. [8]

593

strike (v.)

打

Finger . . . spike. [5]

594

finger (N.)

指

This is the full character for **finger**. Its elements: *Finger . . . pur-pose.* [9]

595

support (v.)

持

Fingers . . . Buddhist temple. [9]

596	assume
担	*Fingers . . . daybreak.* The sense of the key word **assume** is to take on or shoulder responsibility for something. [8]

597	include
括	*Fingers . . . tongue.* [9]

598	bring up
提	The sense of this character is to mention or put forward, as when one **brings up** an idea, topic for discussion, and the like. Its elements: *fingers . . . be.* [12]

599	brandish
挥	*Fingers . . . army.* [9]

600	push
推	*Fingers . . . turkey.* [11]

601	stir ^(v.)
搅	*Fingers . . . senses.* [12]

602	clench
执	*Fingers . . . bottle of pills.* [6]

603	heat ^(n./v.)
热	*Clench . . . cooking fire.* [10]

604	welcome ^(v.)
接	*Fingers . . . vase . . . woman.* [11]

605	hang
挂	*Fingers . . . bricks.* [9]

606 按	press down on
	Fingers . . . peaceful. [9]

607 掉	drop (v.)
	Fingers . . . eminent. [11]

608 拉	pull
	Fingers . . . vase. [8]

609 啦	!!
	This character can be used at the end of a sentence to express exclamation, more or less the way an exclamation mark works. Its elements: *mouth . . . pull.* [11]

610 找	look for
	Fingers . . . fiesta. [7]

611 无	nothing
	"**Nothing** comes from **nothing**," sings Julie Andrews in *The Sound of Music* (disclosing her training in medieval theology). That's the way it went with Eve, at least, who wasn't made out of **nothing**, but out of Adam's rib. If you compare this character to that for *beginning* (FRAME 59), you will see that the only difference is that here the third stroke extends up to the top of the first stroke. Could the added portion be Adam's missing rib? [4]

612 抚	comfort (v.)
	Fingers . . . nothing. [7]

613 开	open (v.)
	Let this character represent *two* hands pushing on a gate to **open** it. [4]
	一 二 干 开

❖ As a primitive element, this character will take the meaning of *two hands*. When it appears at the bottom of another primitive, the drawing is not consistent. Sometimes it looks as if the first stroke is omitted (廾), and at other times, the second (开). Since this is largely a function of font differences, there is no need to adjust the primitive meaning.

---

614 **grind away** (v.)

研

Stone . . . two hands. As the key word suggests, this character means both to grind things to a fine powder and to study—when you **grind away** at the books. [9]

---

615 **play with**

弄

King/ball . . . two hands. [7]

---

616 **different**

异

Snakeskin . . . two hands. [6]

---

617 **nose**

鼻

Let us share a rather grotesque image to help with this character. Imagine taking your *two hands* and reaching up into someone's *nostrils.* Once inside you grab hold of the *brain* and yank it out. At the end, you would have a picture something like that of this character, the full character for **nose**. [14]

自 畠 鼻

---

618 **punishment**

刑

Two hands . . . saber. [6]

---

619 **mold** (v.)

型

Punishment . . . soil. Once again, you might find it easier to break the character up into its more basic elements, like this: *two hands . . . saber . . . soil.* [9]

刑 型

620	genius

才 Whatever one is particularly adept at—one's special "**genius**"—one can do very easily, "with one finger" as the phrase goes. This character is a pictograph of that one finger. Note how its distinctive form is created by writing the final stroke of the element for *fingers* backwards. [3]

一　十　才

❖ The primitive meaning, *genie*, derives from the roots of the word *genius*. Use the *genie* out in the open when the primitive appears to the right of or below another primitive; in that case it also keeps its same form. At the left, the form is altered to 扌, and the meaning becomes a *genie in the bottle.*

621	riches

财 *Clam . . . genie.* [7]

622	troupe

团 *Pent in . . . genie.* [6]

623	deposit [v.]

存 *Genie in the bottle . . . a child.* The sense of the key word is to place something somewhere for safekeeping. [6]

一　ナ　𠂇　存

624	at

在 The key word **at** is used to initiate an expression indicating location. Its elements: *genie in the bottle . . . soil.* [6]

625	only then

乃 This pictograph of a clenched fist is another of the "hand" primitives. Take note of its rather peculiar drawing. Begin by drawing a *fist* (the primitive meaning) and **only then** struggle to come up with a concrete connotation for this otherwise abstract key-word phrase. [2]

ノ 乃

❖ The primitive meaning we will assign it is taken from the pictograph: a *fist*.

---

626 milk (N.)

奶 *Woman ... fist/only then.* [5]

---

627 catch up with

及 The addition of a final stroke transforms this character from the primitive for a clenched *fist* into the character for **catch up with**. Observe how eliminating the hook in the second stroke and slanting it to the left gives the character a more elegant form.

 Sometimes our emotions get ahead of us and it takes a little time for us to **catch up with** them. In this character, all it took was one "stroke" of kindness to turn a *fist* clenched in anger into a hand reaching out in reconciliation. [3]

乃 及

❖ As a primitive, this shall stand for *outstretched hands*. Only take care not to confuse it with *beg* (FRAME 470).

---

628 inhale

吸 *Mouth ... outstretched hands.* [6]

---

629 extreme (N.)

极 *Tree ... outstretched hands.* [7]

❖ tucked under the arm

乂 The picture of an arm dangling from the trunk of the body gives us the element for **tucked under the arm** (relative to the element below it). [2]

丿 乂

630		history
史	*A mouth . . . tucked under the arm.* [5]	

口　　史

631		even more
更	*Ceiling . . . sun . . . tucked under the arm.* [7]	

一　　曰　　更

632		hard
硬	*Rocks . . . even more.* [12]	

633		again
又	You should have no trouble remembering this short two-stroke character, since you will meet it **again** and **again** in its primitive meaning. [2]	

フ　　又

❖ Etymologically, this character is said to be a pictograph of the right hand, hence its inclusion in this lesson. You can always take *right hand* as its primitive meaning, as we will see in the next frame. More commonly, however, we will try to avoid confusing it with other primitives of similar meaning by assigning it the meaning of *crotch*, as in the *crotch* of an arm or a tree. Or whatever.

634		holy
圣	*Right hand . . . soil.* [5]	

又　　圣

635		friend
友	*By one's side . . . crotch.* [4]	

一 亠 方 友

636	pair
双	*Crotch . . . crotch.* [4]

637	Han
汉	*Water . . . right hand.* The key word refers to the **Han** people who gave the name "hanzi" to Chinese characters. [5]

638	frolic [v.]
戏	*Crotch . . . fiesta.* [6]

639	observe
观	*Crotch. . . see.* [6]

640	joyous
欢	*Crotch . . . yawn.* [6]

641	peculiar
怪	*State of mind . . . holy.* [8]

642	that's right
对	This character's key word indicates a judgment that what someone has said is accurate. *Crotch . . . glue.* [5]

643	timber
树	This character really has the same meaning as the pictograph for *tree* that we learned in FRAME 202. Since this character is more elaborate, we choose a more sophisticated key word to represent it. The elements: *tree . . . that's right.* [9]

644	difficult
难	*Crotch . . . turkey.* [10]

| 645 | vendor's stand |
| 摊 | *Fingers . . . difficult.* [13] |

| ❖ 殳 | missile |

Although modern connotations are more suggestive, this primitive simply refers to something thrown as a weapon. Its elements: *wind . . . crotch.* [4]

几 殳

| 646 | throw (v.) |
| 投 | *Fingers . . . missile.* [7] |

| 647 | not have |
| 没 | *Water . . . missile.* [7] |

| 648 | establish (v.) |
| 设 | *Words . . . missile.* [6] |

| 649 | thigh |
| 股 | *Part of the body . . . missile.* [8] |

| 650 | offshoot |
| 支 | *Needle . . . crotch/right hand.* This key word is used to indicate a "branch" of an institution or organization, which helps us assign it a primitive meaning. [4] |

十 支

❖ Used as a primitive this character will have the full range of meanings associated with the word *branch.*

| 651 | skill |
| 技 | *Fingers . . . branch.* [7] |

652 枝	branch
	Tree . . . branch. [8]

653 叔	uncle
	Above . . . small . . . right hand. [8]
	上　才　叔

654 督	superintend
	Uncle . . . eye. [13]

655 寂	lonely
	House . . . uncle. [11]

❖ 厂	drag [v.]
	Although not a pictograph in the strict sense, this primitive depicts one stroke **dragging** another along behind it. Note that the drawing of the first stroke goes from right to left, which naturally helps its appearance to differ from that of *cliff.* [2]
	一　厂

656 反	against
	Drag . . . crotch. [4]
	厂　反

657 板	plank
	Tree . . . against. [8]

658 返	go back
	Against . . . road. [7]

659 后	behind
Drag . . . ceiling . . . mouth. [6]	

660 质	quality
Drag . . . ten . . . shellfish. [8]	

661 派	faction
Water . . . drag . . . bandana. [9]	

氵　氵　沪　沪　派　派

662 乐	music
Drag . . . pole. Notice how the element for *drag* is curtailed here, and use it in your story. [5]	

丿　匚　乐　乐　乐

663 爪	claw (N.)
This character is a pictograph of a bird's **claw**, and from there comes to mean animal **claws** in general (including human fingernails). Since the first two strokes are the same as the element for *drag*, you can imagine a cat *dragging* its claws across a blackboard to get you started. [4]	

丿　厂　爪　爪

❖ When this character is used as a primitive, we shall sometimes give it the graphic image of a *vulture*, a bird known for its powerful *claws*. It generally appears above another primitive, in which case it gets squeezed into the form ⺥.

664 抓	grab
Fingers . . . claws. [7]	

665   **pick** (v.)

采

This character is used to **pick** fruits from trees. Its elements: *vulture . . . tree.* [8]

666   **vegetable**

菜

Flowers . . . pick. [11]

❖   **birdhouse**

爫

The *claw* and crown of the roof of a *house* (whose chimney is displaced by the *claw*) combine to give us a **birdhouse**. [6]

667   **accept**

受

The key word carries the meaning of to receive or take on and does not carry the connotation of "agree with." Its primitives: *birdhouse . . . crotch/right hand.* [8]

668   **confer**

授

This key word has the sense of "bestow" and not "consult with," each of which has its own character (FRAMES 1007 and 481) The elements: *fingers . . . accept.* [11]

669   **love** (N./v.)

爱

Birdhouse . . . friend. [10]

❖   **elbow**

厶

This pictograph of an arm bent at the **elbow** is obvious. Once again, there is some font variation in the way this character is written. [2]

670		(suffix)
厶	*Drop . . . elbow.* [3]	

671		grand
雄	*By one's side . . . elbow . . . turkey.* [12]	

ナ 厷 雄

672		platform
台	*Elbow . . . mouth.* [5]	

673		govern
治	*Water . . . platform.* [8]	

674		commence
始	*Woman . . . platform.* [8]	

675		go
去	*Soil . . . elbow.* [5]	

676		method
法	*Water . . . go.* [8]	

❖		wall
厶	The *elbow* hanging under a *ceiling* will become our element for a **wall**. [3]	

一 厶

677		meeting
会	*Meeting . . . rising cloud.* This is the full character for **meeting**, from which the abbreviated primitive that we met earlier (page 117) gets its name. [6]	

678	until
至	W*all . . . soil.* Be sure to give this key word a concrete image, perhaps in connection with a commonly used expression. [6]

679	room
室	The key word **room** refers to a room in a house or building, not to the abstract sense of "space." Its elements: *house . . . until.* [9]

680	arrive
到	*Until . . . saber.* [8]

681	mutual
互	When you draw this character think of linking two *walls* together, one right side up and the other upside down. [4]

一　エ　厅　互

❖	infant
云	Sudden **Infant** Death Syndrome (SIDS) has been responsible for the death of more babies under the age of one year than any other single cause. Here we see a kind of memorial to the fallen **infants** in the form of a great marble *wall* into which a small *drop* is carved with a name beneath it for each life cut short, creating the image of an ocean of innocents. When you use this primitive, however, think of a healthy toddler on all fours. [4]

丶　亠　宀　云

682	sufficient
充	*Infant . . . human legs.* [6]

683	education
育	The key word has to do with raising children to be strong both in mind and body. The elements are: *infant . . . flesh.* [8]

❖ baby Moses

充

This primitive is a combination of two elements, *infant* and the waters of a *flood*. We give it the meaning of **baby Moses** because of the image of Miriam placing her child in a basket and entrusting it to the swift waters of the Nile River. [7]

云　充

684　flow (v.)

流　*Water . . . baby Moses.* [10]

685　comb (n.)

梳　*Tree . . . baby Moses.* [11]

❖ cast

勾

The primitive for a **cast** is a perfectly logical combination of *bound up* and *elbow*. If you've ever had one on your arm you will remember what it does to your poor *elbow*. [4]

勹　勾

686　purchase (v.)

购　*Oyster . . . cast.* [8]

687　frame (v.)

构　*Tree . . . cast.* The key word **frame** covers a range of meanings: to compose, construct, falsely incriminate, and so forth. [8]

LESSON 23

AFTER THAT LONG excursus into arm and hand primitives, we will take a breather with a much shorter lesson, beginning with a group built up from the character for *exit*.

688	mountain
山	Note the clear outline of a triangular **mountain** here. [3]

$$丨\quad 屮\quad 山$$

689	exit (v.)
出	The character for **exit** pictures a range of mountain peaks coming out of the earth. Note how the drawing runs counter to what you might expect from the previous frame. [5]

$$乚\quad 凵\quad 屮\quad 岀\quad 出$$

690	foundation
础	This character depicts a corner*stone*, which was not—as it is today—a decorative slab of marble set in a corner of a finished building. Rather, it was the first *stone* laid as a guide for the rest of the structure. It was, quite literally, a **foundation** *stone*. What better motive for a *stone* with cathedral ambitions to *exit* the quarry and head downtown! [10]
691	years of age
岁	*Mountain . . . evening.* [6]
692	secret (ADJ.)
密	Think of something that is **secret** to preserve the adjectival form of the key word. *House . . . certainly . . . mountain.* [11]

693   enter

入

Now that we know *exit*, we might as well learn the character for **enter**. This character is meant to be a picture of someone walking to the left, putting one leg forward in order to **enter** someplace. [2]

ノ 入

694   part (N./V.)

分

Here we combine the character for *eight* and the element for *dagger* to give the key word **part**. [4]

ノ 八 分

695   impoverished

贫

Part . . . shells/clams. [8]

696   public (ADJ.)

公

Eight . . . elbows. Use the key word in its adjectival sense, not as a noun. [4]

697   pine tree

松

Tree . . . public. [8]

698   valley

谷

Look closely at the character in this frame and the one right above it and you will see the difference between the primitive element for *eight* and that for *animal legs*: the second stroke in *eight* bends gracefully outwards, while in *animal legs* it just kind of drops down.

But this doesn't tell you what *animal legs* are doing on top of an *umbrella*. The answer lies in the *mouth* of the **valley**, which is what you should think of when you see this key word. In order to stop the illegal immigration of all sorts of critters from the surrounding territories, a gigantic *umbrella*, obviously made of a material tough enough to resist the trampling of the *animal* *legs* trying to creep across the border, has been laid over the *mouth* of the **valley**. [7]

ハ　父　谷

699 浴	bathe
	Water . . . valley. [10]
700 欲	desire (N./V.)
	Valley . . . yawn. [11]
701 容	contain
	This character depicts a *house* so large that it can **contain** an entire *valley*. [10]
702 溶	dissolve
	Water . . . contain. [13]

LESSON 24

THE FOLLOWING GROUP of characters deals with primitive elements having to do with human beings. We shall have more to add to this set of primitives before we are through, but even the few we bring in here will enable us to learn quite a few new characters. We begin with another "roof" primitive.

❖ 尚	**outhouse**
	The combination of the element for *small*, the basic "roof" structure here (in which the chimney is overwritten, as in the element for *birdhouse*), combined with the "window" (*mouth*) below, gives this element its meaning of **outhouse**. Although the window is not an essential part of an **outhouse**, we think you will agree that its inclusion is a boon to the imagination, greatly simplifying the learning of the characters in which it appears. [8] <div align="center">⺍　⺌　尚</div>

703 賞	**prize** [N.]
	Outhouse . . . shellfish. [12]

704 党	**political party**
	This key word refers to the actual group of people that make up a **political party**, not to the kind of gala affair they are famous for throwing. Its elements: *human legs* . . . sticking out of an *outhouse* window. [10]

705 常	**often**
	Outhouse . . . towel. [11]

706 堂	**main room**
	Outhouse . . . soil. [11]

| 707 皮 | covering (N.) |

The simplest way to remember this character is to see it as built up from the primitive element for *branch*. Besides the "barb" at the end of the first stroke, the only other change is the second stroke, which can stand for something "hanging" down from the *branch*, namely its bark or **covering**. Merely concentrating on this as you write the following small cluster of characters should be enough to fix the form in your mind. [5]

〜 厂 广 戌 皮

| 708 波 | waves |

Water's . . . covering. [8]

| 709 婆 | old woman |

Waves . . . woman. [11]

| 710 破 | break (V.) |

Rock . . . covering. [10]

| 711 被 | quilt (N.) |

Cloak . . . covering. [10]

| 712 歹 | malicious |

This character is meant to be a pictograph of a bone attached to a piece of flesh (or vice versa). The key-word meaning, **malicious**, should not be far behind. Note how the first stroke serves to keep this character distinct from the one for *evening* (FRAME 115). [4]

一 歹

❖ When this character is used as a primitive, its meaning will be *bones*.

713

列   *Bones . . . saber.* [6]

line up

714

烈   *Line up . . . cooking fire.* [10]

intense

715

死   *Bones . . . spoon.* Note how the first stroke is extended to the right, forming a sort of "roof" overhead. [6]

death

716

葬   *Flowers . . . death . . . two hands.* Do not confuse with *bury* (FRAME 181).[12]

inter [v.]

艹   苑   葬

717

耳   To the newcomer to Chinese characters, the pictograph for **ear** might look like that for *eye*, but you are far enough along now that the differences stand out dramatically. [6]

ear

一   厂   丌   丌   斤   耳

718

取   *Ear . . . right hand.* [8]

take

719

趣   The sense of this key word is one of curiosity or concern; it has nothing to do with finance. Its elements: *walk . . . take.* [15]

interest

720

最   *Sun . . . take.* Note how the top stroke of the *ear* stretches out to give the *sun* something to rest on. [12]

most

721

职

job

The key word refers to one's occupation or employment. Its elements: *ear . . . only*. [11]

722

敢

brave (ADJ.)

Thumbtack . . . ear . . . taskmaster. [11]

723

曼

drawn out

Sun . . . net . . . crotch. The sense of the key word is not restricted to time, as the English expression suggests, but can also refer to space. [11]

曰　昌　曼

❖ Used as a primitive, this character will change its meaning to a brightly colored *mandala*. As always, the key-word meaning can also be used as a primitive meaning.

724

慢

slow (ADJ.)

State of mind . . . mandala. [14]

725

漫

overflow (V.)

Water . . . mandala. [14]

726

夫

husband

The character for a **husband** or "head of the family" is based on the character for *large* and an extra line near the top for the "head." Recall the character for *heavens* already learned back in FRAME 436, and be sure to keep your story for this character different. [4]

一　二　夫　夫

727

规

regulations

Husband . . . see. [8]

728	replace
替	Two *husbands ... day.* [12]

729	lose
失	"To **lose**" here takes the sense of "misplace," not the sense of *defeated*, whose character we learned in FRAME 64. It pictures a *husband* with a *drop of* something falling from his side as he is walking along, something he **loses**. [5]

丿　失

730	iron[(N.)]
铁	*Metal ... lose.* Note that this character refers to the metal, not to the household appliance. [10]

731	feudal official
臣	This character is actually a pictograph for an eye, distorted to make it appear that the pupil is protruding towards the right. This may not be an easy form to remember, but try this: Draw it once rather large, and notice how removing the two vertical lines gives you the pictograph of the eye in its natural form.
	As for what this has to do with the meaning, the "pop-eye" image belongs to a **feudal official** standing in awe before his Emperor. [6]

一　丁　丏　丐　予　臣

732	power
力	With a little imagination, one can see a muscle in this simple, two-stroke character meaning **power**. [2]

フ　力

❖ When used as a primitive, this character can mean either *muscle* (not to be confused, of course, with the character of the same meaning in FRAME 63) or *power*.

733 边	border
Power . . . road. [5]	

734 势	force (N.)
Fingers . . . bottle of pills . . . muscle. This key word should be associated with things like the **force** of habit or the negative **forces** influencing events. [8]	

735 动	move (V.)
Rising cloud . . . muscles. [6]	

736 励	encourage
Cliff . . . ten thousand . . . muscles. [7]	

737 历	experience (N./V.)
Cliff . . . muscles. [4]	

738 另	another
Mouth . . . muscle. [5]	

739 别	don't
Another . . . sword. [7]	
另　别	

740 拐	turn (V.)
Fingers . . . another. [8]	

741 男	male (N.)
Rice fields . . . power. This character is reserved for human beings only. [7]	

742 功	achievement
	Work/I-beam ... power. [5]

743 办	manage
	Muscles with two *drops* of sweat. [4]
	❖ As a primitive, this character will take the meaning of *sweat*.

744 协	cooperate
	Needle... sweat. [6]

745 苏	revive
	Flowers ... sweat. [7]

746 为	act (v.)
	"Think before you **act**," goes the conventional advice. This character embodies that little piece of wisdom by showing two *drops* of sweat associated with the *muscle* it takes to **act**: the *drop* of cold sweat you shed when thinking about what you are about to do, and the *drop* of hot sweat resulting from the exertion it takes to actually do it. [4]

$$` \quad 为 \quad 为$$

747 奴	slave (N.)
	Woman ... crotch. [5]

748 努	toil (v.)
	Slave ... muscle. [7]

749 加	add
	Muscles ... mouth. [5]

750 贺	congratulate
	Add ... shells. [9]

751 架	shelf(N.)
	Add ... trees. [9]

752 务	tasks
	Walking legs ... power. [5]

753 雾	fog
	Weather ... tasks. [13]

754

行

line of business

The key word refers to the work or **line of business** one is engaged in, but to make it easy to remember think of queues of people lining up to buy whatever your **line of business** has to sell them. First look at the left side of the character. Let the first two short lines represent the first two people in line, followed by a long line of others (the third stroke). As always, there are those who try to cut in line, as you can see from the next two strokes. More often than not, this starts a precedent as others try to creep in after them (the final stroke). [6]

丿 彳 彳 彳 彳 行

❖ As a primitive, this character has two forms. Reduced to the left side only, 彳 it can take the meaning of a *queue,* from the above explanation. When the middle is opened up to make room for other elements, it becomes a *boulevard.*

755 律	law
	Queue ... brush. [9]

756 得	must (AUX. V.) *Queue ... daybreak ... glue.* [11]
757 待	treat (V.) This key word has to do with how one deals with others or **treats** them. The elements: *queue ... Buddhist temple.* [9]
758 往	toward *Queue . . . candlestick.* This character has the special sense of moving or journeying in the direction of or **toward** (or **towards**, if you come from the British Isles) something. [8]
❖ 悳	10 commandments Think of Moses coming down the mountain with the tablets of the **10 commandments** in hand and fire in his eyes. Now look closely at the tablets and you will notice that there is a small safety *net* attached to the bottom. This is just in case Moses gets it into his head to smash them a second time. The people's gaze is fixed on the tablets and once again they are of *one heart.* [12]
759 德	morality *Queue ... 10 commandments.* [15]
760 微	tiny *Queue ... mountain ... ceiling ... wind ... taskmaster.* [13]
761 街	street *Boulevard ... bricks.* [12]

LESSON 25

WE RETURN ONCE AGAIN to the world of plants and growing things, not yet to complete our collection of those primitives, but to focus on three elements that are among the most commonly found throughout the Chinese writing system.

Now and again, you will no doubt have observed, cross-reference is made to other characters with similar key words. This can help avoid confusion if you check your earlier story and the connotation of its respective key word before proceeding with the character at hand. While it is impossible to know in advance which key words will cause confusion for which readers, we will continue to point out some of the likely problem cases.

762 禾	**standing grain** This character depicts stalks of **grain** that have not yet been harvested but are **standing** at attention in the field awaiting the farmer's sickle. [5] 丿　二　千　禾　禾 ❖ When this character is used as a primitive element, its meaning will change to *wild rice*.
763 程	**journey** (N.) *Wild rice . . . submit.* [12]
764 和	**harmony** This key word has to do with peaceful co-existence and, by extension, with all sorts of **harmony**. Its elements: *wild rice . . . mouth.* [8]
765 积	**accumulate** *Wild rice . . . only.* [10]

766 种 Wild rice ... middle. [9]	species
767 移 Wild rice ... many. [11]	shift (v.)
768 秋 Wild rice ... fire. [9]	autumn
769 愁 Autumn ... heart. [13]	gloomy
770 揪 Fingers ... autumn. [12]	hold tight
771 利 Wild rice ... saber. [7]	profit (n.)
772 香 Wild rice ... sun. [9]	perfume (n.)
773 季 Wild rice ... child. [8]	seasons
774 委 Wild rice ... woman. [8]	committee
775 秀 Wild rice ... fist. [7]	elegant
776 透 Elegant ... road. [10]	penetrate

777	entice
诱	*Words . . . elegant.* [9]

778	rice
米	This character has a pictographic resemblance to a number of grains of **rice** lying on a plate in the shape of a star. [6]

丶　丷　丷　半　半　米

779	powder^(N.)
粉	*Rice . . . part.* [10]

780	lost
迷	*Rice . . . road.* [9]

781	riddle
谜	*Words . . . lost.* [11]

782	kind^(N.)
类	*Rice . . . St. Bernard dog.* [9]

783	come
来	*One . . . rice.* The character is drawn in the order of the primitives. [7]

❖	bride
娄	The *woman* coming down the church steps at whom onlookers are throwing *rice* is a **bride**. (She had better watch out for the two little boys at the back of the crowd holding the bucket of *rice* pudding.) [9]

784	number^(N.)
数	*Bride . . . taskmaster.* [13]

785	multistory building
楼	*Tree . . . bride.* [13]

786	bamboo
竹	**Bamboo** grows upwards, like a straight *nail*, and at each stage of its growth (which legend associates with the arrival of the new moon) a new joint forms (the first stroke). Two such **bamboo** stalks are pictured here. [6]

丿　𠂉　𠂉　竹　竹　竹

> ❖ When this character is used as a primitive, the meaning remains the same, but the vertical lines are severely abbreviated so that they can take their place at the top where, like *flowers*, they are always to be found.

787	laugh (v.)
笑	*Bamboo . . . die young.* [10]

788	box (N.)
箱	*Bamboo . . . one another.* [15]

789	etc.
等	*Bamboo . . . Buddhist temple.* [12]

790	calculate
算	If you have ever used an abacus to **calculate**, you should have no trouble with this character. The *bamboo* sticks provide the frame, and in place of beads you have *eyeballs*. Now all you need to do is add your *two hands* to do your gruesome calculations. [14]

791	answer (v.)
答	*Bamboo . . . fit.* [12]

792   strategy

策   *Bamboo . . . thorn.* [12]

Lesson 26

This lesson will take us beyond the halfway mark. From there on, it will all be downhill. The final uphill push will involve what appears to be the simplest of primitive elements. It was withheld until now because of the difficulty it would have caused earlier on.

---

793   **person**

人   The character for *enter* (FRAME 693) showed someone walking to the left. The one for **person**, shown here, represents someone walking to the right. [2]

     ❖ Used as a primitive, this character keeps its character form except when it appears to the left (its normal position), where it is made to stand up in the form 亻.

        The primitive meaning is another matter. The general idea of *person* is already implied in many of the characters in which the primitive appears. But so many of the previous stories have also included people in them that simply to use *person* as a primitive meaning would be risky. We need to be more specific, to focus on one particular *person*. Try to choose someone who has not figured in the stories so far, perhaps a colorful member of the family or a friend whom you have known for a long time. That individual will appear again and again, so be sure to choose someone who excites your imagination.

---

794   **recognize**

认   *Words ... person.* [4]

---

795   **price**

价   *Person ... introduce.* [6]

796		portion
份	*Person . . . part.* [6]	

797		bogus
伪	*Person . . . act.* [6]	

The following three frames all have the same meaning, but need to be kept distinct—something not easily done in English. Be sure to create a distinct context for each of the key words so that they do not get confused.

798	you (literary)
尔	The primitive for *small* in this character tells us that we have to do with something on a smaller scale than the full-fledged *yawn* (see page 181). The head is still tilted back and the arm is still bent at the elbow so the hand can cover the mouth, but the intake of air is short and abrupt. Voilà, le hiccup!

In order to associate all of this with the key word, a **literary** form of **you**, you need only picture an Oxford don addressing you in affected courtesy as he tries to disguise his hiccups and the fact that he is completely shellacked from the after-dinner Port. "My good man… My good fellow… There now, dear chap…." This should give you some sense, even if slightly twisted, of the character for **you (literary)**. [5]

丿　　厶　　尔

❖ As a primitive, this character will mean a *hiccup* in connection with the explanation above.

799		you
你	*Person . . . hiccup.* [7]	

800		you (respectful)
您	*You . . . heart.* [11]	

801 称	weigh
	Wild rice . . . hiccup. [10]
802 什	what?
	Person . . . needle. [4]
803 值	value [N.]
	Person . . . straight. [10]
804 做	make
	Person . . . deliberately. [11]
805 但	however
	Person . . . daybreak. [7]
806 住	dwell
	Person . . . candlestick. [7]
807 位	position [N.]
	Person . . . vase. [7]
808 件	piece
	Person . . . cow. The key word here refers to things like an "article" of clothing or an "item" of furniture. [6]
809 仍	still [ADV.]
	Person . . . fist. [4]
810 他	he
	Person . . . scorpion. [5]
811 仅	merely
	Person . . . crotch. [4]

812 休	rest (v.) *Person ... tree.* [6]
813 体	body *Person ... notebook.* [7]
814 信	faith *Person ... words.* [9]
815 依	depend on *Person ... clothing.* [8]
816 例	example *Person ... line up.* [8]
817 健	healthy *Person ... build.* [10] 亻　律　健
818 停	halt (v.) *Person ... pavilion.* [11]
819 倒	upside down *Person ... arrive.* [10]
820 仁	benevolence Confucius used this character to refer to the fullness of humanity that can only be achieved in a relationship between *two persons* that is characterized by **benevolence**. [4]
821 优	excellent *Person .. Frankenpooch.* [6]

| 822 伤 | wound (N.) |
| Person . . . reclining . . . muscle. [6] | |

| 823 保 | safeguard (V.) |
| Person . . . dim-witted. [9] | |

| 824 堡 | fort |
| Safeguard . . . soil. [12] | |

| 825 付 | pay (V.) |
| Person . . . glue. [5] | |

| 826 府 | government office |
| Cave . . . pay. [8] | |

| 827 俯 | bow one's head |
| Person . . . government office. [10] | |

| 828 代 | substitute for |
| Person . . . arrow. [5] | |

| 829 袋 | bag (N.) |
| Substitute for. . . clothing. [11] | |

| 830 化 | transform |
| Person . . . spoon. [4] | |

| 831 华 | splendor |
| Transform . . . needle/ten. [6] | |

| 832 哗 | clamor (N.) |
| Mouth . . . splendor. [9] | |

833	flower (N.)
花	*Flower . . . transform.* This is the full character from which we derived the primitive element of the same meaning. [7]

834	commodities
货	*Transform . . . shells.* [8]

835	whatwhichwhowherewhy?
何	This character is an all-purpose, all-weather interrogative made up of the primitives *person* and *can.* [7]

836	convenient
便	*Person . . even more.* [9]

837	100 Chinese inches
丈	We already met the *Chinese inch* (FRAME 166). To remember how to write the character for a hundred of them, draw the three strokes in the order shown below, saying as you go "10 times 10." If you think it helps, you can use the element for *tucked under the arm* that appears in the final two strokes. [3]

丿 ナ 丈

838	use (V.)
使	*Person . . . 100 Chinese inches . . . mouth.* [8]

839	long time
久	This character uses the diagonal sweep of the second stroke to double up for *bound up* and a *person.* Think of a mummy, and the key word will not be far behind. [3]

丿 ク 久

840	internal
内	*Glass cover . . . person.* [4]

冂　内

841 呐	holler ^(v.)

Mouth ... internal. [7]

842 丙	third

Ceiling ... internal. As we have seen often enough in these pages, you can always break a complex primitive up into its component parts. For example: those no-frills flights the airlines offer with only **third**-class seating to attract customers should help create an image from *ceiling ... person ... belt.* [5]

843 柄	handle ^(n.)

Tree ... third. [9]

844 肉	meat

Here see why the character for *moon* was also assigned the primitive meaning of *flesh* and *part of the body*: over time the character for **meat** shown here often converged with that for *moon* (月) when it appeared as a part of other characters. The only difference in drawing the character in this frame is that the two horizontal strokes are replaced with two *persons*, one atop the other. [6]

冂　内　肉

845 腐	rotten

Government office ... meat. [14]

846 从	follow

The image of one *person* **following** another could hardly be clearer than it is in this character. [4]

❖ Used as a primitive, this character will take the meaning of an *assembly line.*

847	multitude
众	The character for **multitude** uses a pattern we met first back in Lesson 2, the triplication of a single element to indicate large numbers of something or other. In this case, it gives us *persons, persons* everywhere. Note how it is the *person* at the top who gets a little squashed this time around. [6]

848	sit
坐	*Assembly line . . . soil.* [7]

从　丛　坐　坐

849	seat (N.)
座	*Cave . . . sit.* [10]

850	witch
巫	*I-beam . . . assembly line.* [7]

丁　丌　巫　巫

❖	siesta
曷	Conjure up the classic portrait of a Latin **siesta**: a muchacho (your *person*) propped up against something or other, *bound up* from neck to ankles in a sarape fastened with a *fishhook*, one of those great, broad-rimmed mariachi hats pulled down over his face, and the noonday *sun* beating down overhead. [9]

日　匃　曷　曷

851	drink (V.)
喝	*Mouth . . . siesta.* [12]

852	thirsty
渴	*Water . . siesta.* [12]

LESSON 27

IN THIS LESSON we pick up a *small* group of unconnected characters and elements that have fallen between the cracks of the previous lessons, mainly because of the rarity of the characters themselves, of their primitive elements, or of the way in which they are written. Later, in Lesson 50, we will do this once again.

❖ 壬	**porter** Let the extended dot at the top represent the load that the *soldier* is carrying as part of his secondary role he has been asked to take on: the drill sergeant's **porter**. [4] ノ 二 千 壬
853 任	**appoint** *Person . . . porter.* [6]
854 廷	**royal court** *Porter . . . stretch.* [6]
855 庭	**court of law** *Cave . . . royal court.* [9]
856 头	**head**[N.] Try to think of a situation in which you might need the **head** of a *St. Bernard dog* carved out of *ice*. [5] ❖ The meaning of this character when used as a primitive will be a sculpted *bust*, in keeping with the image above.
857 实	**reality** *House . . . bust.* [8]

	beret
一	The *crown* that is missing the first stroke is a perfect image of a French **beret**. [1]

858 买	buy
	Beret ... bust. [6]

859 卖	sell
	Needle ... buy. [8]

860 读	read
	Words ... sell. [10]

	plow
レ	Take this as a pictograph of a **plow**. [1]

レ

861 以	by means of
	Picture a *person* dragging a *plow* behind, and the *drop of* sweat which falls from his brow as he does his work. Think of him (or her, for that matter) making a living "**by means of** the sweat of his/her brow." [4]

レ　レ　以

862 似	similar
	Be sure to keep this key word distinct from *likeness* (FRAME 1452). Its elements: *person ... by means of.* [6]

863 并	combine (v.)
	Animal horns ... two hands. [6]

丷 并

❖ Try creating an image that fits in with the meaning this character takes as a primitive: a jigsaw *puzzle*.

864 拼	**piece together**
	Fingers . . . puzzle. [9]

865 吕	**spine**
	This character is a clear pictograph of a **spine** with two vertebrae on it. [6]

866 侣	**associate** (N.)
	The sense of this key word is that of a colleague or co-worker. *Person . . . spine.* [8]

❖ 艹	**greenhouse**
	The **greenhouse** shows—what else?—a *house* with *flowers* all over the roof instead of a chimney. [5]

艹 芦

867 荣	**glory** (N.)
	Greenhouse . . . tree. [9]

868 劳	**labor** (N.)
	Greenhouse . . . power. [7]

869 营	**camp** (N.)
	Greenhouse . . . spine. [11]

870 善	**virtuous**
	Sheep . . . horns . . . mouth. Pay special attention to the writing of this character. [12]

羊 羊 羊 盖 善

871   year

年

In an odd fashion, the character for **year** joins together the element for *stick horse,* on the top, and half of what looks to be a pair of glasses—or as we shall call it, a *monocle.* [6]

　ノ　　ト　　ヒ　　ヒ　　午　　年

872   night

夜

First of all, be sure not to confuse the connotations of **night** with those of *evening* (FRAME 115), *nighttime* (FRAME 196), and *daybreak* (FRAME 30). The elements: *top hat . . person . . . walking legs . . . drop.* Take care in drawing the last two strokes. [8]

　亠　　宀　　疒　　夻　　夜　　夜

873   liquid

液

Water . . . night. [11]

Lesson 28

WE COME NOW TO a rather simple group of primitives, built up from the three elements that represent *banners*, *knots*, and *flags*.

❖ 方	**banner** Here we have a unique enclosure made up of two elements: *compass* and *reclining*. Think of the **banner** as a standard for rallying around. When the **banner** is upright and fluttering in the breeze, it serves as a *compass* to give direction to soldiers following it. In defeat, however, it is retired and made to *lie down* as a symbol of surrender. [6]

方　方

874 旅	**travel** (v.) *Banner . . . bandana.* [10]

方　方　旂　旅　旅

875 施	**execute** *Banner . . . scorpion.* The key word has nothing to do with capital punishment. It means rather "to carry out." [9]

876 游	**go swimming** *Water . . . banner . . . child.* [12]

877 勿	**not** Think of this character as the *piglet* minus its body (the horizontal stroke), leaving the curly tail that looks like a "knot"—a homonym that, by way of exception, we will use to remember the abstract key word, **not**. [4]

丿　勹　勹　勿

❖ As a primitive element, this shape will mean a *knot*.

878 忽	suddenly
	Knot . . . heart. [8]

879 物	thing
	Cow . . . knot. [8]

880 易	easy
	Sun . . . knot. [8]

881 賜	grant [v.]
	Shells . . . easy. [12]

882 尸	corpse

The pictographic representation of a *"flag"* is obvious. Actually, it is the national flag in which the **corpse** of a dead soldier has been wrapped. [3]

ㄱ　ㄱ　尸

❖ The primitive meaning for this character will be a *flag*.

883 尼	nun
	Flag . . . spoon. [5]

884 呢	woolen cloth
	Mouth . . . nun. [8]

885 泥	mud
	Water . . . nun. [8]

886 屋	habitation

Flag . . . until. The key word **habitation** is meant to cover a wide range of meanings, from a house and a room to a roof over your head. [9]

887 握	grip (v.)
	Fingers . . . habitation. [12]

888 居	reside
	Flag . . . ancient. Do not confuse with dwell (FRAME 806). [8]

889 锯	saw (N.)
	Metal . . . reside. [13]

890 剧	drama
	Reside . . . saber. [10]

891 据	certificate
	Fingers. . . reside. [11]

892 层	story
	The **story** referred to here is a floor of a building. Its elements: flag . . . rising cloud. [7]

893 局	bureau
	Flag . . . sentence. Note how the flag's long stroke doubles up with (and elongates) the first stroke of sentence. [7]

894 尺	ruler
	Let the final stroke be a tape-measure added to the flag to give a rather patriotic **ruler**. [4]

895 尽	exhausted
	Ruler . . . ice. [6]

896 户	door
	A drop of . . . flag. [4]

897	domicile
房	*Door . . . compass.* [8]
898	hire ^(v.)
雇	*Door . . . turkey.* Be sure to keep distinct from *employee* (FRAME 55). [12]
899	protect
护	*Fingers . . . door.* [7]

LESSON 29

IN THIS LESSON WE pick up a series of primitives related pictographically to one another and based on the image of a seed. But first we include a stray element that does not really fit into any of our other categories but is very useful in forming some common and elementary characters: the *altar*.

900	show [v.]
示	Although the elements *two* and *small* are available for the using, it may be easier to remember this character as a picture of an altar. Something is placed on the altar to **show** it to those gathered around or to the deity above in whose honor it is placed there. [5]

> ❖ As a primitive, this character means *altar*. The abbreviated form this element takes when it stands at the left is almost identical to that for *cloak* (衤), except that it lacks the short stroke: 礻.

901	society
社	*Altar . . . soil.* [7]

` 亍 礻 礻 社

902	ceremony
礼	*Altar . . . fishhook.* [5]

903	inspect
視	*Altar . . . see.* [8]

904	happiness
福	*Altar . . . wealth.* [13]

905 标	mark (N.) *Tree. . . altar.* This character figures in a variety of compounds for everything from road signs to trademarks. [9]
906 禁	prohibit *Woods . . . altar.* [13]
907 襟	front of a garment *Cloak . . . prohibit.* [18]
908 宗	religion *House . . . altar.* [8]
909 崇	worship (V.) *Mountain . . . religion.* [11]
910 祭	offer sacrifice *Flesh . . . crotch/right hand . . . altar.* Note how both the top two elements get distorted to fit into the space available. [11]
911 察	scrutinize *House . . . offer sacrifice.* [14]
912 擦	scrub *Fingers . . . scrutinize.* [17]
913 由	wherefore (N.) Think of the phrase "whys and **wherefores**" to capture the key word's sense of the reason for something. The character does this graphically by depicting a seed in a *rice field* sending up a single sprout, which is the whole why and **wherefore** of the seed's existence. [5] 丨 冂 日 由 由

❖ Used as a primitive, in conformity to the explanation above, this character will be taken to mean a *shoot* or a *sprout*.

914

take out

抽

Fingers . . . sprout. The sense of the key word is "draw out." It has nothing to do with dating. [8]

915

oil

油

Water . . . sprout. [8]

916

first

甲

This character reverses the element for *sprout*, giving the image of roots being sent down into the earth by a seed planted in the *rice field*. To connect this to the key word, remember that the **first** root in many plants is the taproot from which other roots spread out.

This the **first** of the series for which we have already learned *second, third,* and *fourth* (FRAMES 95, 842, 90). [5]

❖ Keeping with the image of roots in the story above, we shall assign this primitive the meaning of *radish* (which has the same "root" as the obsolete word "radix").

917

pawn (v.)

押

Fingers . . . radish. Compare and contrast with *take out* (FRAME 914). [8]

918

express

申

The sense of this key word is to **express** in words as opposed to gestures, actions, or art. Its primitives are a *tongue wagging in the mouth* . . . with a *walking stick* rammed through it and coming out at both ends. [5]

❖ While this character has obvious affinities to the "seed" group, it also happens to be the zodiacal sign of the *monkey*, which we will take as its primitive meaning.

919 伸	extend

Person . . . monkey. [7]

920 神	gods

Altar . . . monkey. [9]

921 果	fruit

The final stage of the seed is reached when the plant has reached its full growth (the *tree*) and comes to fruition, producing **fruit** full of new seeds that can return to the earth and start the process all over again. The main thing to notice here is the element for *brains* at the top, which might prove more helpful than *rice field* for creating an image. [8]

丶　冂　冂　日　旦　甲　杲　果

922 课	lesson

Words . : . fruit. [10]

923 颗	granule

Fruit . . . head. [14]

LESSON 30

By NOW YOU WILL have learned to handle a great number of very difficult characters with perfect ease and without fear of forgetting. Some others, of course, will take review. But let us focus on the ones you are most confident about and can write most fluently, in order to add a remark about what role the stories, plots, and primitives should continue to play even after you have learned a character to your own satisfaction.

This course has been designed to move in steps from the full-bodied story to the skeletal plot to the heap of bones we call primitive elements. This also happens to be roughly the way memory works. At first the full story is necessary (as a rule, for every character, no matter how simple it appears), in that it enables you to focus your attention and your interest on the vivid images of the primitives, which in turn dictate how you write the character. Once the image has strutted through the full light of imagination, it will pass on, leaving its footprints on the interstices of the brain in some mysterious way. And those footprints are often enough of a clue about the nature of the beast to enable you to reconstruct the plot in broad outlines. Should you need to, you can nearly always follow the tracks back to their source and recall your whole story, but that is generally unnecessary. The third stage occurs when even the plot is unnecessary, and the key word by itself suggests the meaning of the primitives; or conversely, when seeing a character at once conjures up a specific key word. Here again, the plot is still within reach if needed, but not worth bothering with once it has fulfilled its task of providing the proper primitive elements.

There is yet a fourth stage to be reached, as you have probably realized by now, but one you ought not trust until you have completed the full list of the characters given here. In this stage, the primitive elements flow naturally one into the other, without any need to associate them with their meanings. Quite early on, you will recall, we insisted that visual memory of the character as a whole is to be discarded in favor of imaginative memory of its component parts. It may now be clear just why that is so. But it should also be becoming clear that visual memory of the whole will take over as a matter of course once recall of the parts has become automatic. This is a process not to be rushed, however appealing its rewards in terms of writing fluency.

Insofar as you have experienced these things in your own study, fears about the inadequacy of the key words should be greatly allayed. For in much the same way that the character slowly finds its way into the fabric of memory and muscular habits, the key word will gradually give way to a key concept distinct from the particular English word used to express it. Hence the substitution of a Chinese word—or even a number of words—will prove no stumbling block. Quite the contrary, it will help avoid confusion between key words with family resemblances.

In short, the number of steps required to learn the Chinese writing system has not been increased by what we have been doing. The steps have simply become more pronounced here than in traditional methods of drawing and redrawing the characters hundreds of times until they are learned, and in that way the whole process has become much more efficient. Pausing to think about just what your mind has been doing through this book should make the ideas mentioned in the Introduction much more plausible now than they must have seemed way back then.

But we must be on our way again, this time down a road marked "tools."

924	catty [N.]
斤	A **catty** is exactly one-half kilogram (or a little more than a pound). This character is a picture of a small ax of exactly that weight, a **catty**—the two vertical lines being the handle and the horizontal strokes, the blade. Note the writing order carefully: it begins like the primitive element for *drag*. [4]

′　厂　厂　斤

❖ As a primitive, this character will mean a *tomahawk*.

925	listen
听	*Mouth . . . tomahawk.* [7]

926	place [N.]
所	*Door . . . tomahawk.* Two lessons ago, we saw that the first stroke for *door* was written differently than it is in this character for **place**. Here the element appears as it does in many traditional fonts, preserving a certain balance in the character's form. [8]

户　所

927	near
近	*Tomahawk . . . road.* [7]

928 斩	hew
	Car . . . tomahawk. [8]

929 暂	temporary
	Hew . . . days. [12]

930 渐	gradually
	Water . . . hew. [11]

931 断	sever
	Rice . . . fishhook . . . tomahawk. [11]
	米 迷 断

932 折	discount
	Fingers . . . tomahawk. [7]

933 哲	philosopher
	Discount . . . mouth. [10]

934 逝	pass away
	Discount . . . road. [10]

935 斥	reprimand (v.)
	Tomahawk . . . a drop of. [5]

936 诉	accuse
	Words . . . reprimand. [7]

937 乍	for the first time
	This character is a picture of a saw. We leave it to you to make an association to the key word: **for the first time.** [5]
	ノ ⺊ ⺓ 乍 乍

❖ In line with the above explanation, the primitive meaning of this character will be a *saw*. Keep this element distinct from the character of the same meaning (FRAME 889).

938 怎	how?
	Saw . . . heart. [9]

939 昨	yesterday
	Day . . . saw. [9]

940 作	do
	Person . . . saw. [7]

❖ 彐	broom
	The pictographic representation here is of the bristles on the head of a **broom**. [3]

フ ヨ ヨ

941 雪	snow (N.)
	Rain that undergoes a change so that it can be swept aside with a *broom* is **snow**. [11]

942 灵	spirit
	The **spirit** descends on a crowd of people here in the form of little *brooms* made of *fire,* presumably to sweep their hearts clean. [7]

943 妇	married woman
	Woman . . . broom. [6]

944 扫	sweep
	Fingers . . . broom. [6]

945	seek
寻	*Broom ... glue.* [6]

946	anxious
急	*Bound up ... broom ... heart.* [9]

947	work as
当	*Small ... broom.* The key word has to do with one's job or occupation, that is, what one **works as**. [6]

948	files
档	*Tree ... work as.* The **files** of this character are the kind you find in archives and offices. [10]

949	record (V.)
录	*Broom ... snowflake.* [8]

❖ As a primitive, the elements will combine to give us the meaning of a *snowman* (with a *broom* in his hand, of course).

950	commonplace (ADJ.)
碌	*Stone ... snowman.* [13]

❖	rake
尹	A single vertical stroke transforms *broom* into a **rake**. In this case the second stroke of *broom* is lengthened. When an element comes BELOW the **rake**, the vertical stroke is shortened, as we have seen before with other similar primitives such as *sheep* and *cow*. Moreover, when something comes ABOVE the **rake** and joins to it at the top, the vertical stroke begins at the top horizontal stroke, as in the following two frames. [4]

⼅   ⺻   彐   尹

951 争	**contend** *Bound up . . . rake.* [6]
952 净	**clean** (ADJ.) *Ice . . . contend.* [8]
953 事	**matter** This key word here refers to abstract **matters**. The elements are: *one . . . mouth . . . rake.* Note how the *rake* handle reaches out the top and bottom of the character. [8]
954 唐	**Tang** The key word here refers, of course, to the **Tang** Dynasty in China (and not to the name of the drink astronauts take with them into outer space, though this could be useful for the next frame). Its elements: *cave . . . rake . . . mouth.* [10]
955 糖	**sugar** *Rice . . . Tang.* [16]
956 康	**hale** This key word—which means "in good health"—is half of the "**hale** and hearty" duo (not to be confused with Laurel and Hardy). Its elements: *cave . . . rake . . . snowflakes.* [11]
957 尹	**overseer** The only thing distinguishing this character from a *rake* is the bent handle that does not cut through the top horizontal stroke. It depicts the swish-swash motion of a mop, as demonstrated here by the **overseer** of a group of sanitary engineers. [4] 彐 尹

958 **Queen Elizabeth**

伊 This character is used now chiefly for its phonetic value in proper names like Iraq, Iguaçu, Illinois, and **Queen Elizabeth** (whose predecessor reportedly was not amused). Its primitives: *person . . . overseer.* [6]

959 **monarch**

君 The **monarch** referred to in the last frame may come in handy for this frame and the next two after it. *Overseer . . . mouth.* [7]

960 **skirt** (N.)

裙 *Clothing . . . monarch.* [12]

961 **crowd** (N.)

群 *Monarch . . . sheep.* [13]

962 **and**

而 The character for **and** is a pictograph of a comb. If you have trouble remembering how many "teeth" are in this comb, think of a questionnaire or form that uses vertical lines to insure that each letter is separated from the others around it. As it turns out, if you look at the character you will see that there are just enough spaces to spell out the word **a-n-d**. [6]

一　丆　丆　丙　丙　而

❖ The primitive meaning of this character is a *comb*, to be kept distinct from the character of the same meaning (FRAME 685).

963 **need** (V.)

需 The sense of the key word **need** is best captured by thinking of the economics of supplying what consumers demand. The primitives: *rain . . . comb.* [14]

964	Confucian
儒	*Person . . . need.* [16]

❖	prospector
峬	The primitives suggest an image of someone who is *combing* the *mountains*—in this case, an old **prospector** roaming the hills with his gear strapped to the back of his faithful donkey. He is looking for gold not by panning for it but by literally *combing* the *mountains* with a giant *comb*. [9]

山 峬

965	auspicious
瑞	*Ball . . . prospector.* [13]

966	upright
端	*Vase . . . prospector.* [14]

967	bent
曲	Picture yourself grabbing hold of the two strokes poking out the top of the character and wrenching them apart, thus giving the sense of **bent**. If you think of them as deriving from the element for *brains* beneath (of course, the middle stroke has been reduplicated and pulled out to where it can be grabbed hold of), you can associate the key word with someone's mind that has been **bent** to your point of view. [6]

丨 冂 冃 囲 曲 曲

968	Big Dipper
斗	The **Big Dipper** here is, of course, the constellation of Ursa Major, of which this character is a sort of pictographic representation. The primitive elements (*ice* and a kind of distorted *ten*) are there if you need them. [4]

丶 冫 三 斗

❖ Since we already have a primitive element for a "dipper"—namely, the *ladle*—we shall let this one stand for a *measuring cup*. By the way, it would make a rather large one, since the character is also used for a measure of about a decaliter!

969	material (N.)
料	*Rice . . . measuring cup.* [10]

970	academic discipline
科	Think of the faculty or **academic discipline** you chose at your university using the elements: *wild rice . . . measuring cup.* [9]

971	utilize
用	*Flesh . . . walking stick.* Be sure to keep this key word distinct from that for *use* (FRAME 838). The stroke order is exactly as you would expect it from the order of the primitive elements as given. [5]

丿 冂 冃 月 用

❖ When this character is used as a primitive element, we shall substitute the image of a *screwdriver*, perhaps the most "utilized" of all tools around the house.

972	reliable
确	*Stone . . . bound up . . . screwdriver.* [12]

LESSON 31

IN THIS LESSON WE pick up a few primitives of quantity to complement those we learned in Lesson 7, as well as some others related closely to elements learned earlier.

❖ 卉	salad
	The element for *flowers* joins with the long horizontal stroke beneath it to create the picture of a bowl of **salad**. [4]
	一　ナ　廾　卉

973 昔	times past
	Salad . . . days. This is the character for the **times** that we refer to as **past**. [8]

974 借	borrow
	Person . . . times past. [10]

975 错	mistaken
	Metal . . . times past. [13]

976 散	scattered
	Salad . . . flesh . . taskmaster. [12]

977 撒	scatter
	Fingers . . . scattered. Be sure to keep this and the previous frame apart by attaching different connotations to the key words. [15]

978 廿	twenty
	The two *tens* joined at the bottom by a short line actually make up the old character for **twenty**, which we might as well learn since we need its primitive form. It is written the same as *salad*, except for the shorter final stroke. [4]

一 十 廾 廿

❖   caverns

庐

The primitive for **caverns** differs from that for *cave* by the presence of the primitive for *twenty*, suggesting a maze of underground *caves*. [7]

广 庐

---

979   mat

席

Caverns . . . towel. [10]

---

980   degrees

度

This key word refers to a gradation of measurement, not to academic diplomas. Its primitives: *caverns . . . crotch.* [9]

---

981   ferry (N./V.)

渡

Water . . . degrees. [12]

---

982   half (N./ADJ.)

半

The two **halves** of this character are mirror images of one another, the last stroke dividing it in **half** right down the middle. It is probably easier to draw it with this in mind than to try working directly with the primitives (*horns, two,* and *walking stick*).

When this character appears to the left as a primitive, the final stroke is gently bent toward the left, as we will see presently in FRAME 985. [5]

丶 丷 丷 半 半

---

983   partner

伴

Person . . . half. [7]

---

984   fat (ADJ.)

胖   *Flesh. . . half.* [9]

---

985   judge (V.)

判   *Half . . . saber.* You might recall the famous scene in which King Solomon is called on to **judge** between two harlots claiming to be the mother of a newborn boy. The King offers to slice the baby in two with a *saber* to give *half* to each of the disputing women, when the true mother reveals herself by relinquishing her claim in order to save the life of the child. In his wisdom, the King **judges** her to be the mother and gives her the child. [7]

❖   quarter

半   This character simply splits the vertical stroke of a *half* in half once again, to get a **quarter**. In so doing, it spreads the split stroke out to form a sort of enclosure under which its other primitives will be placed. [6]

        丶   ⸯ   丷   半   半   关

---

986   dependents

眷   Any of you who have ever had to fill out tax forms know what this key word refers to. For those of you yet to experience that thrill, it refers to family **dependents**. *Quarter . . . eyeball.* [11]

---

987   boxing (N.)

拳   *Quarter . . . hand.* [10]

---

988   slice (N.)

片   This character is based on the pictograph of a tree split unevenly down the middle. The right side, shown here, is really no more than a thin **slice**. Note the stroke order. [4]

        丿   丿'   丨'   片

989

版

printing plate

Although this character also carries the sense of an "edition" of a publication, the elements, *slice* and *against*, more readily suggest its other meaning of a **printing plate**, or the thin slice of metal which is covered with ink and pressed *against* the surface to be printed on. [8]

990

之

of

As abstract as this key word sounds, remembering it is simplicity itself. All you need do is think of the famous "sign of Zorro," which is etched exactly like the bottom part of this character, just below the *drop*, of. [3]

` ⼎ 之

❖ Used as a primitive element, this character will take its meaning from the explanation above: *sign of Zorro.*

991

乏

weary

Eyedropper . . . sign of Zorro. [4]

992

眨

blink (v.)

Eyeball . . . weary. [9]

993

不

no

You may play with the primitives of this character as you wish (*ceiling . . . person . . . a drop of*), but you will probably find that its simplicity, and its frequency, make it easy to remember just as it is. [4]

一 丆 不 不

❖ As a primitive element, this character will mean the internationally recognized *no symbol*: ⊘.

994 否	NO symbol... mouth. [7]	negate
995 坏	Soil ... NO symbol. [7]	bad
996 环	Ball ... NO symbol. [8]	ring (N.)
997 杯	Tree ... NO symbol. [8]	cup
998 还	NO symbol ... road. [7]	give back
999 怀	State of mind ... NO symbol. [7]	cherish

LESSON 32

WE TURN NOW TO the weapons that remain to be examined. To the *saber*, the *dagger*, and the *arrow*, we add two more weapons primitives to the list in the course of this lesson: the *spear* and the *snare*.

1000	dart (N.)
矢	When shot high into the *heavens*, the **dart** gets so small it looks like a mere *drop*. Although this character could as well mean "arrow," it has no connection with the primitive of that meaning. Hence the new key word. [5]
1001	tribe
族	*Banner . . . dart.* [11]
1002	know
知	*Dart . . . mouth.* [8]
1003	wisdom
智	*Know . . . sun.* [12]
1004	spear (N.)
矛	The **spear** shown here is from a **spear**-gun, which accounts for the barbs and hooks, and also for the line you use to reel in your catch (the final stroke). [5] ㄱ ㄹ マ ㅋ 予 矛
1005	gentle
柔	*Spear . . . tree.* [9]
1006	knead
揉	*Fingers . . . gentle.* [12]

1007	bestow

予

This character differs from the *spear* shot from a spear-gun (FRAME 1004) by the absence of the final stroke, the line for reeling in one's catch. Imagine an initiation ritual in which a tribal chief **bestows** on a young man a long "ceremonial spear" as a symbol of his coming of age. It is "given" without strings attached. [4]

❖ As a primitive element this character will keep the meaning of a *ceremonial spear* from the story above.

1008	preface (N.)

序

Cave ... ceremonial spear. [7]

1009	beforehand

预

Ceremonial spear ... head. [10]

1010	wild (ADJ.)

野

This character refers to **wild**life or **wild** things. Its elements: *computer ... ceremonial spear.* [11]

1011	class (N.)

班

The key word refers to a group of students gathered in the same **class**room or studying the same subject matter. Its elements: *saber ... two balls/kings.* [10]

❖	fencing foil

刂

Unlike the *spear* and the *saber*, the **fencing foil** is straight and blunted at the end. [2]

1012	be about to

临

Think of a matador at the "moment of truth," when he **is about to** dispatch the bull to his eternal reward. Since he is using a *fencing foil*, with a safety nob at the end, all he can manage is a tiny scratch producing a single *drop of* blood. This sends the bull into a fit of laughter. Can you see it *reclining* on the floor of the arena shaking its legs in the air? Even the setting *sun* can't keep from rolling over on its side with laughter. [9]

丨 丨⺊ 丨⺊ 丨⺊ 丨⺕ 丨⺕ 临

1013   firm ^(ADJ.)

坚

Let the top two components of this character indicate the cry "*Foiled again!*" (from the element for *fencing foil* and the keyword meaning of the character for *again*). Beneath it, *soil*. [7]

1014   **worthy**

贤

Foiled again! . . . shells. [8]

1015   **bow** ^(N.)

弓

This character pictures the bent wooden **bow**. In Book 2 we will learn how to make the *bowstring* that goes with it. If you stretch this character out and see the indentation on the left as its handle, the pictography should be clearer. [3]

⺄ ⺕ 弓

1016   **draw** ^(V.)

引

In addition to the association with *bows* and arrows, this character is also used to **draw** water from a well or **draw** attention or opinions out of people. The elements: *bow . . . walking stick*. [4]

1017   **fill** ^(V.)

弥

Bow . . . hiccup. [8]

1018   **strong**

强

Bow . . . a mouth full of *insects*. [12]

1019   **weak**

弱

Two *bows* . . with *ice* on them. [10]

| 1020 | list ^(N.) |

单

Horns . . . sunflower. We waited to introduce this character here so that it could be learned in connection with the next one. [8]

| 1021 | bullet |

弹

Bow . . . list. [11]

❖ | dollar sign

弗

Composed of a pair of *crutches* running through a *bow*, this character is infrequent as a primitive, and yet easy to remember for what it looks like: the dollar sign, $. When it is written under another element, the first vertical stroke is abbreviated to a short "tail" as the final stroke, and the second vertical stroke is cut off at the top: 弔. Examples follow. [5]

弓 弔 弗

| 1022 | expense |

费

Dollar sign . . . clams. [9]

| 1023 | Buddha |

佛

Person . . . dollar sign. [7]

| 1024 | younger brother |

弟

Horns . . . dollar sign. [7]

| 1025 | No. |

第

The key word **No.** is the abbreviation for "number." Its elements: *bamboo . . . dollar sign.* [11]

❖ | snare

丂

The **snare** of this primitive is drawn something like the last two strokes of a *bow*. [2]

一 丂

1026 巧	I-beam . . . snare. [5]	adroit
1027 号	Mouth . . . snare. [5]	appellation

LESSON 33

ALTHOUGH WE still have a number of primitives left relating to human activities, we may at this point pick up what remains of those having to do specifically with people and parts of the human body, and a few others.

1028	somebody

身 The key word **somebody** was chosen to convey the double meaning of this character: body and person. Its composition is based on the *nose* (which, you will recall, is also the character for *oneself*). The extension of the bottom and far right strokes of that element, together with the unusual diagonal stroke, forms the pictograph of **somebody** with a prominent paunch. [7]

㇒　亻　ㄇ　自　自　身　身

1029	shoot^(v.)

射 Since this character is used to **shoot** guns and bows, we can call to mind the famous verse: "I **shot** an arrow into the air, It fell to earth I know not where." (Poor Henry Wadsworth must have lost a lot of arrows.) This character, however, tells us where it DID land: *glued to . . . somebody.* [10]

1030	thank

谢 *Words . . . shoot.* [12]

1031	old man

老 In the character for an **old man** the element for *soil* is drawn first to indicate that one has come close to the age when "dust to dust" begins to take on a personal meaning; the diagonal *walking stick* is added to help the **old man** get around, and the *spoon* for those times when he needs to be *spoon*-fed. [6]

一　十　土　耂　耂　老

❖ When this character is used as a primitive and its shape adjusted to 耂, the meaning is changed to *Santa Claus*. If the long white beard is not enough, think of this: by some accounts he is already well over 1,700 years old.

❖

与

slingshot

We could not introduce this element in the last lesson, where it rightly belongs, because only now do we have enough pieces to make a character with it. The **slingshot** is like a *bow*, except for the handle that you pull the sling back with. [2]

一 与

1032

考

take an exam

Santa Claus . . . slingshot. Note how the top of the *slingshot* gets absorbed into the final stroke of *Santa Claus*. [6]

1033

烤

roast [v.]

Fire . . . take an exam. [10]

❖

⼅

pointed tail

The two strokes here form an image of a long, **pointed tail** like the kind you see on hunting dogs such as the English pointer. [2]

1034

与

offer [v.]

A *pointed tail* in a *slingshot*. [3]

1035

写

write

Crown . . . offer. [5]

1036

泻

diarrhea

Water . . . write. [8]

1037

孝

filial piety

Santa Claus . . . child. [7]

1038 教	teach
	Filial piety . . . taskmaster. [11]

1039 者	someone
	Santa Claus . . . tongue wagging in the mouth. Think of "that special **someone**" in your life to avoid confusing this key word with *somebody* (FRAME 1028). [8]

❖ As a primitive it means a *puppet*-on-a-string—or if it helps, a *Santa Claus puppet.*

1040 著	author ^(v.)
	Flowers . . . puppet. [11]

1041 猪	pig
	Pack of wild dogs . . . puppet. [11]

❖ 自	maestro
	To remember this primitive meaning, picture a tuxedo-clad **maestro** waving his baton about wildly. The baton is, of course, the little *drop* at the top. And the two boxes attached to the long vertical stroke may represent his tuxedo tails, if you wish. [6]

❜ 丨 丨 丨 丨

1042 追	chase
	Maestro . . . road. [9]

1043 官	bureaucrat
	By replacing the *maestro's* baton (the *drop*) with the roof of a *house*, we have his equivalent in the institutional world of big government: the **bureaucrat.** [8]

1044 管	pipe
	The key word here should be thought of in the sense of a conduit or tubing. Its elements: *bamboo . . . bureaucrat.* [14]

1045	father
父	The kindness and hard work of the ideal **father** are seen in this abbreviation of the *taskmaster* that leaves off his rod or whip (the first stroke) and replaces it with the sweat of the **father's** brow (the two *drops* at the top). [4]

丿　丷　夕　父

1046	mingle
交	*Top hat . . . father.* [6]

1047	effect [N.]
效	*Mingle . . . taskmaster.* [10]

1048	relatively
较	*Cars . . . mingle.* [10]

1049	school [N.]
校	*Tree . . . mingle.* [10]

1050	lower leg
足	This character depicts the lower leg, that is, the part from the kneecap (the *mouth*) to the foot (the part that leaves the *trail of footprints*). [7]
	❖ As a primitive on the left, it is amended to ⻊. Its meaning remains *lower leg*, but should be thought of as a *wooden leg* in order to avoid confusion with other similar elements, namely *human legs*, *animal legs*, and *walking legs*.

1051	run [V.]
跑	*Wooden leg . . . wrap.* [12]

1052	jump [V.]
跳	*Wooden leg . . . portent.* [13]

1053		path
路	*Wooden leg . . . each.* [13]	

1054		dew
露	*Rain . . . path.* [21]	

1055		skeleton
骨	This character and primitive refer to the *part of the body* composed of the bones and their joints. The top part of the character, terminating in the element for *crown*, is a pictograph of a bone joint. We leave it to you to put the pieces together, so to speak. [9]	

丶　冂　冎　冎　咼　骨

1056		slippery
滑	*Water . . . skeleton.* [12]	

LESSON 34

THE NEXT GROUP OF primitives we shall consider has to do mainly with topography and exhausts the list of primitives remaining in that category.

❖

阝

pinnacle

This primitive meaning has been chosen because of its connotation of "the highest point," thereby suggesting the image of the highest point in a village, that is, a hill or mountain on which sacred or festive events take place. If you have a clear image of the Athenian acropolis, you might use it to express this element for a **pinnacle**. Note that this primitive appears only on the left. On the right, as we shall see later, the same form takes a different meaning. [2]

$$ 阝\quad 阝 $$

1057

阿

Apollo

Transcribing the word **Apollo** into Chinese requires three characters, of which the character in this frame is the first. Since this character is used primarily for its sound value, the choice of a key word has nothing to do with the meaning of the character, as was the case earlier with *Queen Elizabeth*. Its elements are: *pinnacle . . . can.* [7]

1058

啊

aah!

Mouth . . . Apollo. Like the English "oohs and **aahs**," this character is a particle which is used for expressing admiration, among other things. [10]

1059

随

as you wish

Pinnacle . . . possess . . . road. [11]

1060	Yang
阳	*Pinnacle . . . sun.* Here we meet the second of the Yin-**Yang** couple. As you would guess from the inclusion of the *sun,* **Yang** is the bright element, literally the "*sunny* side of the slope." [6]

1061	Yin
阴	*Pinnacle . . . moon.* As you probably guessed from the last frame, **Yin** refers to the "shady side of the slope." [6]

1062	shady
荫	**Shady** as opposed to "sunny." The primitives: *flowers. . . Yin.* [9]

1063	ward off
防	*Pinnacle . . . compass.* [6]

1064	attach
附	*Pinnacle . . . pay.* [7]

1065	occasion [N.]
际	*Pinnacle . . . altar.* [7]

1066	stairs
阶	*Pinnacle . . . introduce.* [6]

1067	Inst.
院	This key word, the abbreviation for **Institution**, represents the use of that word as a suffix affixed to certain buildings and organizations. Its primitive elements: *pinnacle . . . finish.* [9]

1068	battle formation
阵	*Pinnacle . . . car.* [6]

1069	team
队	*Pinnacle . . . person.* [4]

1070	crash (v.)
坠	Team . . . ground. [7]

1071	descend
降	Pinnacle . . . walking legs . . . monocle. Note that the drawing for monocle in the character for year, where it was first introduced (FRAME 871) was somewhat irregular because it doubled up with other strokes. From now on monocle will be written as shown below. [8]

阝　陉　陉　陉　降

1072	hole
穴	House . . . eight. [5]

   ❖ Note that when this character is used as a primitive, the element for eight changes into animal legs, as in the following frames.

1073	research
究	Hole . . . baseball. [7]

1074	abruptly
突	Hole . . . chihuahua. [9]

1075	empty
空	Hole . . . I-beam. [8]

1076	control (v.)
控	Fingers . . . empty. [11]

❖	paper punch
宀冖	This primitive simply discards the first stroke of that for hole to become a **paper punch**. [4]

1077	deep
深	*Water . . . paper punch . . . tree.* [11]

1078	spy (N.)
探	*Fingers . . . paper punch . . . tree.* [11]

1079	hill
丘	Since this supposedly pictographic representation of a **hill** looks like anything but, picture a row of *axes* driven into the ground up to their heads, and see if that doesn't present you with a more memorable image of **hill**—at least a riskier one for sliding down! [5]

1080	troops
兵	*Hill . . . animal legs.* [7]

Lesson 35

THE PRIMITIVE FOR *thread* is one of the most common in all the characters. This means that you are likely to be putting it where it doesn't belong and forgetting to include it where it does—all the more reason to give it a vivid image each time. Fortunately, nearly all the thread-related characters to be covered in this book will appear in this lesson, so you can learn them all at once.

❖

纟

thread

Remember when your granny used to ask you to bend your arms at the *elbows* and hold them out so that she could use them like a rack to hold a skein of yarn (here **thread**) while she rolled it up into a ball? Can you see at the top the two *elbows* (abbreviated here to single strokes), and the stretched out **thread** below? [3]

纟 纟 纟

1081

silk

丝

Silk *thread* is so fine that it needs to be to be twined together ("doubled") to be used in sewing, [5]

丝 丝 丝 丝 丝

1082

weave (V.)

织

Thread . . . mouth . . . animal legs. Note how we broke the character for *only* up into its composite elements, which are more useful for remembering this character. [8]

1083

line (N.)

线

Thread . . . float. [8]

1084

maintain

维

Thread . . . turkey. [11]

1085 统	overall
Thread . . . sufficient. [9]	

1086 给	give
Thread . . . fit. [9]	

1087 结	tie ^(v.)
Thread . . . aerosol can. [9]	

1088 终	end ^(n.)
Thread . . . winter. [8]	

1089 级	rank ^(n.)
Threads . . . outstretched hands. [6]	

1090 纪	epoch
Thread . . . snake. [6]	

1091 红	red
Thread . . . I-beam. [6]	

1092 约	make an appointment
Thread . . . ladle. [6]	

1093 细	fine ^(adj.)
Thread . . . brains. The key word **fine** covers the sense of small and delicate as well as the sense of superb quality. [8]	

1094 纵	vertical
Thread . . . assembly line. [7]	

1095 绿	green
Thread . . . snowman. [11]	

❖

圣 spool

The *I-beam* at the bottom of this element should be taken in this case as a pictograph of a **spool**. At the top, we see something being pulled taut from a *person's* head. What we have here is the record holder for the world's longest tresses—so long, that the poor woman has to wrap them up on a spool to avoid tripping over them. [5]

フ ス 圣

1096 scripture

经 *Thread . . . spool.* [8]

1097 lightweight (ADJ.)

轻 *Car . . . spool.* [9]

1098 continue

续 *Thread . . . read.* [11]

1099 carry on (V.)

继 *Thread . . . rice . . . hook.* Be careful to keep the association for the key word of this frame distinct from that of the previous frame, since the meaning of the two is virtually the same. [10]

纟 纟米 继

1100 medicine

药 *Flowers . . . make an appointment.* [9]

❖

幺 cocoon

The two triangular shapes here and their final stroke are intended as a pictograph of a **cocoon**, spun in circles and tied up at the end. [3]

ㄥ 幺 幺

❖ 糸	**floss** This element shows the *cocoon* with *small* below it. Imagine taking your dental **floss** directly from a *cocoon* stuck on the side of your medicine cabinet. You should be able to picture the *small end of the* **floss** hanging out the bottom of the *cocoon*. [6]
1101 系	**lineage** *Drop of . . . floss.* [7]
1102 紧	**tight** *Foiled again! . . . floss.* [10]

LESSON 36

EARLIER WE CREATED an image for *seal* (FRAME 167). Here we come to a set of primitives based on seals and stamps.

❖ 卩	**stamp** (N.) This character is a kind of pictograph of a **stamp** that may best be imagined as a postage **stamp** to distinguish it from other stamp-like things to come up later. [2] ㄱ 卩
1103 却	**withdraw** The sense of this key word is to step back from something; it has nothing to do with taking money out of the bank. Its primitives: *gone . . . stamp.* [7]
1104 脚	**foot** *Part of the body . . . withdraw.* [11]
1105 服	**apparel** *Flesh . . . stamp . . . crotch.* Note how the *stamp* is stretched out here. [8]
1106 报	**newspaper** *Fingers . . . stamp . . . crotch.* Note how the *stamp* is stretched out here. [7]
1107 命	**fate** This character connotes life in general, but also the particular **fate** meted out to one by virtue of the distinctive character with which one is born. Its elements are: *fit . . . stamp.* The bottom portion of *fit* is nudged to the left in order to make room for the *stamp.* [8]

❖	letter opener

卯 In its full form, this primitive looks like a *stamp* and its mirror image on the left: 卯. This is the form it takes when there is nothing below it. When there is, it is condensed to the shape shown in this frame. Let us take advantage of the fact that the right side becomes a *dagger* and assign this primitive the meaning of a *letter opener*.

If you take care to draw the strokes of this condensed form in the order shown below, the drawing of the full form will follow automatically. [5]

ノ　ㇹ　ㇹ　卯

1108	trade (N.)
贸	*Letter opener . . . shells.* [9]

1109	stay (V.)
留	*Letter opener . . . rice field.* [10]

1110	slide (V.)
溜	*Water . . . stay.* [13]

1111	chat (V.)
聊	*Ear . . . letter opener.* [11]

1112	willow
柳	*Tree . . . letter opener.* [9]

❖	chop

卩 The **chop** is the engraved piece of wood or stone used in the Orient to certify documents, generally using red ink. Unlike the *stamp*, the top stroke here reaches a good distance to the left of its vertical stroke. Note that this primitive is sometimes abbreviated to ㇹ (see FRAMES 1115–1118). Examples of both drawings follow. [2]

フ フ ワ マ

1113 节	holiday
	Flowers . . . chop. [5]

1114 卫	defend
	Chop . . . floor. [3]

1115 令	orders (N.)
	Meeting . . . chop. [5]

人 仝 令

1116 冷	cold
	Ice . . . orders. [7]

1117 零	zero
	Rain . . . orders. [13]

1118 领	collar (N.)
	Orders . . . head. [11]

❖ 甬	sealing wax
	Western *chops* and seals often *utilize* **sealing wax** rather than red ink to leave their impression. [7]

マ 甬

1119 通	communicate
	Sealing wax . . . road. [10]

1120 勇	courageous
	Sealing wax . . . muscle. [9]

❖ 巳	**fingerprint** The primitive for **fingerprint** is like that for *stamp* except that the second stroke bends back towards the right, like an arm. [2]

⁊   巳

1121 仓	**storehouse** *Umbrella . . . fingerprint.* [4]
1122 枪	**gun** *Tree . . . storehouse.* [8]
1123 创	**initiate** (v.) *Storehouse . . . saber.* [6]
1124 犯	**criminal** (N.) *Wild dogs . . . fingerprint.* [5]
1125 危	**danger** *Bound up . . . on a cliff . . . fingerprint.* [6]
1126 脆	**fragile** *Flesh . . . . danger.* [10]
❖ 臣	**staples** This primitive represents a number of small **staples**, like the kind commonly used in an office and at school. Note that when this element stands alone, it is drawn with only 3 strokes, as in the following frame. Both stroke orders are given below. [4]

ノ ᒥ Ᏺ 臣 ノ Ᏺ 臣

1127 印	**print** (N./V.) *Staples . . . stamp.* [5]

LESSON 37

THE NEXT cluster of characters has to do with primitives related to the activities of eating and drinking.

❖ 酉	whiskey bottle
	This primitive will mean *whiskey bottle*. In its pictograph, you can see the loosely corked lid, the bottle, and the contents (about one-third full). You might also think of the Spanish *porrón*, a decanter shaped like a long-necked bird. [7]

一　厂　冂　丙　丙　酉　酉

1128 酒	liquor
	Water . . . whiskey bottle. [10]

1129 配	distribute
	Whisky bottle . . . snake. [10]

1130 酋	chieftain
	Animal horns . . . whisky bottle. [9]

1131 尊	venerate (v.)
	Chieftain . . . glue. [12]

1132 遵	abide by
	Venerate . . . road. [15]

1133 豆	beans
	This character is supposed to depict a pot of **beans**, but in its present form, it looks a lot more like a table on which you might place the pot. [7]

一　口　戸　豆　豆

❖ Used as a primitive, this character will also take the meaning of a *table*. Be sure to avoid confusing this image with the one you have for *small table* (see FRAME 57).

1134

short

短　*Dart . . . table.* [12]

1135

kitchen

厨　*Cliff . . . table . . . glue.* [12]

❖

drum

壴　The element for **drum** shows a *soldier* over a *table*. The top stroke of the *table* appears to be missing, but actually it has doubled up with the final stroke of the element for *soldier*. [9]

1136

drum

鼓　The full character for the *drum* adds a *branch*, apparently to serve as a **drum**stick, to the primitive for *drum*. [13]

1137

joyful

喜　*Drum . . . mouth.* [12]

❖

dish

皿　The primitive for **dish** is, clearly, the pictograph of a painted or carved bowl, seen from the side. [5]

丶　冂　冂　皿　皿

1138

blood

血　The *drop* in the *dish* is **blood**. It is similar to the *drop* we saw earlier on the *dagger* in the character for *blade* (FRAME 84). [6]

1139	lid
盖	*Sheep . . . dish.* [11]

1140	temperature
温	*Water . . . sun . . . dish.* [12]

1141	supervise
监	*Fencing foil . . . reclining . . . drop . . . dish.* [10]

❖ The primitive meaning changes to *hidden camera.* Keep this in mind when creating your story for the key word.

1142	basket
篮	*Bamboo . . . hidden camera.* [16]

1143	blue
蓝	*Flowers . . . hidden camera.* [13]

❖	silver
艮	We give this element the meaning of **silver** from the character in the following frame. Both the original pictographic representation and the primitive elements that make it up are more trouble to hunt out than they are worth. It is best simply to learn it as is. In doing so, take careful note of the stroke order, and also the fact that when this element appears on the left, the penultimate stroke is omitted, giving us simply 艮. [6]

ㄱ　ㄱ　ㅋ　尸　尸　艮

1144	silver
银	*Metal . . . silver.* [11]

1145	heel (N. / V.)
跟	*Wooden leg . . . silver.* Although this character is used as a noun for **heel**, it can also take the verbal meaning of "follow" (close on another's **heels**). [13]

1146 **very**

很 *Queue . . . silver.* [9]

1147 **root** (N.)

根 *Tree . . . silver.* [10]

1148 **immediately**

即 *Silver . . . stamp.* [7]

1149 **retreat** (V.)

退 *Silver . . . road.* [9]

1150 **leg**

腿 *Flesh . . . retreat.* [13]

1151 **limit** (N./V.)

限 *Pinnacle . . . silver.* [8]

1152 **eyelet**

眼 *Eye . . . silver.* [11]

1153 **high-quality** (ADJ.)

良 *Drop of . . . silver.* [7]

❖ When using this character as a primitive, take the image of a saint's *halo*. As with *silver*, when this element is drawn on the left, the penultimate stroke is omitted, giving us 艮.

1154 **breakers**

浪 *Water . . . halo.* These are waves that crest or break into foam, not electrical **breakers** or people who do "break dancing." [10]

1155	mom
娘	*Woman . . . halo.* [10]

1156	food
食	If *halo* and *umbrella* aren't enough, break the *halo* down into *drop* and *silver*—or "silverware," an additional primitive. [9] ❖ As a primitive this character keeps its meaning of *food*, but, as with *silver* and *high-quality*, on the left it is abbreviated. In this case, there are three strokes: 饣.

1157	meal
饭	*Food . . . against.* [7]

1158	dine
餐	*Magic wand . . . evening . . . crotch/right hand . . . food.* [16]

1159	Bldg.
馆	The abbreviation of **Building** suggests that this character is used in proper names, as indeed it often is. Keep your connotation distinct from *Inst.* (FRAME 1067) when working with the elements: *food . . . bureaucrat.* [11]

❖	waitress
无	If you can doodle with the first two strokes on your own, the addition of the *human legs* will give you this primitive's meaning of **waitress**. [4]

一　二　尹　无

1160	since
既	*Silver . . . waitress.* The key word **since** should not be used as a preposition or adverb to indicate "from a point in the past," but as a conjunction meaning "now that." [9]

1161   approximate (ADJ.)

概   *Root . . . waitress.* It is also possible to divide the character up into *tree* and *since.* [13]

Lesson 38

A NUMBER OF primitives relating to plant life remain to be considered, and we shall devote the next few pages to doing so. If it seems that new primitives with only limited use are piling up, remember that they will be needed when you move on to Book 2.

1162   even (ADJ.)

平   This character is easiest remembered as a pictograph of a water lily floating on the surface of the water, which gives it its meaning of **even**. The fourth stroke represents the calm, smooth surface of a pond, and the final stroke the long stem of the plant reaching underwater. [5]

            一   厂   亇   立   平

     ❖   As a primitive, this character can keep its pictographic meaning of a *water lily*.

1163   evaluate

评   *Words . . . water lily.* [7]

1164   level ground

坪   *Ground . . . water lily.* [8]

1165   ooh!

乎   This character is an "exclamatory particle" and it is written as a *water lily* except for its stylishly tilted hat at the top and chic hook at the bottom. **Ooh!** la la. [5]

1166   shout (V.)

呼   *Mouth . . . Ooh!* [8]

❖		sheaf
乂	These two strokes are a crude drawing of a bundle of stalks bound together into a **sheaf**. [2]	

ノ 乂

1167		hope (v.)
希	*Sheaf . . . cloth.* [7]	

1168		scarce
稀	*Wild rice . . . hope.* [12]	

1169		kill
杀	*Sheaf . . . pole.* [6]	

1170		wind (N.)
风	*Wind . . . sheaf.* This is the full character from which the primitive element of the same meaning derives. [4]	

1171		mock
讽	*Words. . . wind.* [6]	

1172		ridge of a hill
冈	*Glass cover . . . sheaf.* [4]	

1173		just now
刚	*Ridge of a hill . . . saber.* This character is used to refer to things that have just happened. [6]	

1174		net (N.)
网	This is actually the full character whose abbreviation (the *eye* lying on its side, ⬚) we have been using as a primitive element. Its components: *glass cover . . . two sheaves.* [6]	

❖

pit

凵

The primitive meaning **pit**, whose drawing is perfectly picto-graphic, shows a trap hole made to catch animals. Do not con-fuse your image with that for the character in FRAME 323. [2]

∟   凵

1175

drawing

画

Ceiling . . . brains . . . pit. [8]

1176

cruel

凶

Sheaf . . . pit. [4]

乂   凶

1177

bosom

胸

Part of the body . . . bound up . . . cruel. [10]

❖

Fagan

㐫

The *top hat* and *cruel* by themselves suggest the villainous figure of Charles Dickens' **Fagan**, the unscrupulous arch-thug who uses Oliver Twist and his companions as pickpockets. [6]

亠   㐫

1178

brain

脑

Flesh . . . Fagan. [10]

1179

annoyed

恼

State of mind . . . Fagan. [9]

1180

leave (v.)

离

Fagan . . . belt . . . elbow. [10]

卤   离   离

1181	fowl
禽	Umbrella . . .leave. [12]

1182	righteousness
义	This character associates **righteousness** with those who have truly earned their bread by the sweat of their brow in the rustic image of a bouquet made of a dried *sheaf* carried in from the cornfield and set on the dining room table. The missing fragrance is supplied with the first stroke, a single *drop* of Eau de Dubuque. [3]

丶　ソ　义

❖ The primitive element retains the meaning of a *bouquet* from the above explanation.

1183	deliberate [v.]
议	*Words . . .righteousness.* The sense here is to discuss or exchange views on something. The primitives: *words . . . righteousness.* [5]

1184	ant
蚁	Insect . . . bouquet. [9]

1185	peppery
辛	The character in this frame pictures food whose taste is so hot and **peppery** that it makes the hairs on your body *stand up* as straight as *needles.* [7]

立　辛

❖ When this character is used as a primitive, it can take the added meaning of *chili pepper.*

1186	dispute [v.]
辩	Two *chili peppers . . . words.* [16]

辛　辡　辩

1187	repudiate

辟　*Flag ... mouth ... peppery.* [13]

尸　　居　　辟

❖ As a primitive, this character will mean *hot sauce*. The sense comes from the fact that the best way to *repudiate* unacceptable tastes is to smother the food with *hot sauce*.

1188	partition [N.]

壁　*Hot sauce ... ground.* [16]

1189	evade

避　*Hot sauce ... road.* [16]

1190	relatives

亲　The combination of the *chili pepper* with the element for *small* should be enough to suggest a way to dispose of some particularly disagreeable, high-maintenance **relatives**. [9]

1191	new

新　*Relatives ... tomahawk.* [13]

1192	fuel

薪　*Flowers ... new.* [16]

1193	good fortune

幸　Simply by turning the dot at the top of the primitive for *peppery* into a cross shape, we move from things bitter and *peppery* to **good fortune**. [8]

❖	cornucopia

凵　Considering the lack of circular lines in the Chinese writing system, this character is not a bad pictograph of a **cornucopia**. Despite the appearance of the printed form, what looks like the first two strokes is actually written as one. [2]

乚　丩

| 1194 | call [v.] |
| 叫 | Mouth . . . cornucopia. [5] |

| 1195 | receive |
| 收 | Cornucopia . . . taskmaster. [6] |

| 1196 | sign of the hog |
| 亥 | This character is the 12th sign of the Chinese zodiac: the **sign of the hog**. It is best learned by thinking of an acorn-eating **hog** in connection with the primitive meaning given below. [6] |

亠　亡　歺　歺　亥

❖ The *top hat* represents the external shape of the *acorn*, and the unusual but easily written complex of strokes beneath it (which you might also see as distortions of an *elbow* and *person*) stands for the mysterious secret whereby the *acorn* contains the oak tree in a nutshell.

| 1197 | nucleus |
| 核 | Tree . . . acorn. [10] |

| 1198 | tot |
| 孩 | Child . . . acorn. [9] |

| 1199 | carve |
| 刻 | Acorn . . . saber. [8] |

| 1200 | should |
| 该 | Words . . . acorn. [8] |

1201   **art**

术

This work of **art** is super avant-garde: a single *drop* drawn on an empty canvas with a full-sized tree. [5]

1202   **narrate**

述

Art . . . road. [8]

---

                                         wire mesh

圭

This primitive for **wire mesh** looks very close to that for *salad*, except that an extra horizontal line has been included. [5]

1203   **aid** (v.)

襄

Top hat and scarf . . . chatterbox . . . wire mesh. To put this all together, think of a flock of well-educated, upper-class carrier pigeons (hence the *top hats and scarves)* who are employed to **aid** you in sending messages. Instead of transporting little notes tied to their legs, they communicate verbally. Here we see them in their *wire mesh* cage on the roof, gabbing away at each other as they await their next assignment, *chatterboxes* that they are.

    As is so often the case—too often to mention each time—this character is commonly used as a family name. [17]

    ❖ As a primitive, this character will take the meaning of a *pigeon coop,* from the explanation above.

1204   **territory**

壤

Ground . . . pigeon coop. [20]

❖	hamster cage
寒	The image of a **hamster cage** should be easy to compose from the elements: *house . . . wire mesh . . . animal legs.* [10]

宀　　宔　　寒

1205	frigid
寒	*Hamster cage . . . ice.* [12]

1206	competition
賽	*Hamster cage . . . oysters.* [14]

LESSON 39

THE REMAINDER OF plant-related primitives are built up from combinations of vertical and horizontal lines, representing respectively plants and the earth from which they spring. Accordingly, it would be a good idea to study the remaining elements of this section at a single sitting, or at least to review them before passing on to the next grouping.

❖	**grow up**
圭	As the plant **grows up** it sprouts leaves and a stalk, depicted here as a single horizontal stroke added to the element for *soil*. Think of something (its accompanying primitive) **growing up** in a flash to many times its normal size, much like little Alice in Wonderland, who **grew up** so fast she was soon larger than the room in which she was sitting. [4]

一　二　キ　主

1207	**poison** (N.)
毒	*Grow up . . . mother.* [9]

1208	**wheat**
麦	*Grow up . . . walking legs.* [7]

1209	**vegetarian diet**
素	*Grow up . . . floss.* [10]

1210	**blue or green**
青	This character can be used for either **blue or green**. The primitives suggest a 300-foot telescope on your roof, all *grown up* (stretched out as far as it will go) and fixed on the moon, that orb of **green** cheese in the evening sky. Once in a **blue** *moon*, you might actually see the cheesemaker! [8]

❖ When used as a primitive element, this character will take the meaning of a *telescope*.

1211 精	refined *Rice . . . telescope.* [14]
1212 请	invite *Words . . . telescope.* [10]
1213 情	feelings *State of mind . . . telescope.* [11]
1214 睛	eyeball *Eye . . . telescope.* By this time there shouldn't be any confusion between this key word and the primitive meaning earlier associated with *eye* (page 24). [13]
1215 清	pure *Water . . . telescope.* [11]
1216 静	quiet *Telescope . . . contend.* [14]
1217 责	responsibility *Grow up . . . clams.* Since this character will be used as an element in several others (one example follows immediately), it would be good to give it as concrete an image as possible. Perhaps you can think back to the first heavy **responsibility** you had in your first summer job when you were *growing up* and where you earned your first *clams*. [8]
1218 绩	accomplishments *Thread . . . responsibility.* [11]
1219 表	surface (N.) *Grow up . . . scarf.* To make this key word more concrete, think of the **surface** of a watch or a meter (secondary meanings of this character, by the way.) [8]

1220		life
生	Think of the microscopic *cell*, that miraculous *drop* of **life**, that *grew up* to become you. [5]	

ノ 生

❖ Used as a primitive, this character will keep the meaning of a *cell*.

1221		star (N.)
星	*Sun . . . cell.* [9]	

1222		surname
姓	*Woman . . . cell.* [8]	

1223		sex
性	*State of mind . . . cell.* [8]	

1224		victory
胜	*Flesh. . . cell.* [9]	

1225		plentiful
丰	The character for **plentiful** may be thought of as a doodle of a row of **bushes**. It differs from the primitive for *grow up* only in the extension of the single vertical stroke beneath the final horizontal stroke and in the order of writing. [4]	

三 丰

❖ When used as a primitive, this character will mean **bushes** in accord with the explanation above.

1226		harm (N.)
害	*House . . . bushes . . . mouth.* [10]	

1227 割	cut off (v.)
	Harm . . . saber. [12]

1228 慧	intelligent
	Two *bushes . . . broom . . . heart.* [15]

1229 韋	tanned hide

The only difference between this character for **tanned hide** and that for *plentiful* is the downward hook on the third stroke. Recalling that the primitive meaning for the latter is *bushes*, we should think of this as *bushes* with hooks—that is, a briar patch. To remember the association, think of putting on the best **tanned hide** jacket you have ever owned and having someone push you down into a briar patch. As you struggle to pick yourself up and avoid the brambles, your prize coat gets scratched beyond repair.

This is another of those characters commonly used in family names and transliterations. [4]

$$= \quad 弓 \quad 韋$$

❖ The primitive meaning of this character, following the above explanation, is a *briar patch*, the kind that Br'er Fox was tricked into letting Br'er Rabbit escape into.

1230 围	surround
	Pent up . . . briar patch. [7]

1231 伟	great
	Person. . . briar patch. [6]

❖ 夆	bonsai

The element for *bushes* has an extra stroke added to give the image of the crutches Japanese gardeners use to hold up a tree that is being bent into shape. From there it is but a short leap to the art of cultivating miniature **bonsai** plants, which began in China and was further developed in Japan. [5]

三 丰 夫

1232 春	springtime
	Bonsai . . . sun. [9]

1233 泰	tranquil
	Bonsai . . . snowflakes. [10]

❖

丰　　cornstalk

The element for *bushes* extended the vertical stroke beneath the final horizontal stroke; the **cornstalk** omits that final stroke altogether, leaving only the **stalk** and the leaves bursting forth on all sides. [3]

二 丰

1234 奉	proffer (v.)
	The sense of the key word **proffer** is to "offer respectfully." *Bonsai . . . cornstalk.* Use a ritualistic, religious meaning. [8]

1235 棒	cudgel (N.)
	Tree . . . proffer. [12]

1236 击	beat (v.)
	Cornstalk . . . mountain. [5]

1237 陆	land
	Pinnacle . . . beat. [7]

1238 专	specialty
	Cornstalk . . . chop. [4]
	❖ As a primitive, this character will take the meaning of a *corncob pipe.*

二 专 专

1239

传

spread (v.)

Person . . . corncob pipe. [6]

1240

转

rotate

Car . . . corncob pipe. [8]

❖

堇

spinach

You no doubt recognized the top primitive of this element as *twenty*. We could use it, of course, but prefer to look at it as the element for *salad*, in this case a healthy **spinach** *salad*. The reason the last stroke is shorter than normal is that it is being shoved down a little boy's *mouth* from above, the excuse being that it will help him *grow up* healthy and strong. [11]

艹 苢 堇

1241

勤

diligent

Spinach . . . muscle. [13]

1242

谨

careful

Words . . . spinach. [13]

❖

丳

silage

The drawing of this element is difficult to do smoothly, and should be practiced carefully. It is a pictograph of all sorts of plants and grasses thrown together to make **silage**. The vertical stroke will always double up with another primitive element's vertical stroke. [6]

一 二 三 开 丑 丳

1243

droop

垂

Porter . . . silage. Note how both the third stroke and the final two strokes of this character double up for the two primitives. This is clearer in the hand-drawn form. [8]

1244

hammer [N.]

锤

Metal . . . droop. [13]

1245

sleep [V.]

睡

Eyes . . . droop. [13]

LESSON 40

THIS LESSON will cover the final few characters relating to time and direction to be treated in Book 1. Only a few will remain, and they will be taken up in Book 2.

1246	now

今

The final stroke of this character is a rare shape, a close but not exact replica of the first stroke in the element for *spool*. It may help to think of it pictographically as the two hands of a clock pointing to what time it is **now**. The element above it, *meeting*, should easily relate to that image. [4]

$$人 \quad 今$$

❖ We shall use *clock* as the primitive meaning of this character, in line with the above explanation.

1247	harbor [v.]

含

Clock . . . mouth. The key word is used for **harboring** things like grudges and resentment. [7]

1248	miss [v.]

念

Not "miss a train," but **miss** one's friends. *Clock . . . heart.* [8]

1249	east

东

The character for **east** looks very much like that for *car*, except that the final horizontal stroke turns into two *drops*. Think of it as a rickshaw, those traditional taxis found in the **East**. Start drawing *car* and think of the drops of sweat pouring off the poor driver as he runs through the streets pulling his passenger. [5]

$$一 \quad 七 \quad 乍 \quad 东 \quad 东$$

❖ We shall use *rickshaw* as the primitive meaning of this character, in line with the above explanation.

1250 栋		building
	Tree . . . rickshaw. [9]	

1251 冻		freeze (v.)
	Ice . . . rickshaw. [7]	

1252 陈		exhibit (v.)
	Pinnacle . . . rickshaw. [7]	

1253 练		practice (v.)
	Silk . . . rickshaw. [8]	

1254 拣		opt for
	Fingers . . . rickshaw. [8]	

1255 西 — **west**

In our way of naming off the directions, **west** always comes fourth. So it is convenient to find the character for *four* in this character. But since we want only *one* of the *four* directions, the **west** adds the *one* at the top and sucks the *human legs* a bit out of their *mouth* in the process. [6]

一　厂　冂　丙　丙　西

❖ When this character is used as a primitive, the meaning of *west* can be expanded to refer to the *Old West* of cowboy-movie fame. Note, however, that in its primitive form the *legs* are straightened out and reach down to the bottom of the *mouth*. Hence, we get the shape 覀.

1256 要		want (v.)
	Old West . . . woman. [9]	

1257 腰		waist
	Part of the body . . . want. [13]	

1258	ticket
票	*Old West . . . altar.* [11]

1259	drift (v.)
漂	*Water . . . ticket.* [14]

1260	merchant
贾	*Old West . . . clams.* [10]

1261	south
南	*Belt . . . good fortune.* Note how the *belt* runs through the middle of *good fortune*, which affects the stroke order. [9]

$$十 \quad 内 \quad 南$$

LESSON 41

THIS NEXT COLLECTION OF characters is based on the primitive for *gate*. From there we shall go on to consider other elements related to entrances and barriers in general.

1262	gate
門	The pictograph of a swinging **gate** with a latch at the top is so clear in this character that only its stroke order needs to be memorized. The **gate** usually serves as an enclosure, and is written BEFORE whatever it is it encloses. [3]

ˋ   ⲅ   門

> ❖ As a primitive, we shall continue to give it the meaning of *gate*, but recommend the image of a swinging door to distinguish it from the primitive for *door*.

1263	(plural)
们	*Person . . . gate.* Here again, the parentheses around the key word indicate this character's grammatical function rather than its meaning. [5]

1264	leisure
闲	*Gate . . . tree.* [7]

1265	ask
问	*Gate . . . mouth.* [6]

1266	interval
间	*Gate . . . sun / day.* This **interval** applies to time and space alike, but the latter is better for creating an image. [7]

1267	simple
简	*Bamboo . . . interval.* [13]

1268	hear
闻	*Gate . . . ear.* Compare the story you invented for the character meaning *listen* (FRAME 925). [9]

1269	non-
非	This key word, a negating prefix, is a doodle of a heavy iron pole with bars extending in both directions, to create the picture of a jail cell. From there to "**non-**" is but a short step. [8]

丨 丿 刌 刌 刲 非 非 非

❖ When this character serves as a primitive, we shall draw on the explanation above for the meaning of *jail cell*.

1270	row (N.)
排	*Fingers . . . jail cell.* [11]

1271	guilt
罪	*Eye . . . jail cell.* [13]

1272	lean on
靠	*Declare . . . jail cell.* [15]

❖	key
乚	This element gets its name and meaning from the pictographic representation of a **key**. The shape should be familiar: the third and fourth strokes of the character for *five*. [2]

㇇ 乚

1273	marquis
侯	*Person . . . key . . . dart.* Hint: the pun suggested by the pronunciation of the key word and the primitive for *key* may come in helpful. [9]

1274	wait ^(v.)
候	*Marquis . . . walking stick.* Note where the *walking stick* is positioned in this character. [10]

❖	guillotine
夬	This element depicts a large, sharpened *key* coming down on the head of a criminal *St. Bernard.* [4]

コ　ユ　尹　夬

1275	decide
决	The etymology of **decide** (de-cidere = cut off) will help here; the elements are: *ice . . . guillotine.* [6]

1276	fast ^(ADJ.)
快	*State of mind . . . guillotine.* [7]

1277	lump ^(N.)
块	*Soil . . . guillotine.* [7]

1278	chopsticks
筷	*Bamboo . . . fast.* [13]

Lesson 42

The next few primitives are only loosely related in the sense that they all have to do with qualities of material objects in one way or another.

| 1279 | dry |

(ignore)

1279   dry ^(ADJ.)

干

It is best to see this character as a pictograph of a revolving circular clothesline (viewed from the side). Spin it around quickly in your mind's eye until the wet clothes are good and **dry**. [3]

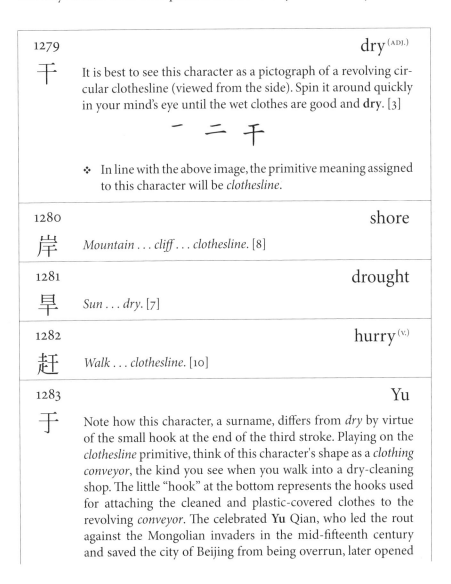

❖ In line with the above image, the primitive meaning assigned to this character will be *clothesline*.

1280   shore

岸

Mountain . . . cliff . . . clothesline. [8]

1281   drought

旱

Sun . . . dry. [7]

1282   hurry ^(V.)

赶

Walk . . . clothesline. [10]

1283   Yu

于

Note how this character, a surname, differs from *dry* by virtue of the small hook at the end of the third stroke. Playing on the *clothesline* primitive, think of this character's shape as a *clothing conveyor*, the kind you see when you walk into a dry-cleaning shop. The little "hook" at the bottom represents the hooks used for attaching the cleaned and plastic-covered clothes to the revolving *conveyor*. The celebrated **Yu** Qian, who led the rout against the Mongolian invaders in the mid-fifteenth century and saved the city of Beijing from being overrun, later opened his own string of dry-cleaning establishments named You Soil—**Yu** Clean. [3]

一　二　于

❖ From the above explanation, the primitive meaning of this character will change to *clothing conveyor*.

1284 eaves

宇 *House . . . clothing conveyor.* [6]

1285 excess

余 *Umbrella . . . clothing conveyor . . . small.* The last stroke of *clothing conveyor* and the first of *small* coincide here. [7]

❖ Since the keyword is overly abstract, we shall take the image of a *scale* whose indicator spins round and round on the dial because *excess* weight has been set on it. It will help to use this image in learning the character itself.

1286 eliminate

除 *Pinnacle . . . scale.* [9]

1287 route (N.)

途 *Scale . . . road.* [10]

1288 bundle up

束 *Tree . . . mouth.* When people **bundle up** in cold weather, the only thing they have to leave exposed is their face. Since *trees* don't have eyes and noses, when you **bundle up** your favorite *tree* in scarf, overcoat, leggings, and mittens, the only thing you have to be sure to leave exposed is that little *tree mouth* that the squirrels run in and out of. [7]

❖ When used as a primitive, this character will add the meaning of a *bundle*.

1289 速	quick *Bundle . . . road.* [10]
1290 辣	spicy hot *Chili pepper . . . bundle.* [14]
1291 整	entire *Bundle up . . . taskmaster . . . correct.* [16]
1292 重	heavy *Thousand . . . li.* Note how the long vertical stroke doubles up to serve both elements. [9]

ノ ニ 台 盲 重 重

| 1293 懂 | understand
State of mind . . . flowers . . . heavy. [15] |

LESSON 43

WE MAY NOW PICK UP the remainder of the enclosure primitives to be treated in Book 1, leaving only a few related to animals, which we will take up toward the end of the book, in Lessons 54 and 55. This lesson should give you a chance to review the general principles governing enclosures.

❖ 疒	sickness

The enclosure shown in this frame is composed of a *cave* with *ice* outside of it. It is used for a number of characters related to **sickness**. If you want to picture a *cave*man nursing a hangover with an *ice*-pack, that should provide enough help to remember the shape of this element and its meaning. [5]

广　疒　疒

1294

病   *Sickness . . . third.* [10]   **illness**

1295

痛   *Sickness . . . sealing wax.* [12]   **ache**[(v.)]

1296

疯   *Sickness . . . wind.* [9]   **insane**

❖ 匚	box

This enclosure, open at the right, represents a **box** lying on its side. When it is not used as an enclosure, its form is cramped to look like this: 匚. You may distinguish its meaning by picturing it then as a very small **box**. [2]

一　匚

1297 区	region *Box ... sheaf.* [4]
1298 枢	hub This key word refers to a center of activity or commerce, not to the center of a wheel. Its primitives: *tree ... region.* [8]
1299 欧	Europe *Region ... yawn.* This character is an abbreviation of the name of the continent of **Europe.** [8]
1300 医	physician *Box ... dart.* [7]
❖ 卯	stamp collection A *box* and *stamps* gives us a **stamp collection.** Take care not to confuse this primitive with that for *letter opener* (page 297). [4] ʿ 卯
1301 仰	look up to *Person ... stamp collection.* [6]
1302 迎	greet *Stamp collection ... road.* [7]
❖ ラへ	teepee The dots at the top of this tent are the wooden poles protruding outside the canvas walls of a **teepee.** This primitive will only be used in one character here, but will prove useful in Book 2. [5] ラ ラ ラʾ ラʾʾ ラへ

1303   **ascend**

登   *Teepee . . . table.* [12]

1304   **send out**

发   Think of "man's best *friend*" (here, the perky little *chihuahua* that shares a stroke with the character for *friend*) being **sent out** to take out the trash and pick up the morning paper, the mail, and the milk. The first half-stroke can be any of those things he is carrying in his mouth.

      The stroke order should come naturally to you by now, but to be safe, pay attention to the sequence below [5]

乚　少　岁　发　发

❖ Though we have only one instance of this character serving as a primitive in Book 1, it will be helpful to assign it the meaning of a *courier* in connection with the above explanation. It will reappear in Book 2.

1305   **discard** (v.)

废   *Cave . . . courier.* [8]

LESSON 44

WE COME NOW to a class of elements loosely associated with shape and form. To these we may append the remaining elements in Book 1 having to do with color.

❖ 彡	rooster tail The three simple strokes of this element depict a **rooster tail**. [3]
1306 形	shape (N.) *Two hands . . . rooster tail.* [7]
1307 影	shadow (N.) *Scenery . . . rooster tail.* [15]
1308 彩	hue *Pick. . . rooster tail.* [11]
1309 须	have to *Rooster tail . . . head.* This is the only time that the *rooster tail* is placed to the left of its relative element, the *head*. [9]
1310 参	participate Our lovable *St. Bernard dog* was invited to **participate** in the short track speed skating event at the Animal Winter Olympics. Unfortunately, he was disqualified early on for excessive roughness, because of all the *elbows* he threw at the captain of the Poultry Team, who lost his balance and had his *rooster tail* cut off by a skate blade. [8] 厶　矣　参 ❖ When this character is used as a primitive, we will take it to mean a knock-down, drag-out *brawl*.

1311	wretched
惨	*A state of mind . . . brawl.* [11]

1312	repair (v.)
修	*Person . . . walking stick . . . walking legs . . . rooster tail.* [9]

❖	cocktail
参	The little *umbrella* used as a garnish in tropical drinks combines with a *rooster tail* to give us a perfect way to remember the primitive for a **cocktail**. [5]

1313	rare
珍	*Jewel . . . cocktail.* [9]

1314	products
产	This element shows you dressed up like a zucchini, *standing up* on the edge of a *cliff* and about to do a bungi-jump to earn a little extra cash by advertising fresh-grown organic farm **products**. [6]

亠　产

❖ The primitive meaning will be a *bungi-jumper*.

1315	erudite
彦	*Bungi-jumper . . . rooster tail.* [9]

1316	countenance (n.)
颜	*Erudite . . . head.* [15]

1317	literature
文	When you think of your first classes in **literature**, your mind no doubt goes back to similes, metaphors, synecdoches, litotes, and all those other figures of speech and highfalutin' language patterns that you had to memorize, with the result that you all but lost your taste for the subject. The *top hat* indicates a connoisseur of fine **literature** who keeps under his hat that whole

tangle of patterns (the "criss-cross" strokes—not really a *sheaf*, but close). [4]

丶　亠　亣　文

❖ To make the criss-cross pattern mentioned above easier to remember, think of the Scottish plaid on a tam-o'-shanter (the *top hat*) and kilt. From there, we get the primitive meaning of this character: a *Highlander*.

1318		mosquito
蚊	*Insect . . . Highlander.* [10]	

1319		this
这	*Highlander . . . road.* In order not to confuse this key word with the literary *this* (FRAME 460), associate the word here with a common phrase such as "**This road** is going nowhere fast." [7]	

1320		identical
齐	*Highlander . . . . crutches.* [6]	

1321		relieve
济	*Water . . . identical.* The sense of the key word is to "bring relief" to someone in need. [9]	

❖   sparkler

丷丷 The four strokes here, which usually come two on each side of another primitive element to tell you what it is that is sparkling, can appear as drops (丷丷), as straight lines (⸚⸚), or as shown in this frame, which is a lot closer to what *sparklers* look like. You can follow the hand-drawn sample below, but you are bound to run into the other two alternatives from time to time.

The only cases in which these shapes do NOT take the meaning *sparkler* is when the element in the middle is a vertical line, as in the shape already learned for *snowflake* (水). [4]

丶　丷　丷ᐟ　丷丶

1322 **rate** (N.)

率 As in a "tax **rate**." *Top hat . . . cocoon-sparkler . . . needle.* [11]

1323 **tumble** (V.)

摔 *Fingers . . . rate.* [14]

1324 **center**

央 The elements depict a *St. Bernard* with its head and paws keeping their stick-like form, but with the middle or **center** of its body filled out in a box-like shape. [5]

1325 **England**

英 *Flowers . . . center.* This is another abbreviation used to identify a country by the pronunciation of the character. [8]

❖ **Victorian lady**

奂 When you think of something *bound up* in the *center* (the elements that make up this primitive), what better image than the classical hourglass figure of the **Victorian lady**. During the last half of the nineteenth century, such women, in quest of a thirteen-inch waist, would lace up their midsections in corsets that all but cut off their breathing and circulation. The idea, apparently, was that when they fainted, they would cut an elegant figure in the arms of the gentleman who stepped in to catch them.

Take note of the fact that the fourth stroke of *center* is cut short here to avoid overwriting the element for *bound up*. [7]

1326 **call out**

唤 *Mouth . . . Victorian lady.* [10]

1327	exchange [v.]
换	*Fingers . . . Victorian lady.* [10]

1328	crust
巴	This character—whose principal use is for its phonetic value in transliterations—is shaped roughly like the *snake*, but pay attention to the difference when writing it. Think of the indentations your grandma made with her thumb on the outer rim of a pie **crust** to beautify it, though it can also refer to the kind of **crust** that sticks to pots and skillets during cooking. [4]

𠃌　　刀　　刃　　巴

❖ Even though the key word is graphic and useful on its own, the added primitive meaning of a *mosaic* or piece of a *mosaic* can also come in handy.

1329	grasp [v.]
把	*Fingers . . . mosaic.* [7]

1330	papa
爸	*Father . . . mosaic.* [8]

1331	bar [N.]
吧	*Mouth. . . mosaic.* The key word refers to the kind of **bar** at which drinks are served. [7]

1332	color [N.]
色	*Bound up . . . mosaic.* [6]

1333	discontinue
绝	*Thread . . . color.* [9]

1334	gorgeous
艳	*Bushes . . . color.* [10]

Lesson 45

A NUMBER OF containers of various sorts can be gathered together here. Most of them have limited use as primitives, but none of them should cause any particular difficulty.

1335　　　　　　　　　　　　　　　　　　　　　　　　　　　　sweet

甘

This character is a pictograph of a small wicker basket. (The extra short stroke in the middle helps keep it distinct from the character for *twenty*.) All one needs to add is the image of something **sweet** carried in the basket, and the union of picture and meaning is complete. [5]

一　十　廿　廿　甘

❖ Used as a primitive, this will mean a *wicker basket*, the small kind you take on a picnic.

1336　　　　　　　　　　　　　　　　　　　　　　　such and such (ADJ.)

某

Wicker basket . . . tree. The key word here refers to an undetermined or unspecified thing or person (a so and so). [9]

1337　　　　　　　　　　　　　　　　　　　　　　　his-hers-its-theirs

其

This container, which is a bit larger than the *wicker basket* and has two *legs* at the bottom, is a clothes hamper filled with towels marked **his, hers, its** (for the cat), and **theirs**. [8]

一　十　廿　廿　甘　苴　其

❖ When used as a primitive, this character will retain the meaning of a *hamper*.

1338　　　　　　　　　　　　　　　　　　　　　　　period of time

期

Hamper . . . month. As the *month* indicates, this has to do with **periods of time**. [12]

| 1339 基 | base (N.) |
| This refers to the foundation of something, not to a chemical substance or the "base" of baseball. Its primitives are: *hamper ... soil*. [11] | |

| 1340 甚 | tremendously |
| *Hamper ... fishhook*. [9] | |

| 1341 斯 | Sphinx |
| This character is used in family names, but also appears as the first and last character of the Chinese word for the mythical **Sphinx**. Its elements: *hamper ... tomahawk*. [12] | |

| ❖ 虫 | purse |
| By adding a single stroke at the bottom of the character for *middle*, we get a sort of pictograph of a **purse**. [5] | |

口　中　虫

| 1342 贵 | expensive |
| *Purse ... shells*. [9] | |

| 1343 遗 | bequeath |
| *Expensive ... road*. [12] | |

| 1344 舞 | dance (N./V.) |
| The top two strokes show someone *reclining*, and the next six are a pictograph of an *oaken tub* ribbed with metal strips, like the kind once used for bathing. At the bottom, *evening* and *monocle* round off the character. This character can be used as a noun or a verb. [14] | |

丿　二　仁　仨　缶　缶　無

舞　舞

Lesson 46

THE SEVERAL PRIMITIVES we turn to next have to do with the position and disposition of things in relation to one another. They are few but deserve special attention, which is why we have set them aside for the shortest lesson in Book 1.

1345	moreover
且	The pictographic representation in the primitive shown here is a small stand with horizontal shelves. (It differs from the character and primitive for an *eye* only in its final stroke, which extends beyond the two vertical strokes at both ends.) Think of the shelves as filled up with knickknacks, so that you can only put **more** "**over**" it on the top, where they risk falling off. [5]

月　且

❖ This character's meaning as a primitive element will remain *shelf*.

1346	older sister
姐	*Woman ... shelf.* [8]

1347	group (N.)
组	*Thread ... shelf.* [8]

1348	ancestor
祖	*Altar ... shelf.* [9]

1349	assist (V.)
助	*Shelf ... power.* The reason the *shelf* appears on the left here is that the right side is the normal position for *power*, the stronger primitive. [7]

❖ 並	side by side This character is a slightly stylized duplication of all three vertical strokes in the character for *stand up*. By lengthening the sixth and seventh strokes, you will see how this is done. [8]

丷　丷　丬　丯　丯　並　並

1350 普	universal *Side by side . . . sun.* [12]

1351 业	profession You might try thinking of beginning your **profession** *side by side* with others of the same aspiration, and then gradually distinguishing yourself and standing apart (*side by side* minus the top three strokes). [5]

1352 显	obvious *Sun . . . profession.* [9]

1353 亚	Asia The key word is chosen because this character is chiefly used for its phonetic value, one of the most common usages being in the term for **Asia**. The elements: *one . . . profession.* [6]

1354 恶	evil (N./ADJ.) *Asia . . . heart.* [10]

1355 严	strict *Asia . . . cliff.* [7]

1356 共	together *Salad . . . animal legs.* We leave it to your culinary imagination to decide what kind of *animal legs* best go **together** with your favorite *salad.* [6]

1357		supply (N./V.)
供	Person . . . together. [8]	

1358		lane
巷	Together . . . snakeskin. [9]	

1359		port (N.)
港	Water . . . lane. [12]	

LESSON 47

THIS NEXT LESSON IS composed of characters whose primitives are grouped according to shape rather than meaning. Each of them makes use, in one way or another, of squares and crossing lines. While this might have brought confusion earlier, we know enough primitives at this stage to introduce them together without risking any confusion.

1360 井	well (N.)

Recalling that there are no circular strokes, and that the shape of the square and the square within a square (FRAME 554) have already been used, it should be relatively easy to see how this character can be consider a pictograph of a **well**. [4]

一 二 丰 井

1361 讲	lecture (V.)

Words . . . well. [6]

1362 进	advance (V.)

Well . . . road . [7]

1363 角	angle

Bound up . . . screwdriver. [7]

ク 角

❖ When this character is used as a primitive, it might be help-ful to think of a *carpenter's square*, a meaning suggested directly by the key word.

1364 解	untie

Carpenter's square . . . dagger . . . cow. [13]

1365	orifice
嘴	This character really has the same meaning as the simple picto-graph for *mouth* that we learned in the very first lesson. Since it is far more elaborate, we choose a more elegant key word to represent it. The elements: *mouth . . . this (literary) . . . carpenter's square.* [16]

1366	once more
再	*Ceiling . . . glass cover . . . soil.* Note how the final stroke of *soil* extends outside of the *glass cover,* unlike the character for *angle* that we just learned. [6]

一　冂　再

❖	tome
冊	If you rip off the cover of a thick **tome,** on the spine you will see stitching and binding that looks pretty much like this char-acter. Caution: this is sure to get you into serious trouble with the librarian. [5]

冂　冃　冄　冊

1367	flat ^(ADJ.)
扁	The *book cover* that you just ripped off the *tome* in the last frame, the "*door*" to the *tome,* is lying **flat** on the floor, right where you let it fall, and where you will soon join it when the librarian comes in to punch your lights out. [9]

❖ When this character is used as a primitive, it takes on the meaning of *book cover* from the explanation above.

1368	piece of writing
篇	*Bamboo . . . book cover.* [15]

1369		compile
编	*Thread . . . book cover.* [12]	

1370	canon
典	We introduce the character for a **canon** (a collection of scriptural or authoritative books) here because of its connection to the characters treated immediately above. It is based on the character for *bent* (FRAME 967), whose last stroke is lengthened to coincide with the first stroke of the element for *tool*. [8]

LESSON 48

A FEW PRIMITIVES HAVING to do with groupings and classifications of people remain to be learned, and we may bring them all together here in this short lesson.

1371 氏	family name
	Pay close attention to the stroke order of the elements when learning to write this character. The elements: *eyedropper . . . plow . . . a one . . . fishhook.* [4]

´　ˊ　ˋ　氏

1372 纸	paper
	Thread . . . family name. [7]

1373 昏	dusk
	Family name . . . sun. [8]

1374 婚	marriage
	Woman . . . family name . . . day. You could, of course, use *dusk* in place of the final two primitives, but this is one of those cases in which breaking a compound primitive up into its original parts is helpful in composing a story. [11]

❖ 氐	calling card
	Family name . . . drop of. The primitive meaning refers to the **calling cards** used by professionals to identify their name and position. [5]

1375 低	low
	Person . . . calling card. [7]

1376 底	**bottom** *Cave . . . calling card.* [8]
1377 民	**people** In place of the *drop* at the start of the character for *family name*, we have a *mouth*, which makes you think of the "vox populi" [5] ㇇　㇆　尸　尸　民
1378 眠	**slumber** (N.) *Eyes . . . people.* [10]
1379 甫	**Fu** This key word is a surname. In case there is no one named **Fu** in your circle of immediate acquaintances, you might take the evil genius with the trademark moustache, Dr. **Fu** Manchu, as a hitching post for the primitives in this character: *needle . . . screwdriver . . . drop.* [7] 一　厂　冂　月　月　甫　甫 ❖ Since the key word refers to a surname, when the character serves as a primitive, you can think of it as a *dog tag*, either the kind you actually hang around the neck of Rover or an identification tag handed out to soldiers.
1380 辅	**supplement** (V.) *Cart . . . dog tag.* [11]
❖ 尃	**gummed label** The elements for *dog tag* and *glue* should be easy enough to associate with the primitive meaning, **gummed label**. [10] 甫　尃

1381 博	knowledgeable
	Needle . . . gummed label. [12]

1382 搏	wrestle
	Fingers . . . gummed label. [13]

❖ 阝	city walls
	On the left, and rather more pressed in its form, this element means the high spot of a village, or its *pinnacle*. On the right side, in the form shown here, it means the lowest part of the city, around which its walls rise up as a protection against invaders. Hence we nickname this element: **city walls**. [2]

1383 都	metropolis
	Puppet . . . city walls. [10]

1384 部	department
	Muzzle . . . city walls. [10]

1385 郎	young man
	Halo . . . city walls. [8]

1386 帮	help (v.)
	Bushes . . . city walls . . . towel. [9]

1387 纟	countryside
	The character for **countryside** is a *cocoon* with a long thread on the end. The association with the key word is left up to you. [3]

LESSON 49

IN THIS SHORT lesson of thirteen characters we introduce three new primitives. They could have been left for the next lesson, but we put them here to give you a breather before you head down the home stretch.

1388	section (N.)
段	The character for **section** shows us a new element on the left: the familiar primitive for *staples* with an additional stroke cutting through the vertical stroke. It is easiest in these cases to make a primitive related to what we already know. Hence, we call it a *staple gun*. To the right, *missile*. [9]

丆 丯 段

1389	forge (V.)
锻	This character has nothing to do with the forgery of documents. It refers, rather, to the tempering of metal and, by extension, of one's physique. Its primitives: *metal . . . section*. [14]

❖	clothes hanger
ㄱ	The primitive for **clothes hanger** looks like its name. [1]

1390	unreal
幻	*Cocoon . . . clothes hanger.* [4]

1391	take charge of
司	*Clothes hanger . . . one . . . mouth.* [5]

1392	word (N.)
词	Here we meet the proper name for all the various images of "words" we used to make the character for *say* more concrete when used as a primitive. Its elements suggest that when you

say things you are *taking charge of* the **words** that a language puts at your disposal. [7]

1393

书

book

This final character of the lesson will take special attention and require some ingenuity on your part. It begins with *key* and *clothes hanger* (note the doubling up of the stroke), and then is followed by a *walking stick* and a single *drop.* You might think of a particular **book** you are fond of when inventing your story. [4]

ㄱ　弓　书　书

1394

舟

boat

After the *drop* and the *glass cover,* we come to a combination of three strokes that we met only once before, in the character for *mother* (FRAME 105). The pictographic meaning we gave it there has no etymological relationship to this character, but use it if it helps. [6]

ノ　丿　几　月　舟　舟

❖

凸

belch

A **belch** is a little more complicated than *wind* in the *mouth,* but the effect is the same. In addition to the example in the following frame, we will meet others in Book 2. [5]

几　凸

1395

船

ship (N.)

Boat . . . belch. [11]

1396

般

sort (N.)

Boat . . . missile. [10]

1397	tray
盘	*Boat . . . dish.* [11]

1398	relocate
搬	*Fingers . . . sort.* [13]

1399	melon
瓜	The only thing that distinguishes this from the *claw* is the *elbow*, made by doubling up the third stroke and adding a fourth. [5]

⺊   厂   几   瓜   瓜

1400	orphan
孤	*Child . . . melon.* [8]

LESSON 50

As we said we would do back in Lesson 28, we now leave the beaten path to gather up characters left aside, either because they form exceptions to the rules and patterns we have been learning, or simply because they fell between the cracks along the way. The list is not large and has a number of repeating patterns.

1401 益	benefit (N.) The bottom part of this character is clearly a *dish*. The top part can be taken in either of two ways: (1) as a *sparkler* with a *one* in the middle, or (2) as *horns* and *animal legs*. [10]
❖ 叚	braces (N.) The primitive for **braces** begins with the *mouth* full of *staples* that you actually pay someone to inflict on you. And as if this weren't enough, the right side of the primitive shows another **brace**, reaching from your *mouth* all the way around your head and back *again*, in order to keep your jaw from growing while your teeth are growing straight. [9] ⼃ ⼕ ⼕ 叚
1402 假	vacation (N.) *Person ... braces.* [11]
1403 暇	spare time *Day ... braces.* [13]
1404 气	air (N.) This character refers to the changeable moods and **airs** of one's personality as well as to the **air** that we breathe. It is also used for that mysterious vital energy or life force that the Chinese call *qi*. Its elements are: *reclining ... floor ... fishhook.* [4]

| 1405 | vapor |

汽 Think of this character as a sibling of that for *air*. Simply add three drops of *water* on the left in order to get *vapor*. [7]

| 1406 | face-to-face |

面 The shape of this character aside, there are really only two elements that make it up: *hundred* and *eyeball*. Look at the first four strokes in the drawing sample below and you will see that they are the start of the character for *hundred*, only drawn more broadly to leave room for the *eyeball*.

Let the key word **face-to-face** suggests two people "facing" each other, but here we see a *hundred* of them, fifty on a side, staring each other down, right up close, *eyeball* to *eyeball*. [9]

一 丆 丆 丂 帀 帀 帀
帀 面

| 1407 | leather (N.) |

革 After the *twenty* at the top, we have a *mouth* and a *needle*. Think of a tanner preparing a fine piece of **leather** to make a belt, with the *twenty mouths* being the holes, and the *needle* a strange replacement for the buckle. [9]

艹 苩 茾 革

| 1408 | shoes |

鞋 *Leather . . . bricks.* [15]

| 1409 | tighten |

勒 *Leather . . . muscle.* [11]

| ❖ | civil war |

殸 Think of any **civil war** you want for this primitive element. The basic ingredients are always the same: *soldiers,* a *flag* split down the middle (the extra vertical line), and *missiles* being cast by countrymen against each other. [11]

士　声　殸

1410　　　　　　　　　　　　　　　　　　　　　　　fragrant

馨　*Civil war ... perfume.* [20]

1411　　　　　　　　　　　　　　　　　　　　　　　voice [N.]

声　This character shows only the civil-war *soldier* standing on the divided *flag*. Since he is not bearing a weapon (no *missile*), we may assume that he is an "embedded journalist" giving a **voice** to those who are sacrificing themselves for their cause. [7]

1412　　　　　　　　　　　　　　　　　　　　　　　undertake

承　The key word suggests a new venture or challenge that one **undertakes**. The elements overlap each other and require care in writing correctly: the second stroke of *-ed* and the first of *water* overlap; and the element for *three* is tucked in the middle of the whole character.

To weave this all together, think of yourself swimming in a 200-meter race. You have just *-ed* (suffer-*ed* or enjoy-*ed*, at any rate complet-*ed*) *three* laps in the *water* and the only thing left to **undertake** is that difficult final lap. The problem is, you have never swum more than *three* laps in your life. Exhausted, but determined to finish, you grab hold of the lane rope and drag yourself along, gasping for breath, into last place—and a cellophane ribbon. [8]

了　手　手　承　承

1413　　　　　　　　　　　　　　　　　　　　　　　steam [V.]

蒸　The *flower* at the top and the *floor* with the *cooking fire* beneath are familiar. The problem lies in between: the character for *-ed*, that doubles up with the first stroke of *water*. [13]

艹　艼　芗　茏　莁　蒸

LESSON 51

THE FINAL grouping of characters revolves about elements related to animals. It is a rather large group, and will take us all of four lessons to complete. We begin with a few recurring elements related to parts of animal bodies.

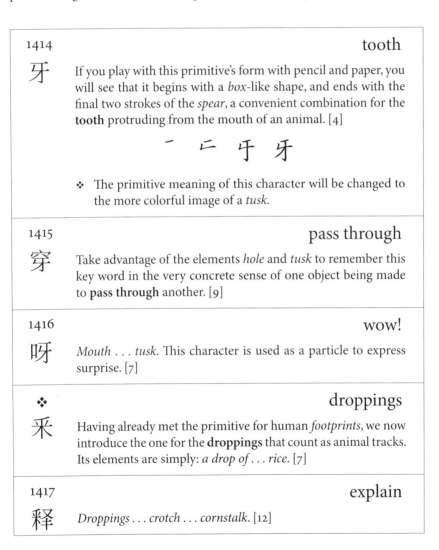

1414		tooth
牙	If you play with this primitive's form with pencil and paper, you will see that it begins with a *box*-like shape, and ends with the final two strokes of the *spear*, a convenient combination for the **tooth** protruding from the mouth of an animal. [4] 一 匚 午 牙 ❖ The primitive meaning of this character will be changed to the more colorful image of a *tusk*.	
1415		pass through
穿	Take advantage of the elements *hole* and *tusk* to remember this key word in the very concrete sense of one object being made to **pass through** another. [9]	
1416		wow!
呀	*Mouth . . . tusk.* This character is used as a particle to express surprise. [7]	
❖		droppings
釆	Having already met the primitive for human *footprints*, we now introduce the one for the **droppings** that count as animal tracks. Its elements are simply: *a drop of . . . rice.* [7]	
1417		explain
释	*Droppings . . . crotch . . . cornstalk.* [12]	

| 1418 | try^(N.) |

番

Droppings ... rice field. This key word carries the sense of taking the time and effort to do something—to have a **try** at something. There are many ways of saying this: as in to have a go, take a whack, a crack, a stab, or a shot at something. [12]

❖ When this character is used as a primitive element, we choose the image of *fertilizer*, from the combination of elements that make it up.

| 1419 | turn over |

翻

Fertilizer ... feathers. [18]

| 1420 | broadcast^(V.) |

播

Fingers ... fertilizer. [15]

| 1421 | fur |

毛

This character simply reverses and elongates the final stroke of *hand* to produce **fur**. If you reverse your *hand* and put it palm down, you will have the side on which **fur** grows. [4]

三 毛

| 1422 | tail |

尾

Flag ... fur. [7]

| 1423 | pen |

笔

Bamboo ... fur. [10]

| ❖ | fur ball |

乇

This element is clearly derived from that for *fur*. By leaving out the second stroke, we get simply a **fur ball**. [3]

| 1424 | entrust |

托

Fingers ... fur ball. [6]

1425 宅	dwelling (N.)
	House . . . fur ball. [6]

❖ 疋	barrette
	Here we have a quasi-pictograph of the colorful and decorated **barrette**, that clip used to bind up long hair. Note its similarity to the *scarf*, which differs only in the way the first stroke is drawn. As we will see, the first stroke of **barrette** frequently doubles up with the final stroke of the primitive above it. [4]

一　　丆　　丁　　疋

1426 展	unfold
	Flag . . . salad . . . barrette. Note that the final stroke of *salad* and the first stroke of *barrette* double up here. [10]

1427 丧	funeral
	Soil . . . animal horns . . . barrette. Note that the final stroke of *soil* and the first stroke of *barrette* double up, and that the *animal horns* are drawn before the final stroke of *soil*. [8]

十　　朩　　查　　丧

We end this lesson with an extremely simple form which, given the approach of this book, turns out to be more difficult to handle than most of the really complex characters.

1428 长	long
	The farmer's *plow* is way too **long**, and when it breaks beneath the surface of the field he is tilling (the *floor*, here), it digs down to the Jurassic Period. If you look closely you can see one loose *animal horn* and one disconnected *animal leg*. [4]

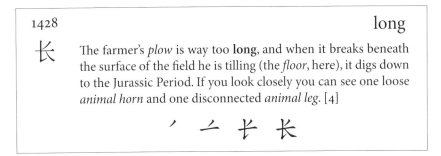

1429		stretch [v.]
张	Bow . . . long. [7]	

1430		swell [v.]
涨	Water . . . stretch. [10]	

LESSON 52

WE TURN NOW to the animals themselves, beginning with a few of our feathered friends. Some of the primitives introduced here and in the remainder of Book 1 come with few examples, but they will prove useful when you get to Book 2.

❖ 隹	**birdman** The combination of the elements for *person* and *turkey* give us a new superhero—**birdman**. [10]
1431 雁	**wild goose** *Cliff . . . birdman.* [12]
❖ ⺍	**owl** We have met these three strokes before. When they come under another stroke, they represent a *claw*, and thence a *vulture*. And when placed atop a roof structure, they create a *schoolhouse*. The **owl** has something to do with both: it is a bird of prey, and it has come to be associated with learning. [3]
1432 応	**ought to** *Cave . . . owl . . . floor.* [7]
1433 兴	**excitement** *Owl . . . floor . . . animal legs.* [6]
1434 挙	**lift up** *Excitement. . . cornstalk.* [9]
❖ 尐	**hootenanny** The *meeting of owls* here will stand for the original **hootenanny** on which the country festivals were based. If you can see the

owls with banjos and a piece of straw in their beaks, their feet stomping out the beat on the *floor*, the image should be simple to remember. [7]

1435   **examine**

检   *Tree . . . hootenanny.* [11]

1436   **face** [N.]

脸   *Part of the body . . . hootenanny.* [11]

1437   **perilous**

险   *Pinnacle . . . hootenanny.* [10]

1438   **bird**

鸟   Logically enough for a **bird**, this character begins with *orientation* (in form, if not in stroke order). It replaces the final *mouth* with a little *drop* (clearly a beak, which is pretty far from a round *mouth*). The long, *pointed tail* belongs to a particularly vindictive breed of "pointer" pheasants used to hunt down the descendent of the dogs that were once used to hunt their ancestors. [5]

1439   **chicken**

鸡   *Crotch / right hand . . . bird.* [7]

1440   **hawk**

鹰   *Cave . . . birdman . . . bird.* [18]

1441   **duck** [N.]

鸭   *First . . . bird.* [10]

1442	island
岛	The *bird's tail* is tucked under here, because it has come to stop on a *mountain* to rest from its journey across the waters. Thus the character comes to mean an **island**. [7]

	Talking Cricket
❖ 禺	Combine the *insect* with a *brain* (observe the writing) and a *belt* to create the **Talking Cricket** who served as Pinocchio's conscience. (The *belt* is there because he pulls it off to give the unrepentant little marionette a bit of "strap" now and again.) [9]

日 禺 禺 禺 禺

1443	encounter (v.)
遇	*Talking Cricket . . . road.* [12]

	tin can
❖ 缶	Although the primitive meaning has no reference to animals, one of the parts does: a *stick horse* on a *mountain*. (The primitive meaning of **tin can** is a fanciful modernization of a now infrequent character that originally meant "clay vessel.") [6]

午 缶

1444	deficient
缺	*Tin can . . . guillotine.* [10]

	can opener
❖ 䍃	The rather unusual **can opener** shown here is something the Flintsones might have dreamed up. It is a simple *vulture's claw*, which is sharp enough to cut through your ordinary household *tin can*. [10]

1445	remote (ADJ.)
遥	*Can opener . . . road.* [13]

1446	shake (v.)
摇	*Fingers. . . can opener.* [13]

1447	rabbit
兔	This character is supposed to be a pictograph of a **rabbit**, but like most such characters it is easier to recognize it as such than to reproduce it. So we revert to playing with the component primitives: *bound up . . . mouth . . . human legs . . . a drop.* Note how the first of the two *human legs* runs through the *mouth*. As the final stroke suggests, this is one of those cute little back-yard bunny **rabbits** that we associate with Easter. [8]

ク　　白　　兔　　兔

1448	flee
逸	*Rabbit . . . road.* [11]

1449	avoid
免	The rabbit becomes a *hare* by taking away the fluffy cotton tail, a trick that evolution has devised to help them **avoid** being so visible to hunters and other critters that prey on them. [7] ❖ The primitive meaning will remain *hare*.

1450	nightfall
晚	*Sun . . . hare.* [11]

1451	elephant
象	A *rabbit's* head and a *sow's* body represents an **elephant**. Little wonder that the character also means "phenomenon"! [11]

ク　　凸　　白　　孚　　象

1452	likeness
像	This key word refers to the kind of **likeness** that a portrait or effigy captures. Its elements: *person . . . elephant.* [13]

Lesson 53

Now that we have come as far as the elephant, we may continue on with more of the larger animals. Fortunately, this group will cause us much less of a headache than the preceding series, since there are fewer new primitives and their use is more frequent.

1453 **horse**

马

Almost everything about this character is odd. The first stroke of this character is not useful as a primitive, so think of it as the head and mane of the **horse**. The element for *snare* that follows does not actually touch the first stroke, as we would expect it to do when "doubling up." Only the final stroke give us some relief: the *pointed tail.* You should not have any trouble with this final stroke, but if you do, think of using a Clydesdale to help you in duck hunting. See the poor beast struggle to run across the swamp, holding his tail out straight and pointing his nose at the prey. [3]

1454 **mama**

妈

Woman . . . horse. [6]

1455 **yes or no**

吗

This character is a particle added to the end of a sentence to turn it into a question that anticipates a **yes or no** answer. Its elements: *mouth . . . horse.* [6]

1456 **scold** (v.)

骂

Chatterbox . . . horse. [9]

1457 **check** (v.)

验

Horse . . . hootenanny. [10]

1458	ride[(v.)]
骑	*Horse. . . strange.* [11]

1459	tiger

虎 The character in this frame recalls the famous Bengali fable about the group of magicians (the *magic wand*) who decided to make a **tiger**. It seems that each of them knew how to make one part of the beast, so they pooled their talents and brought all the pieces (*diced* into pieces) together. A great *wind* swirled around and around assembling the pieces into a full-grown *tiger*—who then promptly ate the magicians. Whatever the parable's significance for modern civilization and its arsenals, it should help with this character.

Oh yes, we should not forget that cliff-like element. Think of it as an abbreviation of the primitive for *zoo* (the first and fourth strokes, actually), in order to fit the **tiger** somewhere into the picture. In fact, the abbreviation is perfectly logical, since the bottom elements usurp the room for the rest of the primitive for *zoo*. [8]

ㄏ 广 虍 虎

❖ As a primitive element itself, the *wind* disappears but the meaning of *tiger* is kept, and the whole serves as a roof for what comes beneath, 尼, giving the *tiger* something to eat.

1460	ponder
虑	*Tiger . . . heart.* [10]

1461	false
虚	*Tiger . . . profession.* [11]

1462	deer

鹿 Drawn on the walls of a complex of *caves* near Niaux in southern France are a number of animal likenesses dating from the Upper Paleolithic period. Among them we find pictures of **deer**, some of them showing men in **deer** masks. By *comparing* their drawings to real **deer**, Stone Age people hoped to acquire power over the animal in the hunt; and by *comparing* themselves to the **deer**, to take on that animal's characteristics. But time has locked with a "double-*key*" (the extra stroke through the element for *key*) the real secret of this art form from us, and we can only surmise such meanings. But more important than the enigmas of the troglodytic mind is the way in which *caves*, a double-*key*, and *compare* give us the character for **deer**. [11]

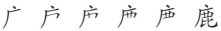

| 1463 | bear (N.) |

熊 *Elbow ... flesh ... spoon* atop a *spoon ... cooking fire.* [14]

| 1464 | ability |

能 Try relating this character to that of the previous frame. For instance, you might imagine that the test of **ability** envisioned here is removing the *bear* from the cooking fire. [10]

LESSON 54

THE GROUPING of characters in this lesson is based on primitives related to fantastical animals and beings. We begin with two animals belonging to the Chinese zodiac.

1465 寅	**sign of the tiger** *House . . . ceiling . . . sprout . . . animal legs.* [11]
1466 演	**perform** *Water . . . sign of the tiger.* [14]
1467 辰	**sign of the dragon** To keep the character for the astrological **sign of the dragon** distinct from the actual dragon, think of someone particularly draconic born in the year of the dragon (2000 and every year a multiple of 12 before and after it). The elements: *cliff . . . two . . . barrettes.* Here again, note that the first stroke of *barrette* doubles up with the second stroke of the primitive above it. [7]
1468 晨	**morning** *Sun . . . sign of the dragon.* [11]
1469 关	**shut** [(v.)] The story is told of the people of the Exodus who, dissatisfied with Moses' leadership, collected their gold ornaments and melted them down to fashion a golden calf for an idol. The *animal horns* and *heavens* here represent that god of theirs, and their way of **shutting** Moses out. [6] ❖ As a primitive element itself, we will keep the graphic image of the *golden calf.*

1470	deliver
送	*Golden calf . . . road.* [9]

1471	unite
联	*Ear . . . golden calf.* [12]

1472	ghost
鬼	*Drop of . . . brains . . . human legs . . . elbow.* Note that the sixth stroke doubles up with the middle vertical stroke of *brains*, which also changes the stroke order for *brains* in this and the following character. [9]

臼　白　白　白　鬼　鬼

1473	demon
魔	*Hemp . . . ghost.* [20]

1474	dragon
龙	This character shows a *pooch* with a long trail of *spoons* attached to his tail. Obviously it has been dressed up to look like a **dragon** in a school drama presentation of Camelot. In order not to confuse this character with the zodiacal *sign of the dragon*, learned earlier in FRAME 1467, you might think here of a parade **dragon**.

The stroke order needs to be paid attention to, though it follows the rules. [5] |

一　ナ　大　龙　龙

1475	raid (v.)
袭	*Dragon . . . clothing.* [11]

LESSON 55

THIS FINAL LESSON, one of the longest in Book 1, is intended to complete this volume and prepare for the transition to Book 2. A number of characters have been reserved for this purpose and arranged into 10 groups, the last of which is a short assortment of stragglers.

❖	razor wire

刃

Razor wire refers to a type of fencing meant to keep people in or out. It is represented by a *dagger* with two razor-sharp metal barbs (the two horizontal strokes) attached to it. [4]

丁 丁 刁 刃

1476   that

那

Razor wire and *pinnacle* suggest a high-security prison like the famous Alcatraz. How do we associate this with the key word? We suggest imagining yourself on a tour-guided cruise around San Francisco Bay. At one point, one of the visitors points to a small island and asks, "What's THAT?" The guide answers theatrically, "**That**, my friends, is the famous Alcatraz!" [6]

❖ The primitive meaning will be *Alcatraz*, from the above explanation.

1477   which?

哪

"**Which** witch wishes?" This is a sentence you might have been asked to pronounce in primary school holding a thin strip of paper under your *mouth* so that it will flutter when the word "which" is properly pronounced and remain still when the words "witch wishes" are spoken. It's a bit of a tongue-twister, but the warden at *Alcatraz*, herself a former third-grade teacher, insisted that inmates pronounce it correctly three times in quick succession or face solitary confinement. [9]

1478	dos
两	Assuming that everyone knows how to count at least uno-**dos**-tres in Spanish, we can use this key word to indicate the number "2" used before a classifier or measure word. The character actually depicts **dos** persons who are "hitched" (the *belt*) to the matrimonial yoke (the top horizontal line). [7]
	❖ As a primitive, we will take this to mean a *yoke*, the kind used to bind a pair of oxen.
1479	duo
俩	*Person . . . yoke.* [9]
1480	full
满	*Water . . . flowers . . . yoke.* [13]
1481	county
县	*Eye . . . wall.* Note how the final stroke of *eye* and the first stroke of *wall* double up. [7]
1482	suspend
悬	In the sense of "hang," not "interrupt." *County . . . heart.* [11]
❖	GPS
囱	The small box with an antenna coming out the top suggests a handheld electronic device. On the screen, we see only a pair of *walking legs.* This suggests a portable Global Positioning System or GPS. [7]
1483	window
窗	*Hole . . . GPS.* [12]
1484	electricity
电	Think of the legend of Benjamin Franklin out in a storm flying a kite with a key on the string. (If he had actually used a key, he would have run the danger of being electrocuted.) This charac-

ter knows better, showing us only a pictograph of the kite as an image of **electricity**. [5]

❖

奄

hang glider

The **hang glider** is like a gigantic kite that is strong enough to support the weight of someone flying around on it. The image of the kite from the last frame and the element for *large* give us just that. [8]

大   奄

1485

掩

conceal

Fingers . . . hang glider. [11]

1486

丑

clown

If you look closely at this character you will see a *needle* being used as a *key*—clearly the sign of a lock-picker at work. We leave it to you to associate this with the key word. [4]

フ   刀   丑   丑

1487

扭

twist (v.)

Fingers . . . clown. [7]

1488

黄

yellow

The only thing that distinguishes **yellow** from the *sign of the tiger* (FRAME 1465) is the top element: *flowers* instead of *house*. Think of a lei made of **yellow** *sign-of-the-tiger* lilies, the kind a Hawaiian astrologer might try to sell you. [11]

1489

横

horizontal

Tree . . . yellow. [15]

1490

赤

crimson

Soil . . . saber . . . animal legs. [7]

1491 亦	**likewise** No doubt your imagination took you to a pretty bloody scene in the last frame for *crimson*. But there are other things that are **likewise** a shade of red—like a fresh, shiny apple. And this immediately conjures up the image of Johnny Appleseed, with his kettle for a *top hat* and surrounded by all the curious animals of the wilderness (the *animal legs*). Apocryphal accounts **likewise** identify him as a master swordsman, but we only know him after he took the biblical prophet's advice and turned his *saber* into a plowshare. [6] ❖ We will take this form to mean a bright red *apple* when it appears as a primitive element. Note the slight change in shape when it appears above another element: the two vertical strokes of the saber are straightened out to give us 亦.
1492 弯	**curved** (ADJ.) *Apple . . . bow.* [9]
1493 湾	**bay** (N.) *Water . . . curved.* [12]
1494 恋	**be enamored of** When we **are enamored of** someone, this character tells us to to refer to that special someone as the *apple* of our *heart*. [10]
1495 变	**change** (V.) *Apple . . . right hand/crotch.* [8]
1496 卑	**lowly** Think of someone of **lowly** origins who has submitted himself to scientific experiments to add a *drop of* income to his meager earnings. After that initial *drop*, we see what looks like *brains*, except that part of them are leaking out to the left—actually not the *brains* themselves, just the data that the *needle* has been stuck in to extract. [8]

白　囱　鱼　卑

1497　　　　　　　　　　　　　　　　　　　　　brand (N.)

牌　*Slice . . . lowly.* The **brand** this key word refers to is the trade-mark of a manufactured product, not the impression a hot iron makes on the backside of a cow. [12]

We conclude this lesson, and Book 1, with three unrelated characters.

1498　　　　　　　　　　　　　　　　　　　　　cover (N.)

套　*St. Bernard dog . . . staples . . . wall.* Note that in this character the first stroke in the element for *staples* is drawn horizontally left to right and not slanted downward right to left. This makes sense if you consider the spatial restrictions imposed by the top element. [10]

大　太　木　本　套　套

1499　　　　　　　　　　　　　　　　　　　　　sayeth

曰　*Pent in . . . one.* The key word refers to famous sayings of famous people, and is the origin for the primitive meaning of a *tongue wagging in the mouth* that we learned in FRAME 12.
　　The size of this character, a relatively rare one, distinguishes it from *day*, but we have used the primitive meanings of the two characters interchangeably. [4]

丨　冂　冃　曰

1500　　　　　　　　　　　　　　　　　　　　　belong to

属　*Flag . . . eyedropper . . . belt . . . insect.* Note that the primitive element for *insect* overlaps and is not drawn in order. [12]

尸　尸　居　属　属

Indexes

INDEX I
Hand-Drawn Characters

This Index presents all the characters in this book in the order of their appearance. They are printed in one of the typical type styles used to teach children how to draw characters with a pen or pencil—the same form used in this book to show proper stroke order. The pronunciation (Mandarin) of the character is given beneath. Some of the characters have multiple pronunciations, which can be found by consulting a dictionary under the pronunciation given here.

一	二	三	四	五	六	七	八	九	十
yī	*èr*	*sān*	*sì*	*wǔ*	*liù*	*qī*	*bā*	*jiǔ*	*shí*
1	2	3	4	5	6	7	8	9	10

口	日	月	田	目	古	胡	叶	吾	朋
kǒu	*rì*	*yuè*	*tián*	*mù*	*gǔ*	*hú*	*yè*	*wú*	*péng*
11	12	13	14	15	16	17	18	19	20

明	唱	晶	品	昌	早	旭	世	胃	旦
míng	*chàng*	*jīng*	*pǐn*	*chāng*	*zǎo*	*xù*	*shì*	*wèi*	*dàn*
21	22	23	24	25	26	27	28	29	30

凹	凸	自	白	百	皂	旧	中	千	舌
āo	*tú*	*zì*	*bái*	*bǎi*	*zào*	*jiù*	*zhōng*	*qiān*	*shé*
31	32	33	34	35	36	37	38	39	40

升	丸	卜	占	上	下	卡	卓	朝	嘲
shēng	*wán*	*bǔ*	*zhān*	*shàng*	*xià*	*kǎ*	*zhuó*	*cháo*	*chǎo*
41	42	43	44	45	46	47	48	49	50

只	贝	贴	贞	员	儿	几	见	元	页
zhǐ	*bèi*	*tiē*	*zhēn*	*yuán*	*ér*	*jǐ*	*jiàn*	*yuán*	*yè*
51	52	53	54	55	56	57	58	59	60

顽	凡	肌	负	万	匀	句	旬	勺	的
wán	*fán*	*jī*	*fù*	*wàn*	*yún*	*jù*	*xún*	*sháo*	*de*
61	62	63	64	65	66	67	68	69	70

首	直	置	具	真	工	左	右	有	贿
shǒu	zhí	zhì	jù	zhēn	gōng	zuǒ	yòu	yǒu	huì
71	72	73	74	75	76	77	78	79	80
贡	项	刀	刃	切	召	昭	则	副	丁
gòng	xiàng	dāo	rèn	qiè	zhào	zhāo	zé	fù	dīng
81	82	83	84	85	86	87	88	89	90
叮	可	哥	顶	乙	飞	子	孔	吼	乱
dīng	kě	gē	dǐng	yǐ	fēi	zǐ	kǒng	hǒu	luàn
91	92	93	94	95	96	97	98	99	100
了	女	好	如	母	贯	兄	克	小	少
le	nǚ	hǎo	rú	mǔ	guàn	xiōng	kè	xiǎo	shǎo
101	102	103	104	105	106	107	108	109	110
吵	孙	大	尖	夕	多	够	外	名	罗
chǎo	sūn	dà	jiān	xī	duō	gòu	wài	míng	luó
111	112	113	114	115	116	117	118	119	120
厂	厅	厉	厚	石	砂	妙	肖	削	光
chǎng	tīng	lì	hòu	shí	shā	miào	xiào	xiāo	guāng
121	122	123	124	125	126	127	128	129	130
太	省	奇	川	州	顺	水	永	脉	求
tài	shěng	qí	chuān	zhōu	shùn	shuǐ	yǒng	mài	qiú
131	132	133	134	135	136	137	138	139	140
泉	原	泳	洲	沼	沙	江	汁	潮	源
quán	yuán	yǒng	zhōu	zhǎo	shā	jiāng	zhī	cháo	yuán
141	142	143	144	145	146	147	148	149	150
活	消	河	鱼	渔	湖	测	土	均	肚
huó	xiāo	hé	yú	yú	hú	cè	tǔ	jūn	dù
151	152	153	154	155	156	157	158	159	160
尘	填	吐	压	哇	寸	封	时	寺	火
chén	tián	tǔ	yā	wā	cùn	fēng	shí	sì	huǒ
161	162	163	164	165	166	167	168	169	170
灭	灰	烦	炎	淡	灯	点	照	里	量
miè	huī	fán	yán	dàn	dēng	diǎn	zhào	lǐ	liàng
171	172	173	174	175	176	177	178	179	180

埋	黑	墨	冒	同	洞	丽	向	响	尚
mái	*hēi*	*mò*	*mào*	*tóng*	*dòng*	*lì*	*xiàng*	*xiǎng*	*shàng*
181	182	183	184	185	186	187	188	189	190
字	守	完	灾	宣	宵	安	宴	寄	富
zì	*shǒu*	*wán*	*zāi*	*xuān*	*xiāo*	*ān*	*yàn*	*jì*	*fù*
191	192	193	194	195	196	197	198	199	200
贮	木	林	森	梦	机	植	杏	呆	枯
zhù	*mù*	*lín*	*sēn*	*mèng*	*jī*	*zhí*	*xìng*	*dāi*	*kū*
201	202	203	204	205	206	207	208	209	210
村	相	本	案	未	末	沫	味	妹	查
cūn	*xiāng*	*běn*	*àn*	*wèi*	*mò*	*mò*	*wèi*	*mèi*	*chá*
211	212	213	214	215	216	217	218	219	220
渣	染	李	桌	杂	若	草	艺	苦	宽
zhā	*rǎn*	*lǐ*	*zhuō*	*zá*	*ruò*	*cǎo*	*yì*	*kǔ*	*kuān*
221	222	223	224	225	226	227	228	229	230
莫	模	漠	墓	苗	瞄	兆	桃	犬	尤
mò	*mó*	*mò*	*mù*	*miáo*	*miáo*	*zhào*	*táo*	*quǎn*	*yóu*
231	232	233	234	235	236	237	238	239	240
厌	状	妆	将	获	默	然	哭	器	臭
yàn	*zhuàng*	*zhuāng*	*jiàng*	*huò*	*mò*	*rán*	*kū*	*qì*	*chòu*
241	242	243	244	245	246	247	248	249	250
狗	牛	特	告	浩	先	洗	个	介	界
gǒu	*niú*	*tè*	*gào*	*hào*	*xiān*	*xǐ*	*gè*	*jiè*	*jiè*
251	252	253	254	255	256	257	258	259	260
茶	合	哈	塔	王	玉	宝	球	现	玩
chá	*hé*	*hā*	*tǎ*	*wáng*	*yù*	*bǎo*	*qiú*	*xiàn*	*wán*
261	262	263	264	265	266	267	268	269	270
狂	皇	煌	呈	全	理	主	注	金	钟
kuáng	*huáng*	*huáng*	*chéng*	*quán*	*lǐ*	*zhǔ*	*zhù*	*jīn*	*zhōng*
271	272	273	274	275	276	277	278	279	280
铜	钓	针	钉	铭	镇	道	达	远	适
tóng	*diào*	*zhēn*	*dīng*	*míng*	*zhèn*	*dào*	*dá*	*yuǎn*	*shì*
281	282	283	284	285	286	287	288	289	290

过	迈	迅	造	逃	巡	选	逊	逛	车
guò	mài	xùn	zào	táo	xún	xuǎn	xùn	guàng	chē
291	292	293	294	295	296	297	298	299	300
连	莲	前	剪	输	逾	条	处	各	格
lián	lián	qián	jiǎn	shū	yú	tiáo	chù	gè	gé
301	302	303	304	305	306	307	308	309	310
略	客	额	夏	洛	落	备	冗	沉	军
lüè	kè	é	xià	luò	luò	bèi	rǒng	chén	jūn
311	312	313	314	315	316	317	318	319	320
辉	冠	坑	亩	高	享	熟	亭	亮	京
huī	guān	kēng	mǔ	gāo	xiǎng	shú	tíng	liàng	jīng
321	322	323	324	325	326	327	328	329	330
景	就	周	士	吉	壮	学	觉	攻	敌
jǐng	jiù	zhōu	shì	jí	zhuàng	xué	jué	gōng	dí
331	332	333	334	335	336	337	338	339	340
败	故	救	敬	敞	言	警	计	让	狱
bài	gù	jiù	jìng	chǎng	yán	jǐng	jì	ràng	yù
341	342	343	344	345	346	347	348	349	350
讨	训	识	话	诗	语	调	谈	式	试
tǎo	xùn	shì	huà	shī	yǔ	diào	tán	shì	shì
351	352	353	354	355	356	357	358	359	360
戈	战	划	或	贼	载	茂	成	城	诚
gē	zhàn	huá	huò	zéi	zài	mào	chéng	chéng	chéng
361	362	363	364	365	366	367	368	369	370
威	咸	钱	浅	贱	尧	烧	晓	止	步
wēi	xián	qián	qiǎn	jiàn	yáo	shāo	xiǎo	zhǐ	bù
371	372	373	374	375	376	377	378	379	380
涉	频	肯	企	武	赋	正	证	政	定
shè	pín	kěn	qǐ	wǔ	fù	zhèng	zhèng	zhèng	dìng
381	382	383	384	385	386	387	388	389	390
走	超	越	是	题	延	诞	建	楚	衣
zǒu	chāo	yuè	shì	tí	yán	dàn	jiàn	chǔ	yī
391	392	393	394	395	396	397	398	399	400

裁 cái 401	装 zhuāng 402	哀 āi 403	袁 yuán 404	初 chū 405	补 bǔ 406	衬 chèn 407	农 nóng 408	浓 nóng 409	巾 jīn 410
帅 shuài 411	师 shī 412	狮 shī 413	布 bù 414	帜 zhì 415	帽 mào 416	幕 mù 417	棉 mián 418	市 shì 419	肺 fèi 420
带 dài 421	滞 zhì 422	刺 cì 423	制 zhì 424	雨 yǔ 425	雷 léi 426	霜 shuāng 427	云 yún 428	运 yùn 429	冰 bīng 430
况 kuàng 431	冲 chōng 432	减 jiǎn 433	凉 liáng 434	冬 dōng 435	天 tiān 436	吴 wú 437	娱 yú 438	误 wù 439	夭 yāo 440
乔 qiáo 441	桥 qiáo 442	娇 jiāo 443	立 lì 444	泣 qì 445	站 zhàn 446	章 zhāng 447	竟 jìng 448	帝 dì 449	童 tóng 450
商 shāng 451	滴 dī 452	匕 bǐ 453	北 běi 454	背 bèi 455	比 bǐ 456	昆 kūn 457	混 hùn 458	皆 jiē 459	此 cǐ 460
些 xiē 461	它 tā 462	旨 zhǐ 463	脂 zhī 464	论 lùn 465	轮 lún 466	每 měi 467	梅 méi 468	海 hǎi 469	乞 qǐ 470
吃 chī 471	复 fù 472	腹 fù 473	欠 qiàn 474	吹 chuī 475	歌 gē 476	软 ruǎn 477	次 cì 478	资 zī 479	姿 zī 480
咨 zī 481	赔 péi 482	培 péi 483	音 yīn 484	暗 àn 485	韵 yùn 486	竞 jìng 487	镜 jìng 488	境 jìng 489	亡 wáng 490
盲 máng 491	妄 wàng 492	望 wàng 493	方 fāng 494	妨 fáng 495	放 fàng 496	激 jī 497	旁 páng 498	兑 duì 499	脱 tuō 500
说 shuō 501	曾 céng 502	增 zēng 503	赠 zèng 504	也 yě 505	她 tā 506	地 dì 507	池 chí 508	虫 chóng 509	虾 xiā 510

独	虽	蛇	蛋	已	起	改	记	已	包
dú	suī	shé	dàn	jǐ	qǐ	gǎi	jì	yǐ	bāo
511	512	513	514	515	516	517	518	519	520
泡	导	顾	逐	家	场	汤	羊	美	洋
pào	dǎo	gù	zhú	jiā	chǎng	tāng	yáng	měi	yáng
521	522	523	524	525	526	527	528	529	530
鲜	样	兰	烂	差	着	养	集	准	谁
xiān	yàng	lán	làn	chà	zhe	yǎng	jí	zhǔn	shéi
531	532	533	534	535	536	537	538	539	540
售	午	许	羽	习	翔	困	固	国	圆
shòu	wǔ	xǔ	yǔ	xí	xiáng	kùn	gù	guó	yuán
541	542	543	544	545	546	547	548	549	550
因	烟	园	回	图	广	店	库	裤	床
yīn	yān	yuán	huí	tú	guǎng	diàn	kù	kù	chuáng
551	552	553	554	555	556	557	558	559	560
麻	庄	心	忘	忍	总	态	志	思	恩
má	zhuāng	xīn	wàng	rěn	zǒng	tài	zhì	sī	ēn
561	562	563	564	565	566	567	568	569	570
愿	意	想	息	恐	感	憾	忧	惊	怕
yuàn	yì	xiǎng	xī	kǒng	gǎn	hàn	yōu	jīng	pà
571	572	573	574	575	576	577	578	579	580
忙	惯	必	手	看	摩	拿	我	抱	抗
máng	guàn	bì	shǒu	kàn	mó	ná	wǒ	bào	kàng
581	582	583	584	585	586	587	588	589	590
批	招	打	指	持	担	括	提	挥	推
pī	zhāo	dǎ	zhǐ	chí	dān	kuò	tí	huī	tuī
591	592	593	594	595	596	597	598	599	600
搅	执	热	接	挂	按	掉	拉	啦	找
jiǎo	zhí	rè	jiē	guà	àn	diào	lā	lā	zhǎo
601	602	603	604	605	606	607	608	609	610
无	抚	开	研	弄	异	鼻	刑	型	才
wú	fǔ	kāi	yán	nòng	yì	bí	xíng	xíng	cái
611	612	613	614	615	616	617	618	619	620

财	团	存	在	乃	奶	及	吸	极	史
cái	tuán	cún	zài	nǎi	nǎi	jí	xī	jí	shǐ
621	622	623	624	625	626	627	628	629	630
更	硬	又	圣	友	双	汉	戏	观	欢
gèng	yìng	yòu	shèng	yǒu	shuāng	hàn	xì	guān	huān
631	632	633	634	635	636	637	638	639	640
怪	对	树	难	摊	投	没	设	股	支
guài	duì	shù	nán	tān	tóu	méi	shè	gǔ	zhī
641	642	643	644	645	646	647	648	649	650
技	枝	叔	督	寂	反	板	返	后	质
jì	zhī	shū	dū	jì	fǎn	bǎn	fǎn	hòu	zhí
651	652	653	654	655	656	657	658	659	660
派	乐	爪	抓	采	菜	受	授	爱	么
pài	yuè	zhǎo	zhuā	cǎi	cài	shòu	shòu	ài	me
661	662	663	664	665	666	667	668	669	670
雄	台	治	始	去	法	会	至	室	到
xióng	tái	zhì	shǐ	qù	fǎ	huì	zhì	shì	dào
671	672	673	674	675	676	677	678	679	680
互	充	育	流	梳	购	构	山	出	础
hù	chōng	yù	liú	shū	gòu	gòu	shān	chū	chǔ
681	682	683	684	685	686	687	688	689	690
岁	密	入	分	贫	公	松	谷	浴	欲
suì	mì	rù	fēn	pín	gōng	sōng	gǔ	yù	yù
691	692	693	694	695	696	697	698	699	700
容	溶	赏	党	常	堂	皮	波	婆	破
róng	róng	shǎng	dǎng	cháng	táng	pí	bō	pó	pò
701	702	703	704	705	706	707	708	709	710
被	歹	列	烈	死	葬	耳	取	趣	最
bèi	dǎi	liè	liè	sǐ	zàng	ěr	qǔ	qù	zuì
711	712	713	714	715	716	717	718	719	720
职	敢	曼	慢	漫	夫	规	替	失	铁
zhí	gǎn	màn	màn	màn	fū	guī	tì	shī	tiě
721	722	723	724	725	726	727	728	729	730

臣	力	边	势	动	励	历	另	别	拐
chén	lì	biān	shì	dòng	lì	lì	lìng	bié	guǎi
731	732	733	734	735	736	737	738	739	740
男	功	办	协	苏	为	奴	努	加	贺
nán	gōng	bàn	xié	sū	wèi	nú	nǔ	jiā	hè
741	742	743	744	745	746	747	748	749	750
架	务	雾	行	律	得	待	往	德	微
jià	wù	wù	háng	lǜ	děi	dài	wǎng	dé	wēi
751	752	753	754	755	756	757	758	759	760
街	禾	程	和	积	种	移	秋	愁	揪
jiē	hé	chéng	hé	jī	zhǒng	yí	qiū	chóu	jiū
761	762	763	764	765	766	767	768	769	770
利	香	季	委	秀	透	诱	米	粉	迷
lì	xiāng	jì	wěi	xiù	tòu	yòu	mǐ	fěn	mí
771	772	773	774	775	776	777	778	779	780
谜	类	来	数	楼	竹	笑	箱	等	算
mí	lèi	lái	shù	lóu	zhú	xiào	xiāng	děng	suàn
781	782	783	784	785	786	787	788	789	790
答	策	人	认	价	份	伪	尔	你	您
dá	cè	rén	rèn	jià	fèn	wèi	ěr	nǐ	nín
791	792	793	794	795	796	797	798	799	800
称	什	值	做	但	住	位	件	仍	他
chēng	shén	zhí	zuò	dàn	zhù	wèi	jiàn	réng	tā
801	802	803	804	805	806	807	808	809	810
仅	休	体	信	依	例	健	停	倒	仁
jǐn	xiū	tǐ	xìn	yī	lì	jiàn	tíng	dǎo	rén
811	812	813	814	815	816	817	818	819	820
优	伤	保	堡	付	府	俯	代	袋	化
yōu	shāng	bǎo	bǎo	fù	fǔ	fǔ	dài	dài	huà
821	822	823	824	825	826	827	828	829	830
华	哗	花	货	何	便	丈	使	久	内
huá	huá	huā	huò	hé	biàn	zhàng	shǐ	jiǔ	nèi
831	832	833	834	835	836	837	838	839	840

呐 nà 841	丙 bǐng 842	柄 bǐng 843	肉 ròu 844	腐 fǔ 845	从 cóng 846	众 zhòng 847	坐 zuò 848	座 zuò 849	巫 wū 850
喝 hē 851	渴 kě 852	任 rèn 853	廷 tíng 854	庭 tíng 855	头 tóu 856	实 shí 857	买 mǎi 858	卖 mài 859	读 dú 860
以 yǐ 861	似 sì 862	并 bìng 863	拼 pīn 864	吕 lǔ 865	侣 lǔ 866	荣 róng 867	劳 láo 868	营 yíng 869	善 shàn 870
年 nián 871	夜 yè 872	液 yè 873	旅 lǔ 874	施 shī 875	游 yóu 876	勿 wù 877	忽 hū 878	物 wù 879	易 yì 880
赐 cì 881	尸 shī 882	尼 ní 883	呢 ne 884	泥 ní 885	屋 wū 886	握 wò 887	居 jū 888	锯 jù 889	剧 jù 890
据 jù 891	层 céng 892	局 jú 893	尺 chǐ 894	尽 jìn 895	户 hù 896	房 fáng 897	雇 gù 898	护 hù 899	示 shì 900
社 shè 901	礼 lǐ 902	视 shì 903	福 fú 904	标 biāo 905	禁 jìn 906	襟 jīn 907	宗 zōng 908	崇 chóng 909	祭 jì 910
察 chá 911	擦 cā 912	由 yóu 913	抽 chōu 914	油 yóu 915	甲 jiǎ 916	押 yā 917	申 shēn 918	伸 shēn 919	神 shén 920
果 guǒ 921	课 kè 922	颗 kē 923	斤 jīn 924	听 tīng 925	所 suǒ 926	近 jìn 927	斩 zhǎn 928	暂 zàn 929	渐 jiàn 930
断 duàn 931	折 zhé 932	哲 zhé 933	逝 shì 934	斥 chì 935	诉 sù 936	乍 zhà 937	怎 zěn 938	昨 zuó 939	作 zuò 940
雪 xuě 941	灵 líng 942	妇 fù 943	扫 sǎo 944	寻 xún 945	急 jí 946	当 dāng 947	档 dàng 948	录 lù 949	碌 lù 950

争	净	事	唐	糖	康	尹	伊	君	裙
zhēng	jìng	shì	táng	táng	kāng	yǐn	yī	jūn	qún
951	952	953	954	955	956	957	958	959	960
群	而	需	儒	瑞	端	曲	斗	料	科
qún	ér	xū	rú	ruì	duān	qū	dǒu	liào	kē
961	962	963	964	965	966	967	968	969	970
用	确	昔	借	错	散	撒	廿	席	度
yòng	què	xī	jiè	cuò	sǎn	sǎ	niàn	xí	dù
971	972	973	974	975	976	977	978	979	980
渡	半	伴	胖	判	眷	拳	片	版	之
dù	bàn	bàn	pàng	pàn	juàn	quán	piàn	bǎn	zhī
981	982	983	984	985	986	987	988	989	990
乏	眨	不	否	坏	环	杯	还	怀	矢
fá	zhǎ	bù	fǒu	huài	huán	bēi	huán	huái	shǐ
991	992	993	994	995	996	997	998	999	1000
族	知	智	矛	柔	揉	子	序	预	野
zú	zhī	zhì	máo	róu	róu	yǔ	xù	yù	yě
1001	1002	1003	1004	1005	1006	1007	1008	1009	1010
班	临	坚	贤	弓	引	弥	强	弱	单
bān	lín	jiān	xián	gōng	yǐn	mí	qiáng	ruò	dān
1011	1012	1013	1014	1015	1016	1017	1018	1019	1020
弹	费	佛	弟	第	巧	号	身	射	谢
dàn	fèi	fó	dì	dì	qiǎo	hào	shēn	shè	xiè
1021	1022	1023	1024	1025	1026	1027	1028	1029	1030
老	考	烤	与	写	泻	孝	教	者	著
lǎo	kǎo	kǎo	yǔ	xiě	xiè	xiào	jiāo	zhě	zhù
1031	1032	1033	1034	1035	1036	1037	1038	1039	1040
猪	追	官	管	父	交	效	较	校	足
zhū	zhuī	guān	guǎn	fù	jiāo	xiào	jiào	xiào	zú
1041	1042	1043	1044	1045	1046	1047	1048	1049	1050
跑	跳	路	露	骨	滑	阿	啊	随	阳
pǎo	tiào	lù	lù	gǔ	huá	ā	ā	suí	yáng
1051	1052	1053	1054	1055	1056	1057	1058	1059	1060

阴	荫	防	附	际	阶	院	阵	队	坠
yīn	yìn	fáng	fù	jì	jiē	yuàn	zhèn	duì	jiē
1061	1062	1063	1064	1065	1066	1067	1068	1069	1070
降	穴	究	突	空	控	深	探	丘	兵
jiàng	xué	jiū	tū	kōng	kòng	shēn	tàn	qiū	bīng
1071	1072	1073	1074	1075	1076	1077	1078	1079	1080
丝	织	线	维	统	给	结	终	级	纪
sī	zhī	xiàn	wéi	tǒng	gěi	jié	zhōng	jí	jì
1081	1082	1083	1084	1085	1086	1087	1088	1089	1090
红	约	细	纵	绿	经	轻	续	继	药
hóng	yuē	xì	zòng	lù	jīng	qīng	xù	jì	yào
1091	1092	1093	1094	1095	1096	1097	1098	1099	1100
系	紧	却	脚	服	报	命	贸	留	溜
xì	jǐn	què	jiǎo	fú	bào	mìng	mào	liú	liū
1101	1102	1103	1104	1105	1106	1107	1108	1109	1110
聊	柳	节	卫	令	冷	零	领	通	勇
liáo	liǔ	jié	wèi	lìng	lěng	líng	lǐng	tōng	yǒng
1111	1112	1113	1114	1115	1116	1117	1118	1119	1120
仓	枪	创	犯	危	脆	印	酒	配	酋
cāng	qiāng	chuàng	fàn	wéi	cuì	yìn	jiǔ	pèi	qiú
1121	1122	1123	1124	1125	1126	1127	1128	1129	1130
尊	遵	豆	短	厨	鼓	喜	血	盖	温
zūn	zūn	dòu	duǎn	chú	gǔ	xǐ	xiě	gài	wēn
1131	1132	1133	1134	1135	1136	1137	1138	1139	1140
监	篮	蓝	银	跟	很	根	即	退	腿
jiān	lán	lán	yín	gēn	hěn	gēn	jí	tuì	tuǐ
1141	1142	1143	1144	1145	1146	1147	1148	1149	1150
限	眼	良	浪	娘	食	饭	餐	馆	既
xiàn	yǎn	liáng	làng	niáng	shí	fàn	cān	guǎn	jì
1151	1152	1153	1154	1155	1156	1157	1158	1159	1160
概	平	评	坪	乎	呼	希	稀	杀	风
gài	píng	píng	píng	hū	hū	xī	xī	shā	fēng
1161	1162	1163	1164	1165	1166	1167	1168	1169	1170

讽	冈	刚	网	画	凶	胸	脑	恼	离
fěng	*gāng*	*gāng*	*wǎng*	*huà*	*xiōng*	*xiōng*	*nǎo*	*nǎo*	*lí*
1171	1172	1173	1174	1175	1176	1177	1178	1179	1180
禽	义	仪	蚁	辛	辩	辟	壁	避	亲
qín	*yì*	*yí*	*yǐ*	*xīn*	*biàn*	*pì*	*bì*	*bì*	*qīn*
1181	1182	1183	1184	1185	1186	1187	1188	1189	1190
新	薪	幸	叫	收	亥	核	孩	刻	该
xīn	*xīn*	*xìng*	*jiào*	*shōu*	*hài*	*hé*	*hái*	*kè*	*gāi*
1191	1192	1193	1194	1195	1196	1197	1198	1199	1200
术	述	襄	壤	寒	赛	毒	麦	素	青
shù	*shù*	*xiāng*	*rǎng*	*hán*	*sài*	*dú*	*mài*	*sù*	*qīng*
1201	1202	1203	1204	1205	1206	1207	1208	1209	1210
精	请	情	晴	清	静	责	绩	表	生
jīng	*qǐng*	*qíng*	*jíng*	*qīng*	*jìng*	*zé*	*jī*	*biǎo*	*shēng*
1211	1212	1213	1214	1215	1216	1217	1218	1219	1220
星	姓	性	胜	丰	害	割	慧	韦	围
xīng	*xìng*	*xìng*	*shèng*	*fēng*	*hài*	*gē*	*huì*	*wéi*	*wéi*
1221	1222	1223	1224	1225	1226	1227	1228	1229	1230
伟	春	泰	奉	棒	击	陆	专	传	转
wěi	*chūn*	*tài*	*fèng*	*bàng*	*jī*	*lù*	*zhuān*	*chuán*	*zhuàn*
1231	1232	1233	1234	1235	1236	1237	1238	1239	1240
勤	谨	垂	锤	睡	今	含	念	东	栋
qín	*jǐn*	*chuí*	*chuí*	*shuì*	*jīn*	*hán*	*niàn*	*dōng*	*dòng*
1241	1242	1243	1244	1245	1246	1247	1248	1249	1250
冻	陈	练	拣	西	要	腰	票	漂	贾
dòng	*chén*	*liàn*	*jiǎn*	*xī*	*yào*	*yāo*	*piào*	*piào*	*gǔ*
1251	1252	1253	1254	1255	1256	1257	1258	1259	1260
南	门	们	闲	问	间	简	闻	非	排
nán	*mén*	*men*	*xián*	*wèn*	*jiàn*	*jiǎn*	*wén*	*fēi*	*pái*
1261	1262	1263	1264	1265	1266	1267	1268	1269	1270
罪	靠	侯	候	决	快	块	筷	干	岸
zuì	*kào*	*hóu*	*hòu*	*jué*	*kuài*	*kuài*	*kuài*	*gān*	*àn*
1271	1272	1273	1274	1275	1276	1277	1278	1279	1280

旱	赶	于	宇	余	除	途	束	速	辣
hàn	gǎn	yú	yǔ	yú	chú	tú	shù	sù	là
1281	1282	1283	1284	1285	1286	1287	1288	1289	1290
整	重	懂	病	痛	疯	区	枢	欧	医
zhěng	zhòng	dǒng	bìng	tòng	fēng	qū	shū	ōu	yī
1291	1292	1293	1294	1295	1296	1297	1298	1299	1300
仰	迎	登	发	废	形	影	彩	须	参
yǎng	yíng	dēng	fā	fèi	xíng	yǐng	cǎi	xū	cān
1301	1302	1303	1304	1305	1306	1307	1308	1309	1310
惨	修	珍	产	彦	颜	文	蚊	这	齐
cǎn	xiū	zhēn	chǎn	yàn	yán	wén	wén	zhè	qí
1311	1312	1313	1314	1315	1316	1317	1318	1319	1320
济	率	摔	央	英	唤	换	巴	把	爸
jì	shuài	shuāi	yāng	yīng	huàn	huàn	bā	bǎ	bà
1321	1322	1323	1324	1325	1326	1327	1328	1329	1330
吧	色	绝	艳	甘	某	其	期	基	甚
bā	sè	jué	yàn	gān	mǒu	qí	qī	jī	shèn
1331	1332	1333	1334	1335	1336	1337	1338	1339	1340
斯	贵	遗	舞	且	姐	组	祖	助	普
sī	guì	yí	wǔ	qiě	jiě	zǔ	zǔ	zhù	pǔ
1341	1342	1343	1344	1345	1346	1347	1348	1349	1350
业	显	亚	恶	严	共	供	巷	港	井
yè	xiǎn	yà	è	yán	gòng	gōng	xiàng	gǎng	jǐng
1351	1352	1353	1354	1355	1356	1357	1358	1359	1360
讲	进	角	解	嘴	再	扁	篇	编	典
jiǎng	jìn	jiǎo	jiě	zuǐ	zài	biǎn	piān	biān	diǎn
1361	1362	1363	1364	1365	1366	1367	1368	1369	1370
氏	纸	昏	婚	低	底	民	眠	甫	辅
shì	zhǐ	hūn	hūn	dī	dǐ	mín	mián	fǔ	fǔ
1371	1372	1373	1374	1375	1376	1377	1378	1379	1380
博	搏	都	部	郎	帮	乡	段	锻	幻
bó	bó	dū	bù	láng	bāng	xiāng	duàn	duàn	huàn
1381	1382	1383	1384	1385	1386	1387	1388	1389	1390

司	词	书	舟	船	般	盘	搬	瓜	孤
sī	cí	shū	zhōu	chuán	bān	pán	bān	guā	gū
1391	1392	1393	1394	1395	1396	1397	1398	1399	1400

益	假	暇	气	汽	面	革	鞋	勒	馨
yì	jiǎ	xiá	qì	qì	miàn	gé	xié	lè	xīn
1401	1402	1403	1404	1405	1406	1407	1408	1409	1410

声	承	蒸	牙	穿	呀	释	番	翻	播
shēng	chéng	zhēng	yá	chuān	ya	shì	fān	fān	bō
1411	1412	1413	1414	1415	1416	1417	1418	1419	1420

毛	尾	笔	托	宅	展	丧	长	张	涨
máo	wěi	bǐ	tuō	zhái	zhǎn	sàng	cháng	zhāng	zhàng
1421	1422	1423	1424	1425	1426	1427	1428	1429	1430

雁	应	兴	举	检	脸	险	鸟	鸡	鹰
yàn	yīng	xìng	jǔ	jiǎn	liǎn	xiǎn	niǎo	jī	yīng
1431	1432	1433	1434	1435	1436	1437	1438	1439	1440

鸭	岛	遇	缺	遥	摇	兔	逸	免	晚
yā	dǎo	yù	quē	yáo	yáo	tù	yì	miǎn	wǎn
1441	1442	1443	1444	1445	1446	1447	1448	1449	1450

象	像	马	妈	吗	骂	验	骑	虎	虑
xiàng	xiàng	mǎ	mā	ma	mà	yàn	qí	hǔ	lǜ
1451	1452	1453	1454	1455	1456	1457	1458	1459	1460

虚	鹿	熊	能	寅	演	辰	晨	关	送
xū	lù	xióng	néng	yín	yǎn	chén	chén	guān	sòng
1461	1462	1463	1464	1465	1466	1467	1468	1469	1470

联	鬼	魔	龙	袭	那	哪	两	俩	满
lián	guǐ	mó	lóng	xí	nà	nǎ	liǎng	liǎ	mǎn
1471	1472	1473	1474	1475	1476	1477	1478	1479	1480

县	悬	窗	电	掩	丑	扭	黄	横	赤
xiàn	xuán	chuāng	diàn	yǎn	chǒu	niǔ	huáng	héng	chì
1481	1482	1483	1484	1485	1486	1487	1488	1489	1490

亦	弯	湾	恋	变	卑	牌	套	曰	属
yì	wān	wān	liàn	biàn	bēi	pái	tào	yuē	shǔ
1491	1492	1493	1494	1495	1496	1497	1498	1499	1500

Primitive Elements

This Index lists all the primitive elements used in this book. Characters used as primitives are only listed where the writing is significantly altered. The primitives are arranged according to the number of strokes. The number refers to the page on which the element is first introduced.

1 画

´	丨	㇄	㇄	㇕	㇔	㇆
31	32	56	56	253	253	349

2 画

八	勹	㇉	刂	刂	㇇	冂	人	川
39	39	40	52	52	54	88	115	115

冖	二	㡀	冂	〻	氵	𠂉	乂	厂
136	137	159	168	170	170	179	217	221

厶	亻	刂	丂	与	ㄱ	阝	卩	卪
223	244	279	281	284	284	288	296	297

ㄱ	巳	乄	凵	丩	工	匸	阝
297	299	307	308	310	325	330	348

3 画

亠	屮	少	巛	川	氵	宀	艹	爿
49	62	63	70	70	71	90	100	107

犭	亼	辶	夂	弋	巴	口	广	忄
108	117	128	132	148	197	205	206	207

扌	廾	开	才	云	彳	彐	糸	幺
212	215	215	216	224	237	267	292	294

采 金
355 359

8画 卓 京 帛 雷 音 隹 尚
37   72   166 169 183 201 230

9画 畐 俞 娄 曷 耑 壹 奂 叚 禺
54   132 241 251 271 301 336 352 361

10画 寅 専 隹 䍃
312   347   359   361

11画 商 菫 殼
175   319   353

12画 惠
238

INDEX III

Characters by Number of Strokes

Here you will find all the characters treated in this book, grouped by the number of strokes. Characters within each group are arranged according to first stroke, of which there are five basic types. Their order is the same as the five strokes of the character 札:

⊖ ─ *horizontal or* ╱ *rising*

① │ *vertical or* ┘ *vertical with left hook*

② ノ ′ *falling to the left*

⊙ 丶 ⸍ *dot or* ╲ *falling to the right*

⊝ 乚乙⌐フ¬ㄑㄥㄟㄣ *etc., sharp turn*

1 画		
⊖ 一	1	
⊝ 乙	95	

2 画		
⊖ 二	2	
十	10	
丁	90	
厂	121	
七	7	
① 卜	43	
② 八	8	
人	793	
入	693	
匕	453	
儿	56	
几	57	
九	9	
乃	625	

⊖ 了	101
刀	83
力	732
又	633

3 画	
⊖ 三	3
干	1279
于	1283
工	76
士	334
土	158
才	620
寸	166
下	46
大	113
丈	837
万	65
与	1034
① 上	45

小	109
口	11
山	688
巾	410
② 千	39
乞	470
个	258
夕	115
久	839
么	670
勺	69
川	134
凡	62
丸	42
及	627
⊙ 广	556
亡	490
门	1262
义	1182
之	990
⊝ 尸	882

己	515
巳	519
弓	1015
子	97
卫	1114
也	505
女	102
飞	96
刃	84
习	545
马	1453
乡	1387

4 画	
⊖ 丰	1225
韦	1229
王	265
开	613
井	1360
天	436

夫	726
无	611
元	59
云	428
廿	978
木	202
不	993
太	131
犬	239
尤	240
支	650
艺	228
友	635
专	1238
车	300
五	5
互	681
歹	712
牙	1414
比	456
切	85

戈	361
厅	122
历	737
区	1297
① 止	379
少	110
水	137
中	38
日	12
曰	1499
内	840
冈	1172
贝	52
见	58
② 仁	820
什	802
化	830
仍	809
仅	811
从	1246
今	259
介	1121
仓	696
公	694
分	1045
父	991
乏	584
手	1421
毛	440
夭	1404
气	542
午	252
牛	474
欠	41
升	1428
长	988
片	924
斤	656
反	663
爪	1371
氏	

勾	66
勿	877
凶	1176
月	13
风	1170
ⓥ 计	348
认	794
六	6
文	1317
方	494
户	896
冗	318
火	170
为	746
斗	968
心	563
㊀ 队	1069
双	636
以	861
引	1016
尹	957
尺	894
办	743
丑	1486
巴	1328
孔	98
予	1007
书	1393
幻	1390

5 画

㊀ 巧	1026
功	742
打	593
节	1113
平	1162
灭	171
丙	842
正	387
玉	266

示	900
古	16
去	675
末	216
未	215
术	1201
本	213
击	1236
世	28
甘	1335
东	1249
厉	123
石	125
布	414
右	78
左	77
龙	1474
可	92
① 旧	37
帅	411
北	454
叶	18
叮	91
叫	1194
号	1027
只	51
兄	107
另	738
史	630
央	1324
占	44
卡	47
出	689
业	1351
旦	30
目	15
且	1345
田	14
由	913
申	918
甲	916

电	1484
四	4
凸	32
凹	31
ⓥ 付	825
代	828
议	1183
们	1263
他	810
令	1115
犯	1124
丘	1079
印	1127
乐	662
禾	762
斥	935
瓜	1399
乎	1165
尔	798
外	118
处	308
冬	435
务	752
乍	937
矢	1000
失	729
生	1220
句	67
包	520
白	34
鸟	1438
用	971
㊀ 讨	351
让	349
训	352
记	518
汁	148
汉	637
立	277
主	419
市	

它	462
穴	1072
永	138
礼	902
写	1035
必	583
头	856
兰	533
半	982
㊀ 加	749
圣	634
对	642
奶	626
奴	747
母	105
召	86
台	672
矛	1004
尼	883
民	1377
皮	707
发	1304
司	1391
边	733
丝	1081

6 画

㊀ 刑	618
动	735
式	359
协	744
地	507
场	526
寺	169
老	1031
考	1032
吉	335
机	206
耳	717
西	1255

INDEX IV
Character Pronunciations

This Index lists alphabetically the pronunciations, with their respective frame numbers, of all the characters treated in this volume. Some of the characters have multiple pronunciations, which can be found by consulting a dictionary under the pronunciation given here.

A

ā	阿	1057
á	啊	1058
āi	哀	403
ài	爱	669
ān	安	197
àn	案	214
àn	暗	485
àn	按	606
àn	岸	1280
āo	凹	31

B

bā	八	8
bā	巴	1328
bā	吧	1331
bǎ	把	1329
bà	爸	1330
bái	百	35
bái	白	34
bài	败	341
bān	班	1011
bān	般	1396
bān	搬	1398
bǎn	板	657
bǎn	版	989
bàn	办	743
bàn	半	982
bàn	伴	983
bāng	帮	1386

bàng	棒	1235
bāo	包	520
bǎo	宝	267
bǎo	保	823
bǎo	堡	824
bào	抱	589
bào	报	1106
bēi	杯	997
bēi	卑	1496
běi	北	454
bèi	贝	52
bèi	备	317
bèi	背	455
bèi	被	711
běn	本	213
bí	鼻	617
bǐ	匕	453
bǐ	比	456
bǐ	笔	1423
bì	必	583
bì	壁	1188
bì	避	1189
biān	边	733
biān	编	1369
biǎn	扁	1367
biàn	便	836
biàn	辩	1186
biàn	变	1495
biāo	标	905
biǎo	表	1219
bié	别	739

bīng	冰	430
bīng	兵	1080
bǐng	丙	842
bǐng	柄	843
bìng	并	863
bìng	病	1294
bō	波	708
bō	播	1420
bó	博	1381
bó	搏	1382
bǔ	卜	43
bǔ	补	406
bù	步	380
bù	布	414
bù	不	993
bù	部	1384

C

cā	擦	912
cái	裁	401
cái	才	620
cái	财	621
cǎi	采	665
cǎi	彩	1308
cài	菜	666
cān	餐	1158
cān	参	1310
cǎn	惨	1311
cāng	仓	1121
cǎo	草	227
cè	测	157

cè	策	792
céng	曾	502
céng	层	892
chá	查	220
chá	茶	261
chá	察	911
chà	差	535
chǎn	产	1314
chāng	昌	25
cháng	常	705
cháng	长	1428
chǎng	厂	121
chǎng	敞	345
chǎng	场	526
chàng	唱	22
chāo	超	392
cháo	朝	49
cháo	潮	149
cháo	嘲	50
chǎo	吵	111
chē	车	300
chén	沉	319
chén	臣	731
chén	陈	1252
chén	辰	1467
chén	晨	1468
chèn	衬	407
chén	尘	161
chēng	称	801
chéng	呈	274
chéng	成	368

jiān	尖	114	jìn	尽	895	kàn	看	585	láo	劳	868
jiān	坚	1013	jìn	禁	906	kāng	康	956	lǎo	老	1031
jiān	监	1141	jìn	近	927	kàng	抗	590	lè	勒	1409
jiǎn	剪	304	jìn	进	1362	kào	靠	1272	le	了	101
jiǎn	减	433	jīng	晶	23	kǎo	考	1032	léi	雷	426
jiǎn	拣	1254	jīng	京	330	kǎo	烤	1033	lèi	类	782
jiǎn	简	1267	jīng	惊	579	kē	颗	923	lěng	冷	1116
jiǎn	检	1435	jīng	经	1096	kē	科	970	lí	离	1180
jiàn	见	58	jīng	精	1211	kě	可	92	lǐ	里	179
jiàn	贱	375	jīng	睛	1214	kě	渴	852	lǐ	李	223
jiàn	建	398	jǐng	景	331	kè	克	108	lǐ	理	276
jiàn	件	808	jǐng	警	347	kè	客	312	lǐ	礼	902
jiàn	健	817	jǐng	井	1360	kè	课	922	lì	厉	123
jiàn	渐	930	jìng	敬	344	kè	刻	1199	lì	丽	187
jiàn	间	1266	jìng	竞	448	kěn	肯	383	lì	立	444
jiāng	江	147	jìng	竟	487	kēng	坑	323	lì	力	732
jiǎng	讲	1361	jìng	镜	488	kōng	空	1075	lì	励	736
jiàng	将	244	jìng	境	489	kǒng	孔	98	lì	历	737
jiàng	降	1071	jìng	净	952	kǒng	恐	575	lì	利	771
jiāo	娇	443	jìng	静	1216	kòng	控	1076	lì	例	816
jiāo	教	1038	jiū	揪	770	kǒu	口	11	liǎ	俩	1479
jiāo	交	1046	jiū	究	1073	kū	枯	210	lián	连	301
jiǎo	搅	601	jiǔ	九	9	kū	哭	248	lián	莲	302
jiǎo	脚	1104	jiǔ	久	839	kǔ	苦	229	lián	联	1471
jiǎo	角	1363	jiǔ	酒	1128	kù	库	558	liǎn	脸	1436
jiào	较	1048	jiù	旧	37	kù	裤	559	liàn	练	1253
jiào	叫	1194	jiù	就	332	kuài	快	1276	liàn	恋	1494
jiē	皆	459	jiù	救	343	kuài	块	1277	liáng	凉	434
jiē	接	604	jū	居	888	kuài	筷	1278	liáng	良	1153
jiē	街	761	jú	局	893	kuān	宽	230	liǎng	两	1478
jiē	阶	1066	jǔ	举	1434	kuáng	狂	271	liàng	量	180
jiē	坠	1070	jù	句	67	kuàng	况	431	liàng	亮	329
jié	结	1087	jù	具	74	kūn	昆	457	liáo	聊	1111
jié	节	1113	jù	锯	889	kùn	困	547	liào	料	969
jiě	姐	1346	jù	剧	890	kuò	括	597	liè	列	713
jiě	解	1364	jù	据	891				liè	烈	714
jiè	介	259	juàn	眷	986		**L**		lín	林	203
jiè	界	260	jué	觉	338	lā	拉	608	lín	临	1012
jiè	借	974	jué	决	1275	lā	啦	609	líng	灵	942
jīn	金	279	jué	绝	1333	là	辣	1290	líng	零	1117
jīn	巾	410	jūn	均	159	lái	来	783	lǐng	领	1118
jīn	襟	907	jūn	军	320	lán	兰	533	lìng	另	738
jīn	斤	924	jūn	君	959	lán	篮	1142	lìng	令	1115
jīn	今	1246				lán	蓝	1143	liū	溜	1110
jīn	仅	811		**K**		làn	烂	534	liǔ	柳	1112
jǐn	紧	1102	kǎ	卡	47	láng	郎	1385	liú	流	684
jǐn	谨	1242	kāi	开	613	làng	浪	1154	liú	留	1109

tàn	探	1078	tuō	脱	500	wú	吴	437	xiāng	乡	1387
tāng	汤	527	tuō	托	1424	wú	无	611	xiǎng	享	326
táng	堂	706				wǔ	五	5	xiǎng	想	573
táng	唐	954	**W**			wǔ	武	385	xiǎng	响	189
táng	糖	955	wā	哇	165	wǔ	午	542	xiáng	翔	546
táo	桃	238	wài	外	118	wǔ	舞	1344	xiàng	项	82
táo	逃	295	wān	弯	1492	wù	误	439	xiàng	向	188
tǎo	讨	351	wān	湾	1493	wù	务	752	xiàng	巷	1358
tào	套	1498	wán	丸	42	wù	雾	753	xiàng	象	1451
tí	题	395	wán	顽	61	wù	勿	877	xiàng	像	1452
tí	提	598	wán	完	193	wù	物	879	xiāo	削	129
tǐ	体	813	wán	玩	270				xiāo	消	152
tì	替	728	wǎn	晚	1450	**X**			xiāo	宵	196
tiān	天	436	wàn	万	65	xī	夕	115	xiǎo	小	109
tián	田	14	wáng	王	265	xī	息	574	xiǎo	晓	378
tián	填	162	wáng	亡	490	xī	吸	628	xiào	肖	128
tiáo	条	307	wǎng	往	758	xī	昔	973	xiào	笑	787
tiào	跳	1052	wǎng	网	1174	xī	希	1167	xiào	孝	1037
tiē	贴	53	wàng	妄	492	xī	稀	1168	xiào	效	1047
tiě	铁	730	wàng	望	493	xī	西	1255	xiào	校	1049
tīng	厅	122	wàng	忘	564	xí	习	545	xiē	些	461
tīng	听	925	wēi	威	371	xí	席	979	xié	协	744
tíng	亭	328	wēi	微	760	xí	袭	1475	xié	鞋	1408
tíng	停	818	wéi	维	1084	xǐ	洗	257	xiě	写	1035
tíng	廷	854	wéi	危	1125	xǐ	喜	1137	xiě	血	1138
tíng	庭	855	wéi	韦	1229	xì	戏	638	xiè	谢	1030
tōng	通	1119	wéi	围	1230	xì	细	1093	xiè	泻	1036
tóng	同	185	wěi	委	774	xì	系	1101	xīn	心	563
tóng	铜	281	wěi	伟	1231	xiā	虾	510	xīn	辛	1185
tóng	童	450	wěi	尾	1422	xiá	暇	1403	xīn	新	1191
tǒng	统	1085	wèi	胃	29	xià	下	46	xīn	薪	1192
tòng	痛	1295	wèi	未	215	xià	夏	314	xīn	馨	1410
tóu	投	646	wèi	味	218	xiān	先	256	xìn	信	814
tóu	头	856	wèi	为	746	xiān	鲜	531	xīng	星	1221
tòu	透	776	wèi	伪	797	xián	咸	372	xíng	刑	618
tū	突	1074	wèi	位	807	xián	贤	1014	xíng	型	619
tū	凸	32	wèi	卫	1114	xián	闲	1264	xíng	形	1306
tú	图	555	wēn	温	1140	xiǎn	显	1352	xìng	杏	208
tú	途	1287	wén	闻	1268	xiǎn	险	1437	xìng	幸	1193
tǔ	土	158	wén	文	1317	xiàn	现	269	xìng	姓	1222
tǔ	吐	163	wén	蚊	1318	xiàn	线	1083	xìng	性	1223
tù	兔	1447	wèn	问	1265	xiàn	限	1151	xìng	兴	1433
tuán	团	622	wǒ	我	588	xiàn	县	1481	xiōng	兄	107
tuī	推	600	wò	握	887	xiāng	相	212	xiōng	凶	1176
tuī	腿	1150	wū	巫	850	xiāng	香	772	xiōng	胸	1177
tuì	退	1149	wū	屋	886	xiāng	箱	788	xióng	雄	671
			wú	吾	19	xiāng	襄	1203	xióng	熊	1463

xiū	休	812	yáng	羊	528	yìn	荫	1062	yuán	袁	404
xiū	修	1312	yáng	洋	530	yìn	印	1127	yuán	圆	550
xiù	秀	775	yáng	阳	1060	yīng	英	1325	yuán	园	553
xū	需	963	yǎng	养	537	yīng	应	1432	yuǎn	远	289
xū	须	1309	yǎng	仰	1301	yīng	鹰	1440	yuàn	愿	571
xū	虚	1461	yàng	样	532	yíng	营	869	yuàn	院	1067
xǔ	许	543	yāo	夭	440	yíng	迎	1302	yuē	约	1092
xù	旭	27	yāo	腰	1257	yǐng	影	1307	yuē	曰	1499
xù	序	1008	yáo	尧	376	yìng	硬	632	yuè	月	13
xù	续	1098	yáo	遥	1445	yǒng	永	138	yuè	越	393
xuān	宣	195	yáo	摇	1446	yǒng	泳	143	yuè	乐	662
xuǎn	选	297	yào	药	1100	yǒng	勇	1120	yún	匀	66
xuán	悬	1482	yào	要	1256	yòng	用	971	yún	云	428
xué	学	337	yě	也	505	yōu	忧	578	yùn	运	429
xué	穴	1072	yě	野	1010	yōu	优	821	yùn	韵	486
xuě	雪	941	yè	叶	18	yóu	尤	240			
xún	旬	68	yè	页	60	yóu	游	876			
xún	巡	296	yè	夜	872	yóu	由	913	**Z**		
xún	寻	945	yè	液	873	yóu	油	915	zá	杂	225
xùn	迅	293	yè	业	1351	yǒu	有	79	zāi	灾	194
xùn	逊	298	yī	一	1	yǒu	友	635	zài	载	366
xùn	训	352	yī	衣	400	yòu	右	78	zài	在	624
			yī	依	815	yòu	又	633	zài	再	1366
Y			yī	伊	958	yòu	诱	777	zàn	暂	929
yā	压	164	yī	医	1300	yú	鱼	154	zàng	葬	716
yā	押	917	yí	移	767	yú	渔	155	zǎo	早	26
yā	鸭	1441	yí	遗	1343	yú	逾	306	zào	皂	36
yá	牙	1414	yǐ	乙	95	yú	娱	438	zào	造	294
yà	亚	1353	yǐ	已	519	yú	于	1283	zé	则	88
ya	呀	1416	yǐ	以	861	yú	余	1285	zé	责	1217
yān	烟	552	yǐ	蚁	1184	yǔ	语	356	zéi	贼	365
yán	炎	174	yì	艺	228	yǔ	雨	425	zěn	怎	938
yán	言	346	yì	意	572	yǔ	羽	544	zēng	增	503
yán	延	396	yì	异	616	yǔ	予	1007	zèng	赠	504
yán	研	614	yì	易	880	yǔ	与	1034	zhā	渣	221
yán	颜	1316	yì	义	1182	yǔ	宇	1284	zhǎ	眨	992
yán	严	1355	yì	仪	1183	yù	玉	266	zhà	乍	937
yǎn	眼	1152	yì	益	1401	yù	狱	350	zhái	宅	1425
yǎn	演	1466	yì	逸	1448	yù	育	683	zhān	占	44
yǎn	掩	1485	yì	亦	1491	yù	浴	699	zhǎn	斩	928
yàn	宴	198	yīn	音	484	yù	欲	700	zhǎn	展	1426
yàn	厌	241	yīn	因	551	yù	预	1009	zhàn	战	362
yàn	彦	1315	yīn	阴	1061	yù	遇	1443	zhàn	站	446
yàn	艳	1334	yín	银	1144	yuán	员	55	zhāng	章	447
yàn	雁	1431	yín	寅	1465	yuán	元	59	zhāng	张	1429
yàn	验	1457	yǐn	尹	957	yuán	原	142	zhàng	丈	837
yāng	央	1324	yǐn	引	1016	yuán	源	150	zhàng	涨	1430
									zhāo	昭	87

INDEX V

Key Words and Primitive Meanings

This Index contains a cumulative list of all the key words and primitive meanings used in this book. Key words are listed with their respective character and frame number. Primitive meanings are listed in italics and are followed only by the number of the page (also in italics) on which they are first introduced.

I

J